G. Muir Mackenzie

Travels in the Slavonic Provinces of Turkey-in-Europe

Vol. 1, Second Edition

G. Muir Mackenzie

Travels in the Slavonic Provinces of Turkey-in-Europe
Vol. 1, Second Edition

ISBN/EAN: 9783337212247

Printed in Europe, USA, Canada, Australia, Japan

Cover: Foto ©Andreas Hilbeck / pixelio.de

More available books at **www.hansebooks.com**

TRAVELS IN

THE SLAVONIC PROVINCES OF TURKEY-IN-EUROPE

SERBIAN BORDER GUARD.

TRAVELS IN

THE SLAVONIC PROVINCES

OF TURKEY-IN-EUROPE

By G. MUIR MACKENZIE and A. P. IRBY

WITH A PREFACE BY

THE RIGHT HON. W. E. GLADSTONE, M.P.

IN TWO VOLUMES.—I.

SECOND EDITION REVISED

LONDON

DALDY, ISBISTER & CO.

56, LUDGATE HILL

1877

LONDON
PRINTED BY VIRTUE AND CO. LIMITED
CITY ROAD

THE SECOND EDITION OF THIS WORK

IS

Dedicated

TO

SOPHIA, LADY MUIR MACKENZIE,

OF DELVINE,

IN TOKEN OF LOVING ESTEEM;

AND IN MEMORY OF HER DAUGHTER,

WHOSE NAME STANDS ON THE TITLE PAGE;

WHO MARRIED, IN 1871, SIR CHARLES SEBRIGHT, BARON D'EVERTON,

AND WHO DIED IN CORFU, JANUARY, 1874.

The Illustrations are from Original Sketches by F. KANITZ, Author of "Serbien," "Bulgarien," &c. The greater portion of the Text of the First Edition was Contributed by G. MUIR MACKENZIE, and has been Revised for this Edition by A. P. IRBY, who has added the Three Chapters: "Bosnia in 1875," "Journey in Bosnia in August, 1875," "Bosnia in 1876-7."

PREFACE.

UNTIL our own day, it has never been possible for the people of one country to obtain trustworthy information respecting the contemporary condition of the people of another. The press, the telegraph, the railway, the large and costly development of diplomatic and consular establishments, and the usages of popular governments, have, in their several manners and degrees, contributed to place within our reach this description of knowledge, in other times substantially inaccessible. In the general absence of it is to be found the best excuse for the seemingly heartless manner in which the statesmen of a bygone generation have argued for the maintenance of the Ottoman Government with a view to the general convenience of Europe, while they have seemingly omitted from the case all consideration of the question, how far the Porte fulfilled or defeated the main purpose for which every government exists—namely, the welfare of those beneath its rule. With the possession, even the partial possession, of such knowledge, we have obtained a great advantage. But we have also come under a new and very grave responsibility. We cannot now escape from the consciousness that we are dealing with questions which greatly involve the happiness or misery of many millions of human beings, whose condition we had formerly omitted from our calculations. In the case of Greece, the recollected glories of the past and the scandal of the servitude of a race once illustrious, were associated with the arguments drawn from the disturbance of the Levant, and probably told more in the production of the result than any keen sense of the specific character of Turkish oppression.

But, although this important change has been effected, it still remains a matter of difficulty, as well as of desire, that this knowledge, in cases with which we have chosen to concern ourselves, should be trustworthy, should be complete, and should be effectual. So to be concerned, is indeed a matter of great inconvenience, and even mischief. Ill able to cope with the problems which appertain to our own affairs, we can yet worse afford to meet drafts upon our care and attention for settling the affairs of others. Happily or unhappily, we have taken upon ourselves a heavy charge of this kind in the case of Turkey. Some found themselves upon British interests, others upon general duty, others upon the specific obligations growing out of our anterior proceedings, and especially out of the Crimean war. But all, or very nearly all, are agreed, that the question of the Ottoman Empire is one from which we cannot wholly withdraw. Very nearly all, whether freely or reluctantly, now confess that in treating it we cannot refuse to look at the condition of the subject races. And if we are to include that element of the case in our view, it is most important that we should see it as clearly and fully as may be possible.

I do not mean to disparage the labours and services of others when I say that, in my opinion, no diplomatist, no consul, no traveller, among our countrymen, has made such a valuable contribution to our means of knowledge in this important matter, as was made by Miss Mackenzie and Miss Irby, when they published, in 1867, their travels in some of the Slavonian Provinces of European Turkey. I shall not now dwell upon the information they have given us with respect to Montenegro: for, although it is highly interesting and instructive, it is subsidiary to the main part of the volume, on which I now dwell. Here, much more than in any other work I have been able to discover, is exhibited to view without passion or prejudice, as well as without reserve, the normal state of life among the subject races, the standing relation both between them and their government, and likewise between them and those Mahommedans, mainly descended from renegades, who are at once their fellow-subjects and their masters. At the time when these ladies undertook a mission of the purest philanthropy with a view to the diffusion of education in the Provinces, the Eastern question did not, among ourselves, wear even in the slightest degree the aspect of a party question. There was nothing from this side to disturb a perfect rectitude of view. It was still more important, that there was then nothing occasional, nothing exceptional, in the condition of the Provinces themselves. They had been, for some time, what would be called in Turkey tranquil. The journey was indeed one which would never have been undertaken except by ladies endowed with a courage and resolution

as remarkable as their discernment and their benevolence.
But they were able at the time to draw, with steady
hand, all the lineaments of a picture, which is the picture
of Ottoman rule over a Christian majority at its best, and
in the absence of all exasperating circumstances. Without
studying pictures so taken, our knowledge of the
Turkish question must be essentially defective, and more
or less misleading. The condition exhibited in it is that
which determines the true measure of happiness or misery,
growth or retrogression, elevation or depression, in the
ordinary human life of these provinces. It shows us
also the point of departure, from which begin the terrible
processes, not indeed without example in former times,
but never so fully exhibited to the view of Christendom
as in the Bulgarian massacres of 1876, now ineffaceable
from the memory of civilized mankind.

We thus come to learn, that there are two distinct
phases of existence for the subject races of Turkey : the
ordinary, and the exceptional. The exceptional phase
comes when the ruling race finds or thinks itself threatened in the key of its position. This is on the rare occasions, when oppression is felt to be absolutely intolerable,
and the down-trodden rayahs, appealing to force, seek to
obtain their rights by the same instrument which has
been the source and the vehicle of all their wrongs.
Other conquerors, such as the Greek or the Roman,
have relied, along with force, upon intellectual superiority, and upon the communication of benefits to the
conquered. The Ottoman Turk, with his satellites, has
relied upon force alone. Whatever intellect he has at
any time displayed, and it has not always been small,

has been intellect addressed to the organisation and
application of force. The rebellious rayah for once
meets him on his own ground. He is in a manner
compelled to develop and apply on these occasions the
whole of his large inventory of the weapons of violence
and torture, and other yet worse and baser means of
inflicting agony upon his subjects. For, if these instruments fail, he has nothing in reserve. It is now, therefore, coming to be understood, that the indescribable
proceedings of last year in Bulgaria were not due to
passion, ignorance, or accident; but to method, policy,
and principle: the ends sought were absolutely vital
to Turkish power as it exists in these Provinces, and
the instruments chosen were admirably adapted to the
ends.

With reference to this, which I have called the exceptional phase of existence under the Ottoman Power,
Miss Irby, in the new edition of her work, has supplied
illustrations of very great interest and importance.
Although a considerable portion of the Metropolitan
daily press systematically suppresses the too copious
evidence of continuing Turkish outrages in Bulgaria,
this portion cannot control its remaining organs, and it
has become generally known that the reign of terror is
still prolonged in that unhappy Province, and that what
was done last May to hundreds and thousands is still,
and daily, done to units, or fives, or tens. If the tem-
pest has passed by, the swell still continues. Ottoman
security is felt to depend upon keeping alive in the
mind of the subject races the memory of the great
massacres; for on the mirror of the past is drawn the

image of the future. The work of Miss Irby, with
the chapters she has added, widens our perspective. I
have myself stated, months back, to the public that,
while we were venting indignation about Bulgaria, the
Turk was doing the very same foul work, though not on
the same imperial scale, in Bosnia. The *Manchester
Guardian* has rendered important public service with
respect to the same afflicted region, through its very
valuable correspondence. But Miss Irby, after her long
and self-sacrificing experience, speaks with a weight of
dispassionate authority, to which neither I nor any
correspondent of a public journal can pretend. She
now discloses, and that down to the latest date, upon
information which she knows to be trustworthy, a state
of things which exhibits a greater aggregate of human
misery flowing from Turkish rule, than even the Bulgaria of 1876 could show. In Bosnia and the Herzegovina more than a third of the population are exiled
or homeless; the mass of these (as we now learn)
reduced to an allowance of a penny a day, but rather
preferring to travel, and that rapidly, the road to famine
and to pestilence, than to descend, by returning, into
the abyss of a suffering which is also shame; and with
this, the constant and harrowing recurrence of the
cruel outrages, which are more and more fastening
themselves, as if inseparable adjuncts, upon the Turkish
name.

" I nunc, et versus tecum meditare cancros."

Teach, you who will, the duty of dealing effectually
with the insurrection, and setting up again that
fabric of Turkish rule over a Serbian people, which,

.

amidst all this misery, we may hope is tottering to its final fall.

Such is the aid Miss Irby gives us towards the attainment not merely of a theoretical, but of a practical and living knowledge with reference to the condition of the Sláv Provinces of Turkey after an insurrection. I however attach not a less, perhaps even a greater, importance to the less exciting picture which is drawn in the older part of the work. By the simple, painstaking communication of the particulars supplied from daily experience, it presents to us in comparatively quiet landscape, rayah life, under Turkish mastery, in the best condition it could attain, after many long years of peace for the Empire abroad, and of reforms promised at home, with facilities for effecting them such as are not likely to return. And what was rayah life under these happier circumstances? It was a life never knowing real security or peace, except when the Government and its agents were happily out of view. A life which never had any of the benefits of law, save when the agents of the law were absent. A life in which no object, that was valued, could be exposed. A life which left to the Christian nothing, except what his Mahommedan master did not chance to want. A life in which wife and daughter, the appointed sources of the sweetest consolation, were the standing occasions of the sharpest anxiety. A life debased by cringing, poisoned by fear, destructive of manhood, shorn of the freedom which is the indispensable condition of all nobleness in man, and shorn too of every hope, except such as might lie in an escape from it to some foreign land; or in the dream of a future redemption, which we may think to be now probably at hand, when acute suffering has been substituted for dull chronic pain, and when a people, too long patient, seems to be at length determined, in vindicating its own rights, to vindicate the insulted laws of the Most High.

W. E. G.

April 10*th*, 1877.

CONTENTS OF VOL. I.

LIST OF ILLUSTRATIONS.

VOL. I.

MAP

of the

SOUTH SLAVONIC

COUNTRIES

Scale of English Miles

Railways shown thus ⌐

Explanation of Colours

Serbian	dark green	
Bulgarian	light green	
Turkish	red	
Greek	blue	
Albanian	yellow	
Roumans	} gray	
North & South of the Danube		
German	purple	

Via Egnatia (Roman) Road now ruined.

15

CHAPTER I.

THE rearguard of Mahommedanism in Europe maintains its last stronghold in the Turkish vilayet of Bosnia. Here, as the religion of the ruling caste, Islam has had a trial of nearly four centuries. What fruits has it borne?

In geographical position the nearest to European civilisation, but in social condition the most barbarous of the provinces of Turkey in Europe, Bosnia, including Turkish Croatia and the Herzegovina, extends to a point west of the longitude of Vienna, and interposes a savage and Oriental aspect between the Dalmatian shores of the Adriatic and the advancing culture of Serbia, Hungary, and Croatia. Cross the frontier from these lands, and you may fancy yourself in the wilds of Asia.

The soil of Bosnia teems with various and valuable minerals, her hills abound in splendid forests, her well-watered plains are fertile and productive, her race, under culture, proves exceptionally gifted. Yet her commerce is contemptible; "*plums*," to quote the report of Mr. Consul Holmes for 1873, being "the most valuable article of trade in the province;" her population is uneducated, not one man in a hundred knowing how to read, and the chief town, Serajevo, which contains from forty to fifty thousand inhabitants, possessing not a single book shop.

One or two English speculators have been tempted to inquire into the mineral riches of the land, but have prudently retired, being unable, on the one hand, to come to satisfactory terms with the government, and, on the other, to find a company to work the mines in face of the vexatious hindrances which baffle all enterprise under the present régime. The immense mineral wealth remains untouched.

An Austrian company has obtained some sort of local concession to work all the mines of coal, lead, and copper, within thirty miles of the proposed line of railway. But this concession has not yet received the needful ratification at Constantinople, and it appears that the Turks have a peculiar disinclination to give their neighbours, the Austrians, any footing in Bosnia. The beautiful marble of the country, white, and white with red streaks, is put to but sorry use in the rough Turkish pavements. Stone for building purposes is plentiful: yet even in Serajevo, wood, rubble and shingles still prevail; only here and there brick and stone houses, roofed with tiles, are beginning to appear.

A road now leads from Brood on the Save to Serajevo, a distance of about one hundred and thirty-eight English miles, along which passes once a week each way the post cart of the Austrian consulate in Bosnia; three places on the hay in the springless vehicle may be hired by those who do not object to jolt on continuously for two days and a night, or more. If a private cart be taken from Brood, at least three nights must be spent on the way, sleeping at khans, the discomfort of which is not to be described. It is necessary to take bed and bedding, or at least a mattress, and moreover to command the immediate expulsion of the carpets, mats and cushions, which form the only furniture of the rooms. A road is in course of completion from Serajevo to the Dalmatian fron-

tier by way of Mostar, the chief town of the Herzegovina.
Two years ago the rough carts of the country might be
driven to Livno, and thence across the Austrian frontier
to Spalato on the Adriatic ; but the Turkish portion of
this road is now impassable. There is a road from
Serajevo by Travnik and Banjaluka to Gradishka on the
Save, and other cart-roads and fragments of roads exist,
but they are constantly out of repair and the bridges in
most uncertain condition.

It is possible to traverse this rude land in many directions, on foot or on horseback, rejoicing in the ever
changing beauty of mountain, wood, and water, which is
enlivened by the rich colouring and picturesque variety
of national costume. But the traveller may journey on
for days, and he will come upon no works of modern
enterprise, no monuments of ancient mediæval art. He
may, indeed, if he search diligently, and if he know
where to look, discover beneath weeds and brushwood,
or scanty tillage, traces of Roman roads, one of which
led across the province from Scissia (Sisseg) on the
Save to Salona on the Adriatic. Such tracks of ancient
passage he may find for the searching, and what is
likely to be more to his purpose, he may come upon
the fragment of a modern railway, lying detached and
unconnected on the Bosnian plains. Along this railway,
without beginning and without end, a train used to
run once a day each way, conveying a ludicrously small
average of goods and passengers between the village of
Novi and the more important town of Banjaluka. The
ideal and fragmentary nature of the achievement was
owing to the collapse of the contract between an Austrian company and the Turkish government ; but the
whole, of which it should form a part, may some day
become our main highway to India. It is to be seen on
the map of the " Continental Guide," where Bradshaw

has traced in anticipation a railway (elsewhere, by-the-bye, prophetically designated a branch of the great Euphrates Valley Railway), which, trending eastward off the well-known Semmering line between Vienna and Trieste, and traversing a part of Croatia, may at some future time cross Bosnia, Old Serbia, and Bulgaria, to Salonica and Constantinople. Such means of passage through the land, viz., lost Roman roads, of which scarce a trace remains, and the projected Turkish railways, of which, save the fragment here noted, not a Bosnian sod has been turned, constitute the chief works —with the exception of the roads, telegraphs, and bridges of the last few years, I should rather say the only works, for which Bosnia is indebted to ancient Roman and modern Turkish enterprise.

But what traces do we find of the intermediate centuries which elapsed before a part of the Roman province of Mœsia became the Turkish pashalik of Bosnia ? Ruined castles of the ancient feudal nobility, ruins of Serb and Latin churches and convents; and the three Franciscan convents of Foinica, Kreshevo, and Sudiska, which, endowed with special privileges, have been maintained from the fifteenth century to the present day. The Paterenes, or Bogomiles, the early Dissidents of Bosnia, were very numerous from the twelfth to the fifteenth centuries, but they were scattered or exterminated with cruel persecutions, and have left visible traces only in graveyards popularly assigned to them.

Before the Turkish conquest at the end of the fifteenth century, the frontiers of Bosnia were repeatedly changed, and its inhabitants were incessantly harassed by the passage and encounters of hostile troops. For Bosnia has ever been the borderland of contending rival states and rival churches. Its history, in the Middle Ages as in later periods, is a distressing and tangled record of

petty warfare, revolting treachery, and terrible crimes.
A gleam of legendary light falls on the times of Ban
Kulin, who held the faith of the Paterenes, and whose
name is still remembered among the people, marking the
era of a distant Golden Age. Its race is identical with
that of Free Serbia, Old Serbia, and Montenegro, and
with the Serbs of Hungary and Dalmatia. The name of
the country is derived from the Bosna, a tributary of the
Save. As in other Serb countries, the early princes of
Bosnia were called *zupans*. At one time nearly all these
lands acknowledged the supremacy of Byzantium. At
another period Bosnia was incorporated in the kingdom
of Hungary. In the middle of the fourteenth century
it formed a part of the empire of Stephan Dūshan, that
great ruler of the house of Nemania, who assumed the
title of "Christloving Czar of all Serbs and Greeks,"
imitated the style and institutions, and aspired to succeed to the sovereignty of Byzantium, but died of fever
on the march to Constantinople (1355).

Before the Turkish conquest, Bosnia was again a
separate state under native *bans* and kings, and had
been partly conquered by and partly reconquered from
the Magyars. The Serbs belonged to the Eastern,
the Hungarians to the Western Church, and then as
now the jealousies of rival hierarchies divided the
Serbian race.

Whatever germs of free institutions may have existed
in the barbarous communities which we trace throughout the Serbian countries, and in Bosnia among the rest,
were here stifled beneath the growth of feudalism, and
the contending claims of the Eastern and Western
Churches. Finally, the accidents of geographical position exposed the Southern Slāvs to the full sweep of the
Turkish deluge. The Osmanli conquered ; the Byzantine
Empire was overthrown ; there suffered also a younger

race, the younger children of the European family, the Southern Slāvs, who, after centuries of repression, are asserting their right to independent existence.

After the conquest of Bosnia by the Turks, those of the nobility who remained alive in the land became Mahommedan. The Bosnian Begs were the offspring of an alliance between feudalism and Islam.

The feudal system, which had been established in Bosnia in the Christian period, was continued after the Mussulman conquest, with this sole difference, that the feudal lords changed their faith and their suzerain. Their own position was confirmed by the change. We have seen that Bosnia was continually the object of attack from Hungary. Now the Turkish policy was acute and masterly; there was also much that was noble and magnanimous in the Osmanli character; tempting terms were offered to the Bosnian nobles. Perceiving that under the shelter of their mighty conquerors, they would be able to preserve their nationality, maintain their caste privileges, and bid defiance to Hungary and the Pope, many of the nobles threw in their cause with that of the Empire of Othman, and the Bosnian Slavonic Mussulman became, in the words of Turkish writers, "the lion that guarded Stamboul." Bosnia was the bulwark of Islam against Western Europe. As in later times the *vis inertiæ* of the Turkish Empire in Europe has been considerably weighted by the Mussulman element in Bosnia, so in the sixteenth and first half of the seventeenth centuries, the days of its aggressive vigour, the spahis or feudal chiefs of Bosnia, led powerful contingents to the Turkish armies, and the ranks of the Janissaries were largely recruited by her sons.

But the tyranny and pretensions of the Begs waxed too great. They assumed entire independence, they coerced or chased away the viziers sent from Constanti-

nople to reside or rule in Bosnia. It became necessary
to subdue it as a rebel province. This subjection was
accomplished in our own days by Omer Pasha, who in
1850-1 put an end to the feudal system in Bosnia,
equalising the Mussulman Bosnian Begs, or magnates,
with all other Mussulmans in Turkey, abolishing the
rank and office of spahis, or military feudal chiefs, and
compelling the tithe hitherto received by them to be
paid into the government treasury.

All Mussulmans being equalised before the law in
1850, and political and social equality among all creeds
and classes having been proclaimed by the Hatt-i-Humayoun of 1856, let us inquire what was the actual condition of the subjects of the Porte in Bosnia in the spring
of 1875, immediately before the outbreak of the revolt.

The population of Bosnia and the Herzegovina, forming part of one Slavonic race, is still commonly spoken
of as three different "nations," so great is the division
marked by difference of creed. I give the following
statistics gathered from Turkish official reports of 1874.
Their accuracy cannot be relied upon: the number of
Mussulmans is enormously exaggerated; the proportion
between Greek and Latin Christians is fairly stated.

Bosnian Mussulmans	442,050
Christians of the Orthodox Eastern Church .	575,756
Roman Catholics	185,503
Jews	3,000
Gypsies	9,537
Total . .	1,216,846

In addition to this native population should be mentioned some 5,000 Austrian subjects, and some hundreds
of Osmanli officials.

It is only in the mutesariflik of Serajevo that the
Mahommedans are in the majority. In the other six

subdivisions of the land the Christians, Eastern Church
Slävs and Roman Catholics being taken together, on the
whole greatly outnumber the Mussulmans.

I. The Bosnian Mussulmans are the owners of the
land, and they reside on their estates, or in houses in
the towns. They are also small merchants, and follow
trades. Some are *kmets*, or farmers of the lands for
richer Mussulmans. The Bosnian Beg par excellence,
the powerful feudal chief of sixty years ago, is a chained
monster with drawn teeth and cut claws. He was
too decidedly a megatherion for our age. The brute
force of the savage is greatly broken, and he has acquired no other force. For, with some possible exceptions, the Bosnian Begs of to-day are ignorant and
corrupt, indolent, and wholly incapable of organization
or combined action. Some have learnt a little Turkish,
Arabic, and Persian, but very few know how to read
and write their own tongue. The spirit of feasting and
merrymaking, banished by Mahomet and his followers,
but ineradicable among the Slävs, still lingers among
the Bosnian Mussulmans. Instead of the annual festival
of the *Krsno imé*, when the friends and relations of
every Serbian house gather to celebrate with feasting the
day of their patron saint, the Begs still in many places
make a festivity of the time of boiling down plums for
bestilj, or plum syrup. But even this lingering opportunity for social union is being relinquished, and scarcely
anything else of the kind remains.

The Mussulmans of Serajevo still keep St. John the
Baptist's day (24th of June, O. S.), when the sun is said
to dance at dawn on the top of the hill Trebovich: on
that day, and on St. Elias's and St. George's days, the
Mussulman population turns out of doors, and the whole
side of Trebovich, especially the neighbourhood of the
Moslem saint's tomb, is bright with red turbans and

jackets and groups of women in white veils. They sit
in separate companies smoking and drinking coffee, and
there is a striking absence of life and gaiety among
them.

Many of the Bosnian Begs are not indisposed to embrace
the Christianity professed by their forefathers. They call
a priest to say prayers over them when they are ill, they
keep the name of the patron saint of their family, and
they preserve with care the patents of nobility of their
Christian ancestors. But on the other hand many of
them are fanatic Moslems, and nourish a blind and
savage hatred against their Christian fellow countrymen.
This hatred finds vent even in quiet times in many a
hidden act of cruelty. At the present moment of licensed
insult and revenge (autumn of 1875), we hear of Christians being impaled and flayed alive, and cruelties of the
worst ages committed on helpless women and children.
In a season of perfect quiet (1871-2) some fierce Mussulmans of Serajevo swore to cut the throats of the Christians
if they dared to hang bells in the tower of their new
church. The conspiracy was discovered, and the leading
Mussulmans held responsible for the quiet of the town.
The pasha confessed the weakness of his authority to
maintain the law when he called the principal merchants
and asked them to give up their legal rights to the bells,
on the ground that if their sound were heard he would
be unable to restrain the fury of the Mahommedans.

The state of political feeling among the Bosnian Mussulmans was described to me before the outbreak by those
who knew them well, as by no means unanimous. At
present they have no leader of preponderating influence who might render them strong and dangerous by
uniting them in one purpose. Some were amicably disposed towards Serbia; others were fanatically jealous of
the Christian principality. The name of the late Prince

Michael of Serbia was not unpopular among them, but
his assassination by men who were his own subjects
greatly injured the Serbian cause, and is regarded by the
Begs of Bosnia, among whom lingers the spirit of their
aristocratic caste, as a crime which condemns the nation.
Dislike to the Osmanlis and to Stamboul is universal
among them, and has been much increased by taxation
and by the obligation to serve in the Turkish army.

The conscription was first enforced by Osman Pasha in
1864. The Bosnian Mussulmans are drawn by lot for
the regular army, or *nizam*, for a term of four years'
service; and likewise for the *redif*, or reserve, in which
they must serve one month in the year for nine years.
Exemption may be purchased from the nizam by the
payment of a hundred ducats, about £50, or a substitute
may be found; but service in the redif is compulsory
on each man on whom the lot may fall. The Bosnians
are not required to serve outside the province. They are
all infantry; the cavalry and artillery stationed in Bosnia
are natives of other provinces of Turkey. Since the
outbreak, robber bands of Turkish volunteers have been
raised in different parts of the country.* The redif (or
reserve) in many places have refused to serve.

The sacerdotal-legal profession is greatly desired by
the Bosnian Mussulmans. Many of their ulemas have
studied at Stamboul. Pilgrimages to Mecca are frequent.
It is a not uncommon sight to see crowds of the Mussulman population sally forth from Serajevo to meet some
returning hadji, or to escort pilgrims setting out for the
Holy Places. Wandering dervishes visit the country, exciting the fanaticism of the faithful. Although no spirit
of proselytism exists in Bosnia, yet renegadism has been

---

* Their method of suppressing suspected insurrection has been amply illustrated in Bulgaria. The like method is to this hour being pursued in Bosnia.
But there are no reporters.

more frequent of late among the Christians. In the course of 1874, in Serajevo alone, ten women and four men, Catholics and Pravoslavs, became Mahommedan, and it is uncertain how many in other parts of the province. The immediate cause is generally the great poverty of the Christians, which often compels them to place their girls in service in Turkish houses.

The difficulty presented by the Mussulman element in Bosnia has been greatly exaggerated, together with its strength and numbers. Any well-organized Christian government would be able to deal with it. But as long as the Mussulmans alone are permitted to bear arms the difficulty is insuperable. With regard to toleration it should be remembered that since Serbia expelled the Turks from her own territory she still maintains a mosque in Belgrade for Mahommedan visitors, the expenses being defrayed by the Serbian government.

II. The Pravoslav Christians of Bosnia are merchants, small tradesmen, and farmers.

Some few Christians have attained to the possession of landed property ; but the Mussulmans cannot endure the innovation, and they do their utmost, usually with success, to prevent a ghiaour from acquiring land, or to dispossess him if he has accomplished the purchase. This can be done in various ways ; whether by bringing in Mussulman evidence—always ready at the call of Mussulmans — to prove that the late owner had no proper title, and that the sale is therefore invalid ; or by making use of the law which exists in Turkey (or at least in Bosnia), that no property can be sold without first giving all the neighbouring owners the right of refusal. It is very seldom that a Mussulman can induce his neighbours to consent that he should sell his land to a Christian, and thus introduce a ghiaour into their midst. Public opinion prevents the sale, even

though no one of the neighbours be able to purchase
instead.

The Bosnian cultivator or farmer (here called *kmet*),
usually a Christian, pays to his landlord, usually a
Bosnian Mussulman, one third of the produce, or one
half, according to the agreement, and as the landlord or
the tenant may supply oxen, seed, and implements. A
tithe, which is now actually the eighth, is paid into the
government treasury, and is collected by the tax-
gatherer, who farms the taxes from the government.
Great and bitter complaints are made of the injustice
and exactions of the tax-gatherer. The cultivator dares
not gather in his crops till the visit of the assessor;
while he is waiting it repeatedly happens that the harvests perish. The tax on the arbitrarily calculated value
is, of course, exacted all the same. In fact the peasants
suffer much less from the Mussulman landlord than
from the government official, for the landowner is interested in the prosperity of his tenant.

The tax in lieu of military service which is paid by all
non-Mussulmans weighs very heavily on the poor, who
have to pay equally with the rich twenty-eight piastres
for every male. In the poorest and most miserable
family this sum must be paid for the male infant who has
first seen the light a few hours before the visit of the
tax-gatherer. This tax on the young children of the
rayah is the most oppressive and galling to him, collected often by house visitations, in which the sanctity of
his hearth is most vilely outraged. Great suffering results
from the forced labour exacted by the government. For
instance, in the making of the new road to Mostar,
Christians were driven by zaptiés from great distances,
and compelled to work for days without pay.

Systematic and legalised extortion has succeeded to the
intermittent violence of former times ; the mass of the

people are ground to the dust under the present régime. They were materially much better off in the days of Begluk (the reign of the Begs). The Christian rayah was often less miserable when more directly under the Beg, or resident landowner, than he is now under the temporary official—the present farmer of the revenue—whose sole advantage lies in pocketing all he can for himself. The position of the landowner and his dependents affords opportunity for the development of much kindly human feeling: the tax-gatherer is by nature a bird of prey. Not long ago the Christian retainers of the Begs used to come into the town to church on the great festivals, decked out in the old-fashioned silver ornaments of the country, but now these ornaments are seldom seen, for their owners have been obliged to sell them.

I will here give a translation of the words of a native Bosnian woman, describing the changes which had taken place in the daily life of the Christian women of Serajevo, within the memory of the present generation and since the residence of the European consuls in that city has restrained the grosser outrages still committed in other parts of the country.

" When the vizier resided at Travnik, thirty years ago, the common people were much better than off than they are now, for then there were no taxes but the *haratch* (in exemption from military service). They were rich, and had horses, oxen, swine, sheep, and poultry; they wore fine clothes with silver ornaments, they had beautiful arms. Although there was no liberty, yet the Begs and Agas, lords of the land, protected and defended their own kmets. The greatest violence was in the days of Mental Pasha and Fazli Pasha, who plundered, killed, raged, tortured, and tormented just as they chose; there was no inquiry made and no evidence taken. This lasted till the time of Omer Pasha. As regards liberty (personal

safety), from that day to this, the difference here is as
great as between heaven and earth; at that time the
women in Serajevo did not dare to go to the charshia
(market place) or along the streets, they did not dare to
stand at the doors; when they went to church, or
wherever they were obliged to go, they went without
ornaments, and covered down to the feet in a white
cloth; the Turkish women rarely went along the streets,
even covered up so that you could not see their eyes.
Now for some time past Christian women and maidens,
wives and daughters of the Pravoslav Serajevo merchants, adorned with ducats and pearls, in their best
dresses, go along our streets, and in our charshia, as in
their own homes, by day or by night without any fear."

With the exception of a few merchants, the Pravoslav population is miserably poor. There has been
no development of the immense material resources of
the country, no means of employment and occupation which might enable the poor to meet the ever
increasing taxation, the extortions of the officials, and
the heavy exactions of their own clergy. But in
spite of all hindrances, the Serb merchants of Bosnia
have advanced steadily, though slowly, in wealth and
position. It was jealousy of their progress which led to
the oppression of the thriving merchants at Gradishka,
opposite the Austrian frontier, in 1873. False accusations
were made against the leading Christians of the place
and some were seized and put in prison; they petitioned
the Porte, and, as usual, a counter-statement was got up
by the medjliss, which Christians were made to sign, not
knowing the contents of the document to which they had
put their names. Fourteen Christian merchants fled over
into Austria, and went to Vienna, declaring they would
never return unless placed under Austrian protection.
Through the initiative of Austria, Mustapha Assim

Pasha, the then governor of Bosnia, too zealous a Turk
for the age, and determined by repression of Christian
progress to restore the waning Mussulman prestige, was
recalled from the province. Had he remained, the inevitable revolt must have broken out sooner. The immediate cause of the insurrection of 1875 may be found in the
iniquitous manner of raising the taxes and the additional
screw which had of late been put on the "naked Bosnian
rayah" to contribute to the payment of Turkish bond-
holders. But this is not all. Far deeper than any temporary accident of increased taxation, lies the innate
strength of Serbian nationality and the immutable determination of the Christian Serb to throw off the foreign
yoke of the Turk—a yoke as foreign now to the Serbs of
Bosnia as it was when first imposed on them four
centuries ago. And it is certain, from the vengeful
temper of the Mussulmans, that should the present insurrection terminate in the pacification of Bosnia as a Turkish
province, the condition of the Christians will be worse
than before, notwithstanding any amount of promises and
professions from Constantinople.*

The Bosnian Christians of the Eastern Orthodox
Church have the same peculiar customs, the same national saints and heroes, the same historic traditions, as
the Serbs of the principality, with whom they count
themselves one nation, though politically separated.
In the house of every Christian Orthodox merchant
you will find pictures or photographs of the princes of
Serbia, and ornaments bearing the Serbian arms. Mari-
novich, some time prime minister at Belgrade, is a
native of Serajevo, and related to the richest houses
there. I know a Serbian family living in Belgrade
which has in Bosnia Mussulman, and in Croatia Roman
Catholic, relations of the same name. In Bosnia and

* Written in 1875.

Serbia there are many families related to one another,
and who interchange visits from time to time. They
call themselves alike Serbs; their religion is the Pravoslav. And the Pravoslav Serb, whether he find himself under Austrian or Turkish rule, or whether he
be a Montenegrin or a native of Free Serbia, is the
citizen of one Serbian fatherland, and nourishes an ideal
national unity.

Considerable confusion has arisen from the term *Greek*
being applied indiscriminately to all Christians of the
Orthodox or Eastern communion. It is sometimes taken
for granted that all the Christians of Turkey in Europe
are Greeks by race as well as by religion. This has
arisen from the habit of French writers describing them
as "les Grees." It is really less reasonable to call the
Orthodox Slāvs *Greeks* than it would be to call the
Roman Catholic English and Germans *Latins*. For
the different branches of the Eastern Church are all
distinctly national in this sense, that they acknowledge
no foreign authority whatever. The Serbs of the Serbian Principality and the Greeks of Free Greece have
their own metropolitans, who reside in Belgrade and in
Athens, and are independent of the Phanariote Patriarch
of Constantinople. The Serb Christians of Turkey
reckon it among their chief grievances, that they are
forced under the jurisdiction of the Greek Patriarch of
Constantinople, and have not their own metropolitan.
Appointed in Constantinople, and Greeks by birth, the
Phanariote bishops placed over Serb flocks are tools of
the Turks and play into their hands. They are the
wolves and not the shepherds of the flock. The name
Pravoslav, the old Slavonic liturgies and Church services,
the Serbs have in common with the Russians; herein
lies their bond of union with Russia.

III. The Roman Catholic Christians, or "Latins," of

Bosnia and the Herzegovina, are more orderly and submissive, but less sturdy and enterprising than the Pravoslavs. They are on a much better understanding with the Turks. Roman Catholic priests are never heard of in the Turkish prisons, Serb priests frequently, and for the most part on accusation or suspicion of political offences. Among the Roman Catholics of Serajevo there is not one single merchant; some follow trades, but for the most part the community are miserably poor. In the villages they are *kmets*, and cultivate the land for the Begs. In Travnik, Livno, and other towns there are "Latin" merchants; here and there they have recently acquired land. Notwithstanding the superior education and intelligence of the priests and the privileges granted to the clergy from the time of Mahmoud the Conqueror, their flocks remain ignorant and benighted. The paucity of schools is astonishing—unparalleled I believe among any other Roman Catholic population in Europe, except the Albanian. There are only from thirty to thirty-four Roman Catholic boys' schools in the whole province. Within the last few years girls' schools have been established in four places by sisters of the society of St. Vincent de Paul, who have their mother house in Croatia. Some improvement may also be expected from the future priests, who are receiving a more national and liberal training in Bishop Strossmayer's seminary at Diakovar in Slavonia. Up to this time they had been educated in Italy or Hungary, and to a great degree had lost sympathy with the spirit of their nation, although their superior learning gave them much influence with the people. They have succeeded in entirely abolishing among the Roman Catholic Bosnians the festival of the *Krsno imé*, on the ground of the expense which it involved to the impoverished people. But whatever are the abuses and the reckless extravagance of these festivals, they have served to keep up the brother-

hood, courage, and sense of national unity among the
Pravoslavs, and made them stronger to resist the Mussulman influence. The Bosnian Roman Catholic is to a great
degree denationalised. He does not call himself Serb,
but Latin. So far as he has any political intelligence
whatever, he has the same aspirations as the Catholic
Slävs of Austrian Croatia and Slavonia. But the unity
which is gradually growing there among the educated
Pravoslavs and Catholics has not yet penetrated Bosnia.
Bishop Strossmayer, however, is hopeful that the Roman
Catholic Bosnians would coalesce with the others under
a fair and free system.

The Jewish community of Serajevo is very prosperous ;
some of its members have grown rich within the last ten
years and have acquired property in land and houses.
Their poor are exceedingly well cared for, and a Jewish
beggar is never seen. No Jew is ever accused of murder,
theft, or violence, or found in the Turkish prisons, except
on account of debt. This is the bright side of the picture ;
there is a dark side : in some respects they are miserably
degraded ; their houses and persons are filthy, they are
small of stature, and the women always undersized.
Their language, I am told by Dr. Thompson of Constantinople, probably the only Englishman who has conversed
with them in their own tongue, continues the same as that
spoken in Spain at the time of their expulsion, and is
very nearly that in which "Don Quixote" is written.
They have a boys' school only. They have many holidays
and feasts, and more merrymakings at home than any
other "nation" in Serajevo.

The wretched condition of education in Bosnia is one
of its greatest misfortunes. Before the insurrection the
Pravoslavs had in the whole province only six girls'
schools, and at the highest estimate forty-seven boys'
schools. The first girls' school was established by the

Bosnian woman Staka, with help from Russia. She travelled to Serbia to find a teacher. The population is carefully kept in ignorance by the Turkish government, the stupidity of the people being a necessary condition for Turkish rule. In the whole province there is not a single book shop, excepting the depôt of the British and Foreign Bible Society in Serajevo, which has been established for about eight or ten years. But no other books are to be bought in the place, save a few elementary school books, the old Slavonic "Book of Hours," and an occasional almanack. A Bosnian merchant, who recently attempted to have a few Serbian books in stock for sale, was obliged to give them up to the Turkish authorities. In fact, Serbian books and newspapers are strictly prohibited at the frontier; whatever enters the country must be smuggled in. So great is the perfectly reasonable jealousy with which newspapers are withheld from the eyes of Bosnian readers, that not long ago a formal complaint was made by the Turkish authorities to the Austrian consulate that one of its officials had shown Slāv newspapers received there to Bosnian merchants. There is a government printing press in Serajevo, but it has sent forth nothing save a few very indifferent elementary school books, a song book, and two newspapers in Turkish and Slavonic, whose contents are of the most meagre description, relating chiefly to the movements and changes of Turkish officials, which, indeed, are so frequent that their record leaves little space for the scanty scraps of news which fill up the remainder of the sheets. It may be supposed that this newspaper has no circulation among the Serb population.

One of the first questions asked by those who have any knowledge of a Turkish province and any human interest in its inhabitants will always be this : " Is the evidence of Christians against Mussulmans received in

Bosnia ?" The evidence of Christians cannot be accepted
in the *mehkeme* or kadi's court, the ancient Turkish court
of justice, whose decisions are based on the Koran alone.
In the modern courts of justice, councils or *medjliss*,
the evidence of Christians against Mussulmans is
admitted by law; their right is now in principle
acknowledged, and even in Bosnia the evidence of Christians against Turks has sometimes been actually taken;
more especially when backed by a bribe, by means of
which, be it remarked, justice or injustice may at any
time equally be obtained. But it is certain that
the evidence of twenty Christians would be out-
weighed by that of two Mussulmans. The Turks have
naturally shown little zeal, except under European pressure, in carrying out the design, which, taking from the
kadis the decision of all disputes between Christians and
Mussulmans, and referring such cases to the medjliss,
threatens to destroy the essentially Turkish institution
of the mehkemes.

In each of the medjliss of Serajevo there are four
or six Mussulmans ; one, sometimes two, Pravoslavs,
one Roman Catholic, and one or two Jews. A knowledge of Turkish is necessary, as the proceedings
are wholly conducted in that language. The influence
of the non-Mussulmans is very small, and the office is
most unpopular among the Pravoslavs, on account of the
contempt with which they are liable to be treated by the
Mussulman majority. Such being the state of things,
the position of the Christian towards the Mussulman
remains intolerable. The hereditary insolence of the
Mussulman Bosnian is met by the hereditary cringing of
the rayah. It will take some generations of another
system than the present to restore to the rayah the
virtues of the free. As an instance of Turkish insolence,
under the eyes of the European consuls in Serajevo,

where the Turks are on their best behaviour, I will give the following anecdote. A dervish, named Hadji Loya, met in the road near the town of Serajevo, a Pravoslav priest on horseback. He ordered him to dismount, telling him, "Bosnia is still a Mahommedan country; do you not see that a Turk is passing? Dismount instantly!" Three different times he met the same priest, and obliged him to get off his horse. This dervish also forced a whole wedding party of Roman Catholics to pass him on foot. This happened in 1871, and that same year, in Serajevo itself, a Christian boy of eighteen was stabbed by a Mussulman, who escaped in the midst of the market-place, in the presence of numerous Turks and zapticś.

I used to find it very difficult to obtain circumstantial accounts of Turkish cruelties which I heard of as perpetrated in the distant parts of the country which I had not visited. I know that so recently as the spring of 1875, in the immediate neighbourhood of Serajevo, a rayah was tied barefoot to an Aga's cart, and made to run behind it. This was told me by a terrified eye-witness under strict promises of secrecy. The wretched Christians were too terrified to speak, for Turkish vengeance would have too surely pursued the reporters. When I complained to one of the more intelligent among the fugitives of the difficulty which I had found in Bosnia in getting the Christians to speak openly to me, he answered: "Why, we dared not complain to one another; how, then, should we tell strangers what happened? I did not dare to tell my friend, lest he should quarrel with me and betray me, or get drunk and repeat what I had said. The Turks would have marked me as a dangerous man, and I should have been imprisoned on some excuse or other, or have been put out of the way." I said to him: "Well, at least you

may tell me now you are on Austrian ground and the
Turks cannot hear you." In the course of our conversation he spoke as follows : " The extortions of
the tax-gatherers and the Begs (land-owners) and the
irregular exactions of the zaptiés (police officers) have
reached a point never known before. What with the
eighth paid to the government, the third or half to the
Beg, the tax in exemption of military service, the taxes
for pigs, cattle, and everything we have and have not,
there remains nothing for us villagers to live upon. I
have seen men driven into pigsties and shut up there in
cold and hunger until they paid, hung up from the
rafters of their houses with their heads downwards in
the smoke, until they disclosed where their little stores
were hidden. I have known them hung up from trees,
and water poured down them in the freezing cold ; I
have known them fastened barefoot to run behind the
Beg's cart ; I have known women and maidens at
work in the fields suffer the extreme of brutal violence, or be forcibly carried off to Turkish houses. If
we complained or reported, we were imprisoned or put
to death."

Now, the same true and horrid tale I have heard
repeated again and again of deeds recurring throughout
the length and breadth of the land. These were causes
enough, indeed, to account for the rising. Encouraged,
no doubt, it was by promises of help from without ; and
by so-called Serbian emissaries and agitators, who,
however, to my certain knowledge, were native Bosnians
and Herzegovinians living in exile in Serbia and Austria.
The inhabitants of the Serbian principality are of the
same race and speech as the Bosnians, and the Serbs
dwelling in Austria are all exiles, of a more or less
recent date, from the countries conquered by the Turks.
In the neighbourhood of Pakrac, in Slavonia, we found

the whole Serb or Pravoslav population mindful of their
Bosnian origin, and for the most part looking forward to
the time when they shall leave the fever-stricken districts between the Save and the Drave, and return to
their own beautiful land, to the "Bosna ponosna," the
"lofty Bosnia," of their songs.

CHAPTER II.

TOWARDS the end of July, 1875, we left England to return to our school established at Serajevo for the purpose of training female teachers. We intended to make a recruiting expedition through some parts of the country which we had not yet visited, our plan being to induce the Serb communities in different parts of the country to send one or more girls to be educated as schoolmistresses, each for her own native place.

At Vienna we saw General Zach, the adjutant of the Prince of Serbia, who apprised us that the revolt in the Herzegovina was likely to become serious, that it would probably extend into Bosnia northward along the Dalmatian frontier into Turkish Croatia, and would spread simultaneously along the Serbian frontier and throughout the mountainous districts. He added that it would be impossible for the princes of Serbia and Montenegro to restrain their subjects from rushing to the aid of their brethren in race and religion. He urged us not to venture into Bosnia at a time when the desperate rising of the crushed and abject Bosnian Christians would call forth a terrible vengeance from the armed and fanatical Mahommedan population.

On the Save steamer we conversed with a Hungarian doctor in the Turkish service, on his way to rejoin the cavalry regiment at Banjaluka. He was of opinion that the rising would become "schrecklich ernst." The causes were deep and widespread. He knew the country too well to repeat fables about foreign instigation; but he related with the freshness of an eye-witness the ever-recurring facts of the intolerable oppression exercised by the farmers of the taxes, of the bribery, corruption, and extortion, systematic among the Turkish officials.

We visited Turkish Gradishka under the guidance of Vaso Vidević, a native Bosnian merchant, and the leader of the deputation to Vienna in 1873 to entreat protection from the Emperor. We were paddled over the river in one of the long narrow Save canoes, hollowed out of the trunk of a tree, and found ourselves once more amid the Oriental barbarism, the dirt, squalor, and misery which everywhere mark the frontier line of the Asiatic encroachments into Europe. The houses are built almost entirely of wood, here and there varied with plaster, and their condition was ruinous. In the tcharsia, or bazaar, were sitting turbaned Turks, cross-legged, in their shops, before the usual paltry stores of water-melons, Manchester cottons, leather shoes, rice, sugar, clay pipes, and little coffee cups. At last we came to a shop of European aspect, with counters arranged within, and the name Bozo Ljubojevićh, painted in bright colours without. This was the shop of the richest Christian merchant in the place, one of those who had been obliged to flee into Austria two years before. He owned the largest house in the village, a very respectable building surrounded by a garden. Here we sat talking with his wife and family, served with coffee and sweetmeats. In 1873 armed Turks surrounded the house, insisting that ammunition was concealed there, and they made a rude but fruitless search. This house has been now completely sacked and demolished; the whole family are in exile in Austria, and Ljubojević is a ruined man. In the poor little church Vaso showed us with pride a bell, which the brave Christians of Gradishka had dared to hang up in accordance with their rights : the only bell in any Orthodox church in Bosnia which could be heard from the outside. The Mussulmans would not tolerate the sound. But Vaso boasted that their bell could be heard even across the Save. Close to the church was a school, and on a plot of ground belonging to the community they were going to build shops, the rent of which would help them with their girls' school. At that time the town contained 150 Orthodox, 50 Latin, and 500 Turkish houses.

The next day we drove to Banjaluka, four hours distant, across a level plain, surrounded by hills, along the best road I have ever seen in Bosnia. At a short distance from the town we crossed the tramway of that fragment of railway which had been completed between Banjaluka and Novi. It has now been wholly destroyed, the bridges thrown down and rails torn up.

We paid a visit to a Bosnian family to whom we had brought a letter. The father, then absent, was one of the principal merchants in the place. The mother was an Austrian Slāv, a native of New Gradishka ; the daughters, who were beautiful girls, had been educated by governesses from Austria, and are now married to Serb merchants, living in Belgrade. It was evident, with all their courtesy and real pleasure at seeing friends, that they were no little troubled at our coming. They told us that any intercourse with strangers rendered them objects of suspicion to the Turks. The father of the family had been seized and imprisoned in 1873, solely because he was on intimate terms with the then Austrian vice-consul, who was known to be friendly to the Christians, and eager to inform himself about their condition. They said that to avoid persecution they had requested the new Austrian vice-consul not to come to the house ; that a Mussulman who had been long in their service had warned them to be exceedingly on their guard, and that they felt their lives and property were not safe. How much worse was it with the poor peasant, fleeced by the Mahommedan landowner, by the tax-gatherer, and by the native priest and Greek bishop, till nothing remains to him but the bare life ! His food is the coarsest black bread, boiled beans, and maize : meat he does not taste once a year. In reply to our inquiries, they told us they had known instances of girls being carried off by Mussulmans in the villages in the neighbourhood of Banjaluka, but the cases were not so frequent now ; though much that happened in the distant villages no one heard of.

Immediately after we left a zaptié came to the house, to inquire who we were and what we had come for. On our way to the inn we were met by another zaptié, who ordered us immediately to appear before the Turkish authorities. I replied that we were English ladies, and should do no such thing ; and, producing our passport, told him to take it to the governor immediately, and to say that we must be supplied with an escort to Travnik the next day. The man said " Peki " (very well), and went off. Just then appeared the Turkish doctor, our friend of the Save steamer, who immediately went to the konak, to secure us a suitable guard for the journey.

Further information, however, as to the detestable condition of the hilly road between Banjaluka and Travnik, reported movements of Turkish redif (land-wehr) about the country, together with the intense heat of the weather, decided us to give up the new route, and return to Gradishka, to take the steamer to Brod ; much as we regretted the loss of a visit to the lake

scenery of Bosnia, and the old historic fortress and castle
of Jaica.

The day after we left Banjaluka, Sunday, 15th August,
commenced the rising in North Bosnia, at Kosarać, in
the district of Priedor, and in the neighbourhood of
Gradishka. We first heard of it on the Monday morning, when at an early hour the two girls of the family we
had visited at Banjaluka appeared at the door of our
room in the inn at Austrian Gradishka, telling us their
mother had sent them away in the middle of the night
with all the children and those of a neighbouring family
to join their relations in Austria. They reported that
"a Christian had killed a Turkish tax-gatherer," and
that "Turks and Christians were now killing one another
in the fields." Vaso Videvich had been with us the afternoon of the preceding day, and he knew nothing then of
what was taking place. He had told me a few days previously that the rayahs in North Bosnia could do
nothing, that they were too weak to join the Herzegovinian example, and that they had no arms and no
Montenegro to help them. Now we saw him earnestly
consulting with some Bosnians in the garden of the
inn. He was going away by the steamer, and he
would never return to Turkish Gradishka. We found
some months afterwards that he was then taking his
whole wealth to purchase guns for the Christians. He
conveyed these guns to Gradishka in Save boats, but the
landing was ill arranged, and as the boats had lain there
two or more days, it being perfectly well known that
arms were on board, the officials were obliged to seize
them. They were confiscated, and are to this day
lying in the Austrian fortress at Gradishka. The same
thing happened again and again. We heard that quan-
tities of ammunition were confiscated, notwithstanding
the readiness of every Slāv official along the Austrian

frontier to wink at the transmission of arms for the
insurgents.   On one occasion the poor fellows had contrived to store some powder on an island in the river.
It got damp; they spread it out to dry, it caught fire,
and several men were killed or badly hurt.   Another
time they had made a wooden cannon, which they
crammed so full of powder that it burst, killing one
man and wounding several.   What could be expected
from peasants who were wholly unaccustomed to the use
of firearms, and absolutely illiterate and unskilled ?   It
is only surprising that the armies of the Porte have not
been able long ago to put down the revolt of unarmed
and ignorant peasants, but the rising is now stronger
than ever,* and the Bosnian rayahs, who are apt to
learn and keen-witted, now know better how to handle
their weapons.

But to return to our own narrative.   On board the
steamer we found the Croatian *avocat*, Dr. Berlić,
returning home to Brod.   He had come that morning
from Sisseg, and he told us that at a short distance from
Gradishka, on the Turkish bank of the Save, he had
seen from the deck of the steamer women and children
hiding in the bushes at the water's edge, and peasants
running to and fro with hoes and spades in their hands.
Certainly the rising had commenced.   Vaso Vidević,
pale as death, called us down into the cabin, and

---

* " The capital error in Europe was the not aiding and encouraging the Turkish
provinces to rise entirely and simultaneously, and helping them even, if necessary,
in their self-liberation, as she has helped the Turks, with arms and means, leaving
the discipline of war and military organization to establish the bases of political
organization.   The process would have been costly, but would have been pro-
fitable in the end; for it would have made of these slaves, men, as it has, to a
certain extent, done in Herzegovina and Bosnia would have brought forward
their natural chiefs and established a moral authority of the highest importance
in the new state of things.   War and death are not so dreadful as slavery and
corruption; and *it remains to be seen if the solution to be adopted will not in the end
cost more bloodshed than the natural solution by a general insurrection.*"—" *Herzegovina and the late Uprising.*"   By W. J. STILLMAN.   Longmans.   1877.

implored us, with tears, not to go to Serajevo; persisting that it was highly dangerous to attempt the journey, and that the Austrian post-cart would very likely be fired at in the night. We told him, encouragingly, it might prove a very good thing for their cause if two English ladies were killed. To which he replied, "Yes; but not you." He was quite right in expecting the disturbances would spread eastward towards Brod. Many women and children were killed a few days afterwards at Kobash, near which place three Christians were impaled* two months later. A fierce Beg, named Osman Aga, from Dervend, on the post-road to Serajevo, sallied forth and effectively checked for a time the rising in that neighbourhood by the massacre of many defenceless men, women, and children. Corpses were seen floating down the Save, and were cast on the sand of the island near Brod. The body of a man was brought on shore at Brod, and was found on examination by the town doctor to be terribly burnt across the chest. This poor victim had suffered one of the well-known Turkish tortures, which consists of heaping burning coals on the breast. These horrors took place a day or two after we reached Serajevo. We left Brod in the post-cart August 17th, travelled through the night and the following day in

---

* "In the month of October, 1875, after the Turks had been two or three times defeated by the insurgents at Srbač and in the hills of Motaica, returning enraged and infuriated, they cut in pieces four peaceful Christian inhabitants, in the villages of Vlamka and Brusnika, named Simo Vrsoika, Marco Guzoica, Stevan Vrovać, and Jovan Lepir; and three they impaled alive on stakes on the banks of the Save above Kobash, opposite the Austrian churchyard and church of Kloster, namely, Mihail Snegotinać and his brother Aleksa Snegotinae, and Luka Drajevic, all three from the village Kaoč, in Bosnia, above Kobash. To this testify Kuzman Skolnik and Bozo Davidovish, who behold it with their own eyes, and there are many others who will not give their names.

"(Signed)   VASO VIDEVIĆ."

The impalement witnessed by Canon Liddon and Rev. M. McColl was no solitary instance on the banks of the Save.

safety, slept at Kiseljak in the khan (where I remember
being awakened at midnight by angry Turkish women
flinging charcoal in at our open window), and reached
Serajevo August 19th.

Our arrival was unexpected, and never had the aspect
of the house, and the garden, and the whole little
establishment been so encouraging. The holidays were
over, and we found pupils and teachers at work in the
school-room, three new girls having been just brought
from Nova Varosh, on the Serbian frontier.

Mr. Consul Holmes was absent, having accompanied
his friend Dervish Pasha to Mostar, the Turkish head-
quarters in the Herzegovina. The aspect of affairs was
considered very grave by the acting-consul, Mr. Freeman. Our Austrian friends held civil war to be
imminent, and the wife of the Austrian consul-general,
on the excuse of the illness of her mother, was on the
point of starting with her little boy. Scarcely any
regular troops were left in the town, every available
man having been sent off to the Herzegovina. The
Mahommedans of Serajevo are three times as numerous
as the Christians, and are many of them exceedingly fanatical. They had sworn that it should go hard with the
Christians in the town unless the rising in Bosnia was
soon quelled. The defence of the place was almost
wholly entrusted to some companies of the redif,
composed of native Bosnian Mussulmans. The redif
were being called out all over the country, and companies of fierce and wild-looking recruits on their way
to the barracks were constantly passing our windows
shouting their war-songs. One of the most cruel Bosnian Begs of Serajevo, Cengić Aga,* who had large
properties in the Herzegovina, had started to form a

* Happily for the Christians, this Cengić Aga was wounded early in the
insurrection, and died of his wounds at Mostar.

troop of Mahommedan volunteers, that is, to collect a band of licensed and fanatical marauders.

The situation was anything but hopeful. We decided to turn these adverse circumstances to the furtherance of our educational plans and to carry off the most promising of the pupils to continue their training at Prague, in' Bohemia. The consuls assured us it would be impossible at that moment to obtain for these girls, or for any Turkish subjects, the necessary teskeré, or passport ; the authorities were refusing the numerous applications now made, and objected even to women and children leaving the country. Mr. Freeman did, however, obtain the requisite permission, in exchange for a written promise, signed and officially witnessed, that we would bring back these subjects of the Porte to the lands of the Sultan. At the same time we received from the representative of the pasha an earnest request to remain, for our going away would give a bad impression of the inability of the Turks to maintain order. We thought matters too serious to admit of our staying for the sake of keeping up appearances for the Turks, and we therefore effected our departure early on the morning of August 23rd.

We were a party of ten in all, occupying four of the springless carts of the country. Three of our drivers were Mussulmans, the other a most miserable Christian boy in their service, who was always blubbering, and seemed literally terrified out of his wits. On the way we were obliged to take on another cart for the luggage. This was driven by its owner, a Jewish khangee. One of our Mussulman drivers, a black man, who went by the name of "the Arab," got frightfully drunk, and behaved so ill that we appealed to the kaimakam at Shebsche to put him in prison. Notwithstanding the order of the kaimakam, at our next halt the Arab appeared again, but he had been frightened into behaving himself better, and we had no further trouble with him. Another of the Mussulman drivers, a Turkish boy of sixteen, the son of a Bosnian Aga, owner of the horses, proved entirely beyond control. He stopped wherever he chose to stop, or he tore recklessly along the road, flogging his miserable horses and firing off pistols in the air. This boy was after the worst type of Bosnian Mussulmans. He was lank and small, with colourless eyes; wisps of his sandy hair escaped from the red handkerchief which was tied round a dirty white linen cap; his weazened boy's face was old with an expression of mingled cruelty, rapacity, and cunning. The day before we reached Dervend, the zaptiés told us the Turks and Christians were fighting there, and that the Turks were cutting the Christians to pieces; but we need not fear, whatever happened, for they had orders to defend us. These rumours referred to the raid of Osman Aga of Dervend, which I have already mentioned, and which had accomplished its cruel work some days previously. When we passed the next day through the Turkish portion of Dervend, which is on the post-road, all was quiet as the grave. Several times the new zaptiés, who seemed to suspect our sympathy with the Christians, volunteered to tell us about the revolt of the rayah; "Nasha rayah" (our rayah) "had actually dared to rebel, but the Sultan would send a great army to Bosnia along the Save."

Before we reached Brod, still expecting some difficulty in getting the Bosnian girls across, we made them put on European costume, which we had prepared for the occasion before leaving Serajevo. It may have been owing to this disguise that their teskeré, or passport, was never asked for, and we were allowed to cross the river with our whole party into Austrian territory, after a few lazy questions as to the contents of our luggage. A peal of bells from the church in Austrian Brod sounded more cheerily than ever across the water, while we were waiting for the ferry-boat in a golden breadth of evening sunlight. The loveliness of the earth and sky had all along uttered a protest against the odious sights and sounds of human degradation which we witnessed on the way, and the cloudless starlit heavens had invited us to forget the dirt and the disgust of the Turkish shelters. We had spent the nights in a cart, guarded by the zaptiés, and knowing even then but little of the terrible scenes enacted in this beautiful land, to which Humanity is faithless.

CHAPTER III.

ANARCHY, insurrection, terror, massacres, "infernal chaos." More than one-third of the whole Christian population fled over the frontier out of Bosnia into the neighbouring lands—Austria, Serbia, and Montenegro. The number of those who have perished by the sword, the famine, and the pestilence within the land is unreckoned and unknown.

A letter which I have just received from a native Bosnian merchant will best describe the present condition of his wretched country. I can vouch for his trustworthiness. He writes from Austria Slavonia, on the northern frontier of Bosnia:—

" GRADISHKA, $\frac{10}{22}$ *March*, 1877.

" When the Bosnian refugees in Austro-Hungary heard that Serbia had made peace with Turkey they were struck dumb, as if a thunderbolt had fallen from the sky. They ask incessantly, 'What will become of us now? Do the Powers want again to force us under the Turkish yoke? Better each one of us should perish than return on the faith of the Turk.' They ask, 'What Power could have the conscience to wish or dare to drive us back under the Turkish sword, to ignore and forget our two years' struggle, and again hand us over into slavery?' I told them, only to see what they would

D 2

reply, that perhaps Austria would send her armies into Bosnia. They answered, ' Why should we go from one slavery into another ? Better we should slay our wives and children, and all seek death among the bands of the *haïduks* (outlaws), than go from slavery to slavery.' I think you will have already heard this sentiment from the Bosnian Serbs. As for Bosnia, and the Serb (Pravoslav) population of Bosnia, this is the condition to-day, as described to me from genuine sources within the province, and also by some who have saved their lives by flight. There is a complete clearing out of the Serb people of Bosnia, for the Turkish authorities themselves hunt them down, and give full licence to the Bashibazouks and Gipsies, also to the Catholics and the Jews ; and every one is free to kill or do any violence to a Bosnian Serb, or to take away his property, and no Serb dares to make a complaint. They are fleeing incessantly out of Bosnia, wherever they are able. Below Brod, near Vuchijak, a hundred families have crossed over. I spoke with them myself, and asked them, ' Why do you fly, brothers, when here you must perish of hunger ?' Weeping and groaning, they replied they would rather jump into the river than suffer what they have to endure. They said there were a hundred families in Gornje, the half of which had fled into Austria, but afterwards returned at the bidding of the Turks and of the Austrian government, who had assured them of perfect safety. They had been left in peace for some months, but now their sufferings were greater than ever before. They were incessantly harassed by Mussulman bands, composed of the worst murderers and evildoers, who violated women, carried off maidens, and seized whatever property they found. The principal inhabitants of the place had been carried off to Dervend, to Teshan, and to Prnjavor, and had never returned.

" These tidings gave me bitter grief. I said what I
could to comfort them and went on my way to Diakovar.
On my return I visited Austrian Brod, in order to get
further information ; and there again I heard terrible
news. It so happened that I met there a merchant who
is still living at Dervend, the first town on the post road
between Turkish Brod and Serajevo. I asked him what
was going on at Dervend and in the neighbourhood.
He looked very anxiously round to see if any one was
within hearing, and when he was satisfied that we were
alone he went on to tell me that in the course of the last
two months forty-two men, the principal Bosnian Serbs
in the neighbourhood, had been murdered at Dervend.
These butcheries had been perpetrated at night, behind
the Turkish barracks. When the relatives of these men
came to visit them in the prison and to bring them bread
(as is the custom), they were driven away, and told to go
home until the time came to shut them up too. Then
they were also accused, and were sent off to Banjaluka.
I hear now that this is the way the Turks are proceeding
throughout Bosnia. Only to-day I heard that thirty
families from Gashitza and other villages tried to escape
into Austria across the Save below Jassenovatz, but the
Turks came up with them, and murdered those who had
not yet got over; a certain Jovo from the village of
Medjedj was cut to pieces, and his two children flung
into the water. Behold those woes upon woes, and
behold the selfishness and inhumanity of Europe, which
keeps us for centuries in slavery, and is resolved still so
to keep us! There remains nothing for us but to fight.
Better die than live in shame and misery. You know
very well what sort of people are gone from Bosnia to
represent the country at Constantinople. Misery, indeed,
for us! Faim Effendi, from Banjaluka ; Petraki, from
Serajevo ; Ephzem and Marotić, from Travnik, are all

men who, together with the pashas, suck out the life of
the rayah. No pen can describe the evil of the Turkish
government, but the Turcophiles will neither see nor
hear.

"In Bosnia the assessment and collection of the taxes
is carried on in the following manner. Turks on horseback, with alibashis, go by twenties about the villages,
demanding lodging, food, and drink for nothing, com-
mitting every sort of violence on men and women.
Cattle worth 300 piastres have to be sold for 150
piastres in caimés (paper notes), on which the loss is
40 per cent., and the tax is to be paid in silver. The
villagers have thus become so impoverished that about
one-third of them have no live stock remaining, and the
prisons are full of those who cannot pay. The various
dues to the Beys and to the government, and other
oppressive levies, are multiplied from day to day. Without excuse the bimbashis send zaptiés into the villages
to terrify the inhabitants, and in some way or other to
collect a few hundred piastres. For all the misery and
wrong which the Christians are suffering at the hands of
the Turks there is no justice and there are no judges, for
none of the courts will give them a hearing. As for
murders, they are happening every day. The last day
or two there are fresh cases. Mahmoud Muftic, in the
middle of the town, cut off the right hand of Pejo
Savanević. Osman Shabio killed Josef Ervachenin in
his own house, and flung the body into the middle of the
road in the wood. Achmet Asnada killed Jovo Uvković
in the village of Timara, together with another whose
name I do not know. Also Sefto Jakupović, whom
Faim Effendi let go that he might kill and rob the
Christians, killed a housefather in his house in the
village of Timar. In the quarters of the Turkish redif
at Gradishka, he killed a peaceful villager from Koba-

tovéa. Ifish Mlicharević killed the son of the Knez
Ristic in his own house in the village of Miljević.
Numerous like atrocities there are everywhere and
in every place, and for all these misdeeds no one is
answerable to anybody, for the government makes no
inquiry, and will not even hear. Faim Effendi, the
most renowned bloodsucker of the Christians, and the
present representative of Bosnia and the Herzegovina at
Constantinople, has spread a secret proclamation to be
read by night to the Bosnian Mussulmans, in which it is
declared that the Mahommedans will on no account
accept any reforms, but that on the contrary they will
everywhere oppose them with all their might, and that
the utmost violence is to be carried out upon the rayah.
The Turkish government has during the last few days
distributed fresh arms to the Bosnian Mussulmans from
12 to 80 years of age. Three considerable encounters
have taken place in the neighbourhood of Banjaluka, in
the village of Verbać, three-quarters of an hour distant;
in Klashonica, three hours distant; and the third at
Mortanza in Zupa, eight hours from Banjaluka. Also
in the Sandjak of Travnik in the villages of Pechko
and Metko, between Livno and Travnik. We hear
of encounters daily. Numbers are escaping to the
mountains and to the camp of Despotović. Some of
the richer villagers had fled from the country into the
towns to be under the protection of the authorities.
Turkish violence is now driving them all out of the
towns, out of Travnik and Banjaluka, and other towns.
They dare not go into the villages, for the Turks have
taken to disguise themselves as insurgents. The Christians from the towns also are now escaping into
Austria."

The rising was joined at the beginning by Roman
Catholics. They were restrained by their priests, who

received orders from Rome to stand aloof. Dread of the success of Serbia has also been a powerful withholding motive. As a rule, the Roman Catholics have aided the Turkish power in the insurrection; they have played into the hands of the Turks; they have acted as spies; they have gone on patrol with the Turkish soldiers. The rule, however, is not without exception, and at this moment Fra Buonoventura, a Roman Catholic priest, is one of the insurgent leaders in South Bosnia, and other priests, besides the well-known Herzegovinian Mussics, have led their flocks against the Turks.

I have just received the following account from Peter Uzelatz, a trustworthy resident on the Austrian frontier, of what is now passing in South Bosnia. He writes under date March 29:—

"In Ochijevo the Turks have massacred the brothers Vaso and Jefto Karanović, have outraged women and girls, plundered 300 head of cattle, and burnt many houses. In the Klechovaca Mountains the Turks have fallen upon a quiet village, have killed three brothers named Kecman, stolen cattle, and exercised all kinds of brutalities. In the neighbourhood of Glamosh the Turks are attacking quiet Christian villages, and are massacring, plundering, and robbing in every direction. Near Glamosh four brothers Govzdonovic were murdered; their heads were cut off and carried to Glamosh.

"Turkish licence is driving numbers of the Christian population to Austria for safety. The help given by the Austrian government was reduced on March 20 from ten to five kreutzers (1d.) per day. From April 1 it will be given only to women and children and sick persons. Ablebodied men will receive nothing. Help is more necessary than ever at this very time, for it is a moment of the greatest poverty."

The diminution of assistance by the Austrian govern-

ment is intended to check the immigration, and to drive
back the fugitives into their own land. But these poor
people, who have seen from the experience of their own
lives and the lives of their forefathers what Turkish
promises are worth, dare not return, knowing their
certain fate to be massacre and outrage. The result
of the Conference at Constantinople was announced to
the Bosnians in the following manner by Kulinevic
Beg at Vakup, in South-western Bosnia. The proclamation of the Constitution* being read in Turkish
was then explained in Slāv, in the style of the
Bosnian Mussulmans : "It is all quite right and
very good; the Turk rules as before, and the rayah
remains rayah. The Sultan, the Brother of the Sun,
the Cousin of the Moon, Bond-brother of the Stars, the
Friend of Allah, the Kinsman of Mahomet, the Son of

* The correspondent of the *Manchester Guardian*, writing from Ragusa under
date February 9th, gives the following anecdote of the election of a Christian
deputy for the Turkish Parliament :—"At Mostar, where consular supervision
has also to be taken into account, these enlightened employés of the Turkish
government have seized on and forcibly elected a Christian merchant as deputy
for the capital of Herzegovina. The unfortunate Bilich, who was anything but
ambitious of this unexpected honour, was so far intimidated that he dared not
refuse it at Mostar, and was accordingly packed off to Stamboul by way of
Ragusa. The instant, however, he set foot on Christian soil he despatched a
letter to Mostar resigning his seat, and, fearing to return, is at present a refugee
at Ragusa. Truly, it remained for the Turks to discover this new form of elec-
toral intimidation." He goes on to say :—"Meanwhile the Mahommedan population of Herzegovina are becoming more and more dissatisfied with the first-
fruits of the new régime. Among the merchants of the towns ruin has been sown
broadcast by an enormous influx of paper money ; Trebinje alone has been flooded
with a new paper currency to the amount of 100,000 piastres. In the district of
Trebinje, indeed, nothing but the neighbourhood of Turkish nizam has prevented
Mahommedan discontent from bursting into open revolt. According to the law
the heads of families are exempted from military service, but the kaimakam of
Trebinje has been attempting to extort large sums of money, in some cases as
much as 1,000 florins, from the heads of the richest Mahommedan families, in lieu
of military service. Upon their appeal the tyrant tried to seize and imprison
them, but has not been able to set hands on more than a dozen. The rest, to the
number of over a hundred, and among them several Begs and influential land-
owners, have fled, and during the last few days no less than seventy Mahommedan refugees have arrived at Ragusa. Even as I write, I hear of fresh
arrivals."

Osman, Emperor of Emperors, King of Kings, Prince of
Princes, Lord of the Earth under the Sky, has commanded
of those kings who came to him at Stamboul that they
shall drive back for us our rayah into our lands again,
and has decreed that whoever is not obedient on his
return shall be put to death." Before the conclusion of
the Conference, Bosnian Mussulmans had begun to
spread the report that the Sultan would decree the
massacre of every Christian in the land, in order that
Bosnia might be preserved intact for the Faithful.

I have related in the last chapter the story of the
beginning of the Bosnian rising in August, 1875, in
North Bosnia. The following account of the spread of
the insurrection was sent me by Herr Fric, in August,
1876 :—

"The Bosnian insurgents, who are extremely numerous, and in some instances well armed, are for the
most part distributed among the following troops and
bands :

"1. The bands in the Rissovać and Grmeć mountains in West Bosnia. 2. In the Vuejak in East Bosnia.
3. In the Pastirevo and Kozara mountains in North
Bosnia.

"The insurgents in the Rissovać and Grmeć mountains are under the leadership of the well-known Golub
Babić, Marinković, Simo Davidović, Pope Karan, and
Trifko Amelić. Latterly the Serb Colonel Despotović
has assumed the chief command, and has formed eight
battalions out of the scattered bands. In Pastirevo and
in Kozara are the bands of Marko Gjenadija, Ostoja,
Spasojević, Marko Bajalica, Igumen Hadzić, and Pope
Stevo. The new camp of Brezovać, not far from Novi,
is held by Ostoja Vojnovic. The former camp of Peter
Karageorgevic in Chorkovać is held by Ilija Sevic.

"The joint object of these bands at the present

moment is so fully to occupy the Turks as to prevent any greater concentration of Mussulman troops or irregulars on the Drina, on the western frontier of Serbia. As there is no possibility of systematically organizing an insurrection in Bosnia, the mode of warfare peculiar to the land is pursued. . . . . that is, by perpetual harassing to drive back the whole Mussulman population into their towns and strong places. Another object of the insurgent bands is the safe conduct, under cover of their protection, up to the frontier of Austria or Serbia, of the Christians who have escaped from the cruelties of the Turks into the forest mountains of Bosnia. Sometimes these poor exiles—unarmed men, women, and children—have been for months hiding in the woods, until the armed bands could open a way for them through the country into neighbouring Christian lands. They were driven from their homes by savage Mussulman soldiery, who suddenly appeared in their peaceful villages, murdering and plundering, and then setting fire to their houses. It is hard to realise the misery of these flights ; the father loses the son, the mother the daughter ; the young and the feeble perish on the way ; weeks or months go by before the scattered members of a family find one another, and the fate of many is never known. No property, hardly the bare life, can be saved.

"It is especially to be observed that these Turkish onslaughts on Christian villages are not made exclusively by the Mussulman rabble of the land on their own account. These murderous raids are frequently ordered and authorised by the Turkish officials, and the regular troops take part in them.

"On my last journey from Kostainitza to the 'dry frontier,' near Novi, Bosnian fugitives who had just crossed over at Kuljani (between Kostainitza and

Podove), from Svinja on the Save, assured me that large
Mussulman bands led by the recently appointed kaima-
kan of Bihac, Vessel Bey, had fallen on the village of
Svinja and burnt it to the ground. The next day this
account was confirmed to me in the presence of the
Austrian authorities at Dvor by many other fugitives,
who had fled before a similar incursion conducted by the
Turkish Miralay. Driven by the kaimakam Vessel
Bey, and this Miralay overrunning the land, 3,000 to
4,000 fugitives have passed over into Austrian territory,
according to official report.

"With a heavy heart I call to mind the passage of
the fugitives over the Unna at Kuljani, protected by a
very large body of insurgents against an expected on-
slaught of the Turks. The miserable exiles this time
reached the Austrian shore in safety in the little canoes
of the river. What a scene of wretchedness! Hundreds
and hundreds dragging themselves along the dusty road
—men, women, and children. In the heavy despairing
countenances of the tall strong men may be plainly read
the hereditary misery of centuries. Weary women and
little children can scarcely crawl along; some of the sick
(for the most part smallpox cases) fall down by the way.
I go up to a group which is gathering round some object
on the road-side; a woman has been overtaken by the
pains of labour, and, surrounded by her children, is
giving birth to an infant. A few steps further on is
another group; here lies in the last agony a woman who
has been wounded; seven wounds on her body . . . .
Here lie some others slightly wounded, who from pain and
fatigue can crawl no further. Many sink down on the
dusty hard roadside to seek on Christian soil the sleep
to which for nights they had not dared to yield. By
degrees the greater number reach the Gemeinde Haus
in Divari. The whole group sit or lie about on the large

grassy space in front of the building. Some begin to
eat the ears of Indian corn which they have brought
with them out of Turkey; for in the fields on the
Turkish side is still lying Indian corn of last year's
harvest, which neither Turks nor Christians, out of
mutual fear, have dared to gather. Fathers of families
go to seek bread in the village. Some have brought
away a few coins, and can pay for it. Now, a father
returns with some bread, which he divides among his
family; the children watch every mouthful with longing
eyes. Another father returns empty-handed; a cry of
distress bursts forth. Alas! there are hundreds upon
hundreds of such scenes; for fresh bands of fugitives
are crossing daily at one or another point on the frontier
into Austrian territory."

I spent the greater part of 1876 on the Croatian and
Slavonian frontiers of Bosnia, engaged, together with
Miss Johnston, in applying for the benefit of the exiles,
the "Bosnian and Herzegovinian Fugitives and Orphan
Relief Fund."*

Near Kostajnica, on the Croatian military frontier,
Pope Mandic, of Meminiski, told us that he had in
his parish over 2,700 fugitives, the number of inhabitants being 2,400. Thus the fugitives exceeded by
300 the number of inhabitants. The parish is extremely
poor, and the house-room insufficient in ordinary
times. In winter, not only one family, but several
families, composing the *zadruga* or house communion, which prevails in this country, all sleep in one
room round a fire made'in the middle, the smoke of

* Some account of this work will be found at the end of the second volume.
Donations are received by Messrs. Daldy, Isbister & Co., 56, Ludgate Hill; at
Messrs. Twinings' Bank, 215, Strand; by the Clydesdale Bank; the London and
Westminster Bank; by Lady Muir Mackenzie, 8, Eaton Place West; by Mrs. De
Noe Walker, 10, Ovington Gardens, S.W.; and by the Hon. Treasurer, Andrew
Johnston, Esq., 158, Leadenhall Street. The profits of these volumes will be
given to the fund.

which escapes through the rafters of the unceiled dwelling. In common winters there may be found in such houses from twenty to thirty persons sleeping on the ground, round the fire, in this manner; when the poor fugitives were taken in there were sometimes upwards of forty. Was it surprising that first smallpox and then typhus had broken out, and that this priest had sometimes ten burial services a day to perform ? Then there were newborn babies for whom their parents had no clothing, and for whom, when born on the flight, their fathers had cut up their stockings to make some sort of little covering for them.

The Bosnians' love of their own country is very great; they remain as close to the frontier as they can, within sight of their own hills. One poor man came from a distant village to Kostajnica, and crossed the bridge on to the narrow strip of land by the Austrian fortress on the other side to breathe his native air. "The air of Bosnia," he said, "smells like a rose." We heard from one and all the fugitives the same story—their houses are burnt, they escaped for their lives from the Turks, and they will never go back so long as the Turk rules there. The Bosnian villages, at a distance from the frontier, which had never risen, were frightfully plundered and maltreated by Turkish soldiers, regular and irregular, and by the native Mussulmans. We were told, on thoroughly trustworthy authority, that the former practice of the Turks was again resorted to of hanging up the rayah to a tree with his head downwards and pouring water over him, in the freezing weather, till he reveals the place where his little hoard of coin is hidden. At the present moment no Christian's life or property is safe in Bosnia, except under the eyes of the European consuls in Serajevo. The land is a desert. We hear from numerous Bosnians that three sowing seasons have passed, and nothing has been sown except in the gardens belonging to the towns. The fields are bare ; the Turkish villages have been destroyed by the insurgents; the Christian villages by the Turks. Large tracts of country are absolutely depopulated. An enormous number of Mussulman widows and children are left, for the Christian Bosnian insurgents do not harm women and children, but let them go safe "in the name of Christ and St. John." On the other hand, the treatment of the Christian women by the Turks is now well known. The "Bulgarian atrocities" have been repeated again and again in Bosnia, from time to time, on a small scale, in different parts of the country ever since the beginning of the uprising.

In January, 1877, we went to the Dalmatian frontier of Bosnia, where the greatest distress prevails, and where there have been many deaths from sheer starvation. At this moment over one third of the whole Christian population of Bosnia and Herzegovina are in most miserable exile; the number of fugitives all round the frontier very considerably exceeds 200,000. The magnitude of the misery has been impressed upon us, eye-witnesses, by the constant repetition of the same scenes all through these many months, and along the extent of so many hundred miles. We found in the neighbourhood of Knin in Dalmatia the same misery, in a still greater degree, which we had left in the distant Slavonian district; we heard the same changes on the same sad story over and over again: "Our homes have been burned by the Turks, our crops destroyed; we fled for the bare life ; we could save nothing, or we have spent all we were able to save. Our children are dying of hunger and sickness, but we will all rather perish here than return to encounter the armed and angry Turks." From whatever quarter you may approach the Bosnian and Herzegovinian boundaries, be it from Serbia or Montenegro, from Slavonia, Croatia or Dalmatia, you will find the same throng of ragged starving fugitives. They are in a worse condition than last winter, and the mortality among them is very great.

Mr. Arthur Evans thus describes a scene on the frontier :—

"We approached the Bosnian frontier by way of the village of Strmica, about which as many as 6,000 refugees are crowded. I had never come in contact with so much human misery before. They crowded round us, these pinched haggard faces, these lean bony frames, scarred by disease and bowed down with hunger; they followed till it seemed a dreadful Dance of Death. There was one lad of twelve, as pale as a spectre, who could not live many hours; and by him another younger child, whose only clothing was a few rags tied together and eked out by the long tresses of a woman's hair. Some English help has already reached Strmica, but in many cases it had come too late, and in this village alone over 500 have died in the last few months. A little further on the mountain side we came upon a new graveyard already well tenanted. We now crossed the Bosnian frontier, and followed a path along a precipitous mountain steep, passing the débris of a stupendous landslip, and beneath some extraordinary rock pinnacles, called "the Hare Stones" by the Bosnians. Near here we saw the first signs of Turkish ravages—the village of Zaseok burnt by the Turks at the first outbreak of the insurrection; and presently found an old Bosnian, who guides us by more difficult mountain paths to a lonely glen, where a torrent divides the Austrian from the Bosnian territory, and where, on the Christian side, we descried a series of caves in the rocky mountain side, to which

we now made our way. Then indeed broke upon
my sight such a depth of human misery as it has
perhaps fallen to the lot of few living men to witness.
We crossed a small frozen cataract, and passed the
mouths of two lesser caverns, toothed with icicles three
feet long and over, and then we came to the mouth of a
larger cave, a great black opening in the rock, from
which, as we climbed up to it, crawled forth a squalid
and half-naked swarm of women, children, and old men,
with faces literally eaten away with hunger and disease.
A little way off was another small hole, outside which
leant what had once been a beautiful girl, and inside,
amidst filth and squalor which I cannot describe, dimly
seen through smoke and darkness, lay a woman dying of
typhus. Others crowded out of black holes and nooks,
and I found that there were about thirty in this den. In
another small hole, going almost straight down into the
rock, I saw a shapeless bundle of rags and part of the
pale half-hidden face of another woman stricken down by
the disease of hunger ; another den with about a dozen, and
then another more horrible than any. A black hole, sloping downwards at so steep an angle as made climbing
up or down a task of some difficulty, descended thus
abruptly about thirty feet, and then seemed to disappear
into the bowels of the earth. The usual haggard crowd
swarmed out of the dark and fœtid recesses below and
climbed up to seek for alms. A woman seated on a
ledge of rock half way up burst into hysterical sobs ; it
was at the sight of old Lazar. The good old fellow had
already discovered these dens of destitution, and had
brought them some food from the English ladies all the
way from Knin. They had tasted nothing then for three
days, and would have all died that day, she said, if he
had not come. Then, slowly tottering and crawling
from an underground lurking place at the bottom of the

pit, there stumbled into the light an old man, so lean, so
wasted, with such hollow sunken eyes, that he seemed
nothing but a walking skeleton ; it was the realisation
of some ghastly mediæval picture of the Resurrection of
the Dead ! He seemed to have lost his reason, but from
below he stretched out his bony hands towards us as if
to grasp our alms, and made a convulsive effort to climb
the rocky wall of his den. He raised himself with difficulty a few feet, and then fell back exhausted and was
caught by a girl in her arms. Poor old man ! It was
not hard to see that he would never leave that loathsome
den alive ; nay, I dare not say that those horrible recesses were not catacombs as well. Not far off we
passed another cave, where the bodies of some women
and children had been found."

Insurgent bands are again making sign from mountain
and forest throughout the land. The rising has acquired
compact strength in a district of South Bosnia, which is
cleared of the Turks and held by Bosnian bands, who are
at present under the command of Despotović, between
the Austrian frontier and the Turkish fortresses of
Kulin Vakup, Kljuc, and Glamosh. This district was
visited, in February last, by Mr. Arthur Evans, who
has fully confirmed, by the evidence of his own eyes,
the accounts I have heard from many native Bosnians.
He says the bulwark of this insurgent territory, to the
east, is the great mountain range of Cerna Gora, or the
Black Mountains, so that there literally exists at this
moment a Bosnian Montenegro. " The fields and fertile
lands of the peasants are circled, like a fortified town,
by mountain walls, and often approachable only by difficult mountain portals. When this fact is appreciated,
you will understand the great capabilities of defence
possessed by a country whose mountain strongholds contain fertile fields, where corn may be sown and harvests

gathered in. Against the Turkish towns the insurgents
may show themselves weak; but, with ordinary leaders,
they could defy the invader for generations in their
mountain fastnesses. They are themselves beginning to
appreciate their defensive strength, and the importance of
dividing their energies between agriculture and defence;
but during the period when the insurrection was confined to a few villages on the Dalmatian frontier, the
Turks had penetrated into their secluded uplands, and
several villages had been burnt." . . . .

"The district of Podić runs apparently in an undefined
manner into that of Vidovoselo, to the north-west of this
polje, and the whole of this district has been ravaged by
the Turks in a most atrocious manner. As I have no
wish to indulge in loose and unsubstantiated charges, I
may say that I have taken down the accounts of three
sets of witnesses. First, of the peasants, a man and a
woman at the hut at Podić; secondly, of two peasants
of Vidovoselo, by name Stojan Vasović and Gavran
Tadić, whom I saw at Unnatz, and who actually witnessed what occurred from a wood above the village
where they had hidden themselves; and lastly, from
Boian Sterbać, who was horribly cut in the neck by a
blow from a yataghan and his left hand nearly severed,
and who lies at present in the insurgent hospital at Knin,
where I saw him, and whose deposition and extraordinary signature I have before me. All these accounts
agree in the minutest particular, and I do not think
that even the Turks themselves would call them in
question. On the 12th July of last year, about two in
the afternoon, the peasants of this district were peace-
fully engaged in their fields, when a large band of
Bashi-bazouks from Glamosh, under the leadership of
Ahmed Beg Philipović, of that place, broke into the
polje. They hunted down and killed—some on the

E 2

plain and some in the houses—twenty-three unarmed peasants, nine of the village of Podić and fourteen of Vidovoselo. I have the names and families of all the victims before me. Among them were two children, one of five years old and the other about ten. The village pope, Damian Sterbać, was hacked to pieces; his wife, Stana Sterbać, was cut with yataghans about the breast; and his daughter Militéa was wounded in the arm. The villages were first plundered and then burnt, and the Turks made off to Glamosh, carrying with them the heads of most of their victims. The hut we were in was saved from burning by the timely appearance of an insurgent band on the height above. A party of Bashibazouks were engaged in plundering the cottage when they caught sight of the enemy, and as unarmed peasants and women were their game, and not armed men, they decamped in a hurry."

I have a list of the names of these victims, and the signatures of some of the eye-witnesses whom I saw at Knin, among others of Boian Sterbać, whose scars are a frightful confirmation of his almost incredible story of escape, after being left for dead on the ground.*

* I give a translation of this statement: "On the 12th of July, 1876, Turks from Glamosh found peaceful villagers at work in the fields. They killed them all with the exception of the undersigned, whom they wounded terribly with a jatagan about the neck and hands. He lay on the ground, the Turks counting him for dead; when they were at a distance hunting other villagers along the fields, his wife and neighbours came, and carried him off, that he might tell it to the world, and relate the names of his murdered companions. The undersigned is the witness of this deed, and he writes with his own wounded and maimed body; other witnesses also sign who beheld the deed with their own eyes. *Murdered*—Pope Damjan Sterbać, Aleksa, Golub, Gliso Ilija, Vid, Nikola, Lazo Sterbać, Todo, Mijat and Stanko Vestica, Vaso and Ilija Knezevic, Sava Srećić Sava Tomic, Luka Mandic, Mijo, Pane, David, Jovan Radanovic, Peter Radun, Gavro Jovic, Vid Radun. *Left Wounded*—Stana Sterbać, wife of the pope, Milica, his daughter, Gliso Srećić, Kuzman Sterbać.

"(Witnesses)
○ BOJAN STERBAC.
+ VASILJ KNEZEVIC.
× JOVAN TOMIC.
× IVAN VJESTICA.

"For the other wounded, above-named who cannot write, signs

"Unatz, 13*th February*, 1877.   T. SUDIEVICH."

No correct estimate can be formed of the numerical and military strength of the Bosnian insurgents. It is said that Despotović can summon 5,000 armed Bosnians, not counting other bands in Kraina, Kosarać, and elsewhere, who are not under his command. It is certain that the whole Pravoslav population would to a man join the insurgent ranks if they had arms. " We cannot fight the Turks with our pipes," said tall strong men whom we saw hanging listlessly and moodily about the frontiers, among the old men, women, and children, who are living on the scanty pittance doled out by the charity of the Austrian government. One of our hardest tasks lay in the absolute necessity we were under to refuse to assist them in any way with arms and ammunition. To have done so would have been to compromise our whole special work of education and relief. But it was impossible to resist the conviction that if the Christians had had arms last spring they would soon have learned to use them and have settled their own affairs for themselves.

In any proposal of Turkish disarmament it should be remembered that the Mussulman Bosnians have been recently supplied by the Porte with fresh arms for the defence of Islam after the approved method, and that it will be practically impossible to disarm them except in the presence of a superior force. The Mussulman population is armed to the teeth, and is even now carrying out the extermination of the Pravoslav inhabitants—that is, of the industrious, enterprising, and independent majority of the population of Bosnia.

CHAPTER IV.

SALONICA IN 1863.

" The admirable situation of Thessalonica, and the fertility of the surrounding country, watered by several noble rivers, still enables it to nourish a population of upwards of sixty thousand souls. Nature has made it the capital and seaport of a rich and extensive district, and under a good government it could not fail to become one of the largest and most flourishing cities on the shores of the Mediterranean."—FINLAY's *History of the Byzantine Empire*, p. 317.

THE reader is now requested to go back into the quiet times of Turkey in Europe, and to start on a journey through Southern Bulgaria, Old Serbia, Northern Albania and Montenegro.

We first reached Salonica at the end of May, 1863, and had our best view of it from the deck of the steamer. But though cities that rise in amphitheatre round a bay are always most favourably seen from the sea, a Turkish city has a charm of its own whatever its situation, and looked at from what point you please. True to the pastoral instinct of his ancestors, the Turk ever seeks to absorb the prosaic town into the poetry of nature; he multiplies spires to atone for roofs, and wherever he builds a house he plants a tree. For the ground indeed he cares not, provided his horse be good, so in roughness his street outdoes a quarry, and in filth exceeds the wallowing-ground of swine. But potent is the magic of outward beauty. After a time one consents that nose and feet should suffer offence; if only, when the labours of the day are over, one may recline on the cool, flat house-roof, and feast one's eyes on masses of white and green, pierced by taper cypresses and glistening minarets.

Salonica has several points that repay a ride; among others the Fortress of the Seven Towers, which stands on the site of the ancient Acropolis, and commands a glorious view, bounded by Mount Olympus. But the citadel itself is in a very tumble-down condition, and the dwelling houses within its walls are mostly deserted.

The Chaoush Monastery stands also on a height above the town and offers healthy quarters for a traveller. Its monks live in somewhat ignoble comfort, for their convent was left standing and endowed with privileges as reward for one of its former inhabitants having betrayed the neighbouring castle to the Turks. The present caloyers are Greeks of that servile type which sets many an Englishman against the whole race; nothing could be more honeyed than their flatteries of England, because it was then popularly expected that she would transfer her patronage from Turkey to Greece.

As the precious things in the convent were almost all presents from Russia, it was necessary to explain this away; the monks did so by saying that the Czar had given them in exchange for relics of inestimable worth. For instance, a service of communion plate and a costly book were said to have been received in exchange for a gourd out of which our Saviour drank at the Last Supper, or, as others say, at the Well of Samaria. "Look!" said the Greek, "they gave us miserable gold for a treasure that kingdoms could not buy; they received from us a skin of oil and in return have sent us a single olive." Finally, it was declared that "if England will only protect us, she may count on our eternal devotion."

On the way down the hill we passed through the burying-place of the city. The Franks have secured themselves graves between those of the Turks and the walls. On the other side of the Turks lie the Jews, "that they may be obliged to carry their dead furthest from the town." The whole ground is unenclosed, and desecrated by asses and dogs. Some time ago a violent thunder shower washed the earth from an ancient sarcophagus which was found by the French consul and sent off to Paris.

The antiquities of Salonica occupied two days' sight-seeing, and no kinder nor more persevering cicerone can be wished than the Scottish missionary. Almost every street, every fountain, shows fragments of coloured marbles and sculptured stones; and on the Vardar Gate and Arch of Constantine* may still be seen the processions of Roman triumphs. Among the principal objects of interest we may enumerate the churches of the Twelve Apostles, St. Sophia, and St. Demetrius; the pulpit wherein St. Paul is supposed to have preached; the so-called Rotunda; the remnants of a sculptured *bema* outside the Rotunda; and the five figures (called by the Jews *incantadas*) which formed the propylæum of the hippodrome. Except the two latter relics, which, though ruined, are not transformed, all that is of the pagan period has been byzantinized, and all that was Byzantine has been mahommedanized; so that while much may be traced to interest the antiquary, there is scarce beauty enough left to delight the unprofes-

---

* "The Egnatian way, which for many centuries served as the high road for the communications between Rome and Constantinople, formed a great street passing in a straight line through the centre of the city from its western to its eastern wall. This relic of Roman greatness, with its triumphal arches, still forms a marked feature in the Turkish city; but the moles of the ancient fort have fallen to ruin, and the space between the sea-wall and the water is disfigured by a collection of filthy huts."—FINLAY's *Byzantine Empire*, p. 317.

sional traveller. Perhaps the Christian who spoilt a classic temple in the attempt to render it cruciform, may be deemed as barbarous as the Mussulman who turned the cathedral of St. Demetrius into a mosque; but the latter achievement has had results so grotesque that we cannot forbear enumerating them.

The nave is supported by columns of precious marble; but these the Turk has painted green, and their capitals strawberry and cream colour. Icons and candles he has banished, and in their stead strings up ostrich eggs to ward off the evil eye; also garlands of little lamps, which look fairy-like by night, but wherein by day the oil floats cold and brown. The altar has been hurled from its site, but thereabouts stands the pulpit of the imaum, with its narrow stair and extinguisher canopy. A little side chapel is purged of its idolatries, and instead crammed with old mats, rubbish, and tools. As for the name and superscription of St. Demetrius, these must be sought on one of the doorsteps, but the tiny cell containing his tomb is respected and ostentatiously shown. This distinction it owes to its miraculous exudations, which attract hosts of Christian pilgrims, and bring to its Mussulman guardian a regular income of bakshish.[*]

But the real curiosity of Salonica is its population, that strange medley of antipathetic races. The Therma of ancient history and the Thessalonica of St. Paul's Epistles yields at present the curious instance of a city historically Greek, politically Turkish, geographically Bulgarian, and ethnographically Jewish.[†] Out of about 60,000 inhabitants some 40,000 are Hebrews;

---

[*] The Sahatli mosque is now notorious as the scene of the massacre, May 6, 1876, of the French and German consuls by a Mussulman mob.

[†] The number of Jews at Salonica is estimated (1863) at 40,000, but with their usual astuteness they contrive to avoid being taxed individually, and the community bribes the Turkish officials to let them pass without scrutiny for no more than 11,500.

and these, the most numerous citizens, are also the most
wealthy and considered. They came, like most of the
Jews in Turkey, from Spain, whence they were expelled
by the Inquisition, and the comparative tolerance
showed them by the Sultan renders them his good
subjects. The Hebrews settled in Salonica are handsome, many of them auburn-haired, and their women
often delicate, and even fair. In beauty the latter
exceed the Hellene, which now-a-days is not saying
so much, for, at least in Europe, the modern Greek
woman falls short alike of the softness and fire of the
Oriental and the refinement and loftiness of the Western
lady.

Like most other numerous communities, the Salonican
Jews are divided into three ranks—the tip-top, the
middle, and the low. Of these the foremost, by their
wealth and luxury, absolutely extinguish their Christian
neighbours. The French consul, Marquis de ——,
told us that for him and his wife society was out of the
question. All the richest people are Jews. If they
give a dinner, friends and relatives lend each other plate
and other trappings, so that the pomp is overpowering,
and in return one cannot receive them in any way that
would not appear *mesquin*. Then, if one gives parties,
the Jewish ladies come so apparelled that the Europeans
feel *gênées* in meeting them : " on finirait par n'avoir que
des Juives chez soi." The opinion of the French consul
was shared by one of our English acquaintances. She
would willingly have shown us some of these Hebrew
dames, whom she described as accomplished and beautiful ; " but the fact is," said she, " that my new summer
gown has not yet come from London ; and though in
you, as a traveller, they might excuse a plain dress, I
should not dare to go among them otherwise than spick
and span."

The middle class of Jews are also rich, but less exacting in matters of toilette, so no obstacle existed to our visiting them. The first family we saw was that of a rabbi, and more interesting than others, as retaining some remnants of traditional habits and costume. The daughters had muslin dresses made in the European style, but their long hair hung loose down their backs. On marriage the hair is cut off, and the matrons wear a small turban fastened with a black handkerchief, which is passed under the chin and tied on the top of the head. The rabbi himself appeared in a sort of long loose coat bordered and lined with fur.

In Salonica, doctors disagree as to the advisability of adopting Frankish fashions, so we sought to learn the ideas of this good man, who is reputed liberal in his views. We alluded to the Jews of Cracow, to their peculiar dress, and to their unwillingness to change it. " Yes," quoth the rabbi, " but in Poland the Jews dress differently from us, and are of very different character. We came here from Spain, and at first all wore black, like Spaniards; what we now wear is Turkish, and some of us are beginning to imitate the Franks." " In that case," said we, " you do not connect any religious feeling with your costume ? " He answered evasively, " Every dress has a religious value in the eyes of the people to whom it belongs." He then asked if we had remarked the curious out-door pelisses of the women. These are of scarlet cloth, lined with fur and bordered with gold. Over the head is worn a long scarf of the white stuff used for Turkish towels.

The rabbi whom we visited is a merchant, and carried on the conversation in Italian ; he is also a rich man. We learned that here most of the rabbis are merchants and also rich ; for wealth is one of the most needful qualications to obtain their office and sustain its influence.

Much of their commercial success is owing to their power
of association, and their willingness to help one another.
Herein they and their brethren excel the local Christians, who seldom seem able to trust each other or work
as one.

Another distinction of our rabbi is that he keeps a
printing-press.   This privilege is not granted to the
Greeks, and was lately denied to a Bulgarian bookseller.
The request of the latter was supported by the English
consul, who regarded it as most desirable that the Slavonic population in the neighbourhood should obtain
books in its own language.   Of course the excuse was
put forward that the press would be used to circulate
Russian proclamations; as if the lack of a printing-
press in their own country were not precisely what
hitherto has forced the Bulgarians to take their books
from Russia.

The next house we visited was that of a rising coal
merchant; a handsome dwelling, cleanly and cool.   We
came rather too near the middle of the day, so the lady
and her daughters were enjoying a siesta, but they sent
us a message so earnestly begging us to stay that we sat
down patiently to wait.   For this we were rewarded by
seeing the maid carry three gowns and three " cages "
upstairs, through the saloon, and past us into her mis-
tresses' chamber.   After the interval necessary for don-
ning them, out came three ladies, elegant and smiling.

While waiting, our attention was directed to the
extraordinary precautions adopted to secure the house
against fire.   The cause of this is that the Jews here
will not touch fire on their Sabbath.   Not only do they
keep their candles ready lighted from the evening before,
and a Gentile servant to do the necessary work ; but
should a conflagration break out among their dwellings,
they must let it burn on, rather than meddle with it.

Jewish servant girls, whose clothes have happened to
catch fire on the Sabbath, have been known to run burning to the nearest Christian house before they could
obtain assistance. When a Salonican Jew sets up to be
"liberal" one of his first symptoms is to smoke a cigar
on the Sabbath. Sometimes the rabbis make an effort
to reclaim him, *e.g.*, they bribe the pasha to put him in
prison.

Another Jewish observance consists in saying prayers
for the departed, a certain amount being sufficient for a
good spirit and a longer time for a wicked one. Hence,
while it would be considered undutiful for a son to omit
having prayers said for his father's soul, he must take
care not to have them said too long, lest he cast a slur
on his father's character.

We were told that many of the poorer Jews are disposed to think that Sir Moses Montefiore will shortly
prove to be their Messiah. The richer are said to be
in no such hurry, "inasmuch as the coming of the
Messiah would involve their own migration to the
Promised Land, and being an exclusively commercial
people they have little fancy to become landholders in
Judea."

We cannot attempt to describe the Turkish residents
in Salonica, as it happened that we saw nothing of them;
but next in interest to the Hebrew comes the Greek
community. Although it cannot vie in number or wealth
with the Jews it counts some rich merchants, who were
building fine houses while we were there. Besides these
there are certain families which, from intermarriage for
generations, are to all intents Greek, yet claim Western
descent, and enjoy the protection of foreign powers.
This, by sheltering them from Turkish interference, gives
them great advantage in trade. In some cases the right
to such protection is rather doubtful, and should a

European agent not prove himself above bakshish great abuses are certain to ensue.

It was with consternation that we heard of so-called British subjects stooping to farm taxation for the Turk. For "a man cannot carry fire in his bosom and his clothes not be burned;" and a tale was told us of the working of this system, in the particulars of which we would fain hope that there may be some exaggeration. Certain Frankish merchants undertook to farm the pig-tax, and hearing that the Christian peasants of a village were suspected of concealing pigs, they called on the Pasha to put five of their principal men into prison, where at the time typhus fever was raging. Out of the five, four took the fever and died.

Among the Greeks of Salonica, as elsewhere in Turkey, prevails the heinous custom of taking up dead bodies after a year spent in the grave, to look whether they be consumed or no. The scene on these occasions was described to us by a native who had often attended—the horrid curiosity, the superstitious terror, the fearful sight, and still more fearful smell, of which many women sicken on the spot. Should the body be preserved, it is taken as a bad sign and prayers must be said, for which of course the priest is paid. Then the corpse is reinterred for another year, and unless decay ensue the ceremonial may be repeated three times. So tyrannical is conventionality in this particular, that wealthy educated mothers—living in intercourse with Europeans—feel obliged to have their children disinterred. We heard of one instance where there was the additional agony of finding the little body in a state which relations and neighbours considered as indicating that the soul was in hell.

From these grim revelations, we turn to a quaint anecdote of the late sultan, Abdul Medjid. He came to

Salonica, and was invited to visit the garden of the rich Mr. John ——. Having walked about for some time, he asked to see "the merchant Jack." The merchant came, and with a profound bow gave utterance to the following Oriental compliment : " When I beautified this garden and planted these flowers I dared to hope that they might one day be honoured with a visit from your Majesty." The Sultan replied, with grave sincerity, " This day then God hath answered thy prayer."

Sight - seeing and visiting being accomplished, we had only to look if there was anything pretty in the shops, and then make preparations for the inland route. The Bazaar of Salonica is the finest in European Turkey next to that of Constantinople, and is far before the best in the interior, viz., those of Adrianople and Serajevo.

We had seen in Athens a dress made of the silk gauze of Salonica, a material stronger, and less like French *gaze de soie* than the gauze of Broussa. It was for this that we sought first, and then for silver bands to trim it; but we had to consume no end of time in collecting enough bits of a few yards each to make up the quantity required for a gown. The reason is, that the silk is made in private houses in pieces, each sufficient for a shirt.

We saw tailors working at splendid embroidery, and in many shops hung long trusses of what looked like golden straw—used to mingle with the locks of a bride.

One article we had made at Salonica, viz., the cover of a box. Our dragoman assigned the task to Jews, and we, soon after coming into the corridor, were startled to behold two venerable patriarchs, looking as if they had walked bodily out of an old picture Bible. These patriarchs seated themselves on the floor with the large chest between them; their bare feet extended on each side of it, their hands holding the ends of a long piece of sacking whereof they purposed to make the cover, and which they wound round and round the box by way of taking the measure.

CHAPTER V.

" The entrance of Russia into the political system of the European nations was marked by an attempt to take Constantinople,—a project which it has often revived, and which the progress of Christian civilisation seems to indicate must now be realised at no very distant date, unless the revival of the Bulgarian kingdom to the south of the Danube create a new Slavonian power in the east of Europe capable of arresting its progress."—FINLAY'S *History of the Byzantine Empire*, p. 223.

"As for the Bulgarians, whether they remain yet awhile under Turkish rule or free themselves from it in our own time, as they must ultimately do sooner or later, it is in them alone that one can see any really hopeful prospect, on taking a broad general view of the probable future of these countries. This is afforded by their numerical preponderance; their utter primitiveness, which has learned nothing, and has nothing to unlearn; their industry and thrift; their obstinacy; and their sobriety of character."—LORD STRANGFORD.

WE have said that Salonica is geographically Bulgarian; in other words, it is one of the ports of that country with a Slavonic-speaking population which stretches from the Ægean to the Danube. Indeed, Salonica itself forms a point on the ethnographical boundary which, in this part of Turkey in Europe, divides the Slavonic population from the Greek. To a certain extent this frontier coincides with the line of the old Roman road between Salonica and the Lake of Ochrida; nevertheless some miles of country, inhabited by Bulgarians, stretch south of the Via Egnatia, Greek colonies lie to the north of it, and in the towns the population is mixed, in part consisting of Osmanli Turks. The other boundary cities are Monastir, Vodena, and Yenidjé; in all of which dwell

few or no Greeks, whereas in Salonica itself there are
only about 500 families of Slāvs.

On its south-eastern frontier, it is worthy of notice,
the mass of the Slavonic population stops everywhere
short of the sea, and leaves (or perforates only with
stragglers) a coast-strip including part of Thrace,
the Chalcidian peninsula, the cities of Constantinople
and Salonica. This district is so variously peopled, so
important for commercial and strategical purposes,—
and it would so ill-suit any one that it should fall into
the grip of any one else—that those who look forward
to a readjustment of the Slāvo-Greek peninsula take it
under their especial care. Among other plans, they
suggest that it be erected into a neutral territory, and
attached to the two great sea-ports, in the same manner
as domains are attached to the Free Cities of Germany.
These modifiers would give Greece her due in Thessaly
and Epirus, and accord native and Christian self-government, as now exercised by the Principality of Serbia, to
all the Slavonic provinces of Turkey.

Without venturing an opinion on this or other political projects, we may remark that any arrangement
which would disincumber the thrifty and well-disposed
Bulgarian of the yoke of his present barbarous master,
would certainly prove a gain to civilisation, and in one
respect especially to ourselves. Its immediate result
would be the development of the resources of the
country, and, among others, of its resources in cotton.
The vast desert plain of Salonica is stated to be pecu-
liarly adapted for the growth of Sea Island cotton; and
a neighbouring district, not far from the town of Seres,
is so favourable to the culture, that a man who planted
the third of an acre with cotton realized a profit of £60.
This cultivation is in the hands of Bulgarians; the
Turkish landlord cares only to clutch half the produce,

and the farmer of the Turkish revenue is the arch-foe of industry.

The labouring, *i.e.*, the Christian Slavonic, population of the country behind Salonica holds land on the following tenure : after a tenth has been paid to the Sultan, seed is put aside for the coming year, and of what produce remains the landlord gets half.

As for the taxation : in Turkey, grievances commence at the point where in other countries they are supposed to culminate ; so we say nothing of the injustice to a population of millions that it should have no voice in the disposal of its money. Granted that the Bulgarians be ready to give all the government calls for, and, moreover, to pay for exemption from the army, that is, for being disarmed and held down by Mussulmans,* still the greatest grievance remains, viz., the waste and iniquity wherewith the revenue is raised.

Hitherto the taxes have been paid in kind, a method which always gives the gatherer much power to extort bribes, since he can refuse to value the peasant's standing corn until half of it be spoiled. But Turkish tax-farmers do not confine themselves to such by-paths of cheating. The following is an instance of what constantly recurs :—

Two men agree to keep a flock between them, the one in summer on the mountains, the other in winter on the plain. The tax-gatherer compels the first to pay for the whole, promising that he will ask nothing of the other ; he then goes to the second, and with a similar promise forces him likewise to pay for all. In like manner, the Christian can be compelled to pay twice over for exemption from the army if the tax-gatherer declare his first

---

* "Exemption from the army" is the name now given to the tribute paid by Christians as such, which formerly was called *haratch*. The people still use the old word, for to them the tax remains the same, and so does its practical signification, *i.e.*, the Christian continues the disarmed tributary of the Mussulman.

receipt forged. The other day a Bulgarian brought his receipt to the British consul, who threatened the official to have it sent up for investigation. Immediately the charge was withdrawn.

A change of system is being introduced which will supersede payment in kind by payment in money. But it is hard to see how this is to prove beneficial without such means of transport and security of communication as would enable the peasant to bring his produce to market. At present, while he must sell it in the neighbourhood wherein it abounds, he is taxed for it at market value. The people declare that the oppression is now worse than before, and that this is one of the many *soi-disant* reforms which tell well, on paper, while unless followed up by other reforms they prove actually mischievous. We ourselves saw the tax-gatherer swooping down on the villages, accompanied by harpy-flocks of Albanians armed to the teeth.

On occasion of the late cotton famine, the British Government instigated the Porte to encourage the growth of cotton, to give the seed for experiments, and, what is more important, to suspend, in favour of cotton, some of the modes of taxation which chiefly harass agricultural industry. The Christian Bulgarians have responded to this encouragement in a manner that gives fair promise of their energies should they ever be entirely free from vexatious interference.

By Bulgaria we understand, not that insignificant portion of the same termed " the Turkish Province of Bulgaria," but the whole tract of country peopled by Bulgarians. The population, usually given as four millions, is estimated by the people themselves as from five to six millions—forming the eastern division of the South Slavonic race. The Bulgarians are distinguished in all essentials from their neighbours—the

BULGARIAN PEASANTS, WITH BULGARIAN MERCHANT AND HIS SON WHO HAS SPENT SOME YEARS. OUT OF TURKEY.

Greek, the Rouman, and the Turk; they differ in a few
points of character from their own western kindred,
the Croato-Serbs. The chief of these latter points is
a deficiency in what is called *esprit politique*, and a
corresponding superiority in the notion of material
comfort. Unlike the Serb, the Bulgarian does not keep
his self-respect alive with memories of national glory,
nor even with aspirations of glory to come; on the
other hand, no amount of oppression can render him
indifferent to his field, his horse, his flower-garden, nor
to the scrupulous neatness of his dwelling.

How strongly difference of race can tell under identical conditions of climate, religion, and government, is
exemplified in towns where Greeks have been dwelling
side by side with Bulgarians for centuries. The one is
commercial, ingenious, and eloquent, but fraudulent,
dirty, and immoral; the other is agricultural, stubborn,
and slow-tongued; but honest, cleanly, and chaste. The
latter quality has from early times attracted respect
towards the South Slavonic peoples. Their ancient
laws visit social immorality with death, and at present
their opinion, inexorable towards women, does not, like
our own, show clemency to men. A lady told us that
in the society of Greeks she could not be three weeks
without becoming the confidante of a *chronique scanda-
leuse;* among Bulgarians she had lived for months, and
never heard a single "story."*

In Bulgarian towns the Mussulmans are Osmanli colonists, who form, as it were, the garrison of the province.
The Slavonians who have become Mahommedan mostly
live in the country and continue to speak Slavonic.

---

* "The Greek cannot overcome the Bulgarian, nor lead him, nor incorporate
him. He is of a less numerous and not of a superior race; his mind is more
keen but less solid; roughly speaking, he is to the Bulgarian as the clever Cal-
cutta baboo to the raw material of the English non-commissioned officer."—LORD
STRANGFORD in *Eastern Shores of the Adriatic.*

In their bravery and warlike disposition the renegade Bulgarians evince the character of the nation before it was betrayed and disarmed, and they themselves adopted Mahommedanism only to avoid falling into the position of rayahs. In some parts they are known by the name Pomak (from *pomegam*, "I help"), and are supposed to be descended from those Bulgarian troops who served in the Sultan's army as "allies," until the Turks grew strong enough to force on them the alternative of surrendering their arms or their creed. Among our guards once happened to be a Bulgarian Mussulman, who allowed us to be told in his presence that he was still at heart a Christian; and in the neighbourhood of Salonica we heard of Mahommedan Bulgarians who excuse their apostasy by the following story. Being hard pressed they fixed a certain term during which they would fast and call on Christ, at the end whereof, if no help appeared, they would submit themselves to Mahommed. Help arrived not, and so Mahommedans they became. Since then, the old hatred of race has caused them to take part against the Greeks in more than one insurrection; but they equally detest the Turk, and thus sympathize with their own Christian countrymen in their national antipathies as well as in tenacity of their native tongue.

The rural population of Bulgaria is Christian, and hereabouts the rayah has a down-look and a dogged stolidity, which give one the impression that heart and mind have been bullied out of him. Of late years, however, he has presented an unflagging resistance to the Porte's imposition of foreign bishops; and those who have instructed him, both in his own country and out of it, assured us that he is of excellent understanding and zealous and apt to learn. The Christian Bulgarian is reproached as timid, but at least his is the timidity

of shrinking, not of servility; he hides from those he
fears, he does not fawn on them. His country, lying
as it does on the road of Turkish armies to the Danube,
has been subject to unceasing spoliation, and nothing
is more melancholy than the tale told by its desolate
highways, and by the carefulness with which villages
are withdrawn from the notice of the passers-by. Cross
the border into Free Serbia, and the cottage of the
peasant reappears.

To give a sketch of Bulgarian history, one must go
back to the end of the fifth and beginning of the sixth
century, when a Slavonic population south of the Danube
is spoken of by Byzantine authors.

Under the old East Roman Empire the people of
Bulgaria appear both as subjects and as rulers. Justinian's birthplace was, as it still is, a Slavonic village,
in the neighbourhood of Skopia, and his Latin name is
the translation of his Slavonic one, Upravda. The great
Belisarius is said to have been the Slavonic Velisar;
Basil, the Macedonian, or, as Finlay calls him, the
Slavonian groom, was the father of the longest line that
ever maintained itself upon the throne of Byzance.

It would appear that the first colonists established
themselves to the south of the Danube gradually, and
recognised the imperial rule; but in the seventh century
they were joined by tribes of a more warlike character,
under whose leadership they rose against Byzance, and
overran the greater part of the peninsula. These newcomers, who were of the same race with the Finns,
adopted Christianity, and amalgamated with the Slāvs.
From them dates the name of Bulgaria, and the first
dynasty of her sovereigns. Though often at war with
the Byzantine Empire, the Bulgarians profited by its
neighbourhood so far as to imbibe a certain amount of
civilisation. In the ninth century they fought covered

with steel armour; their discipline astonished the veterans of the Empire, and they possessed all the military engines then known. Their kings and czars encouraged literature, and were sometimes themselves authors. As almost all accounts of them come from Byzantine sources there can be little doubt that this portrait is not flattered. Under their more powerful rulers the Bulgarians threatened Constantinople; under the weaker they acknowledged the Byzantine Emperor as suzerain, and more than once Byzantine armies effected a temporary subjection of their land; but their monarchy was not finally overthrown till the end of the fourteenth century, when they were conquered by the Turks. Coins of Bulgaria are to be seen in the museum of Belgrade, and a curious chronicle of Czar Asen has lately been published in modern Bulgarian.

At the Turkish conquest, 1390, Shishman, the last king of Bulgaria, surrendered himself and his capital to the conqueror's mercy; but the people submitted only by degrees, and always on the condition that if they paid tribute to the Sultan they should be free to govern themselves. Their soldiers were commanded by their own voivodes,* their taxes were collected, and towns and villages ruled by officers of their own choosing. The Bulgarian Church had native Bishops and a Patriarch, residing first at Tirnova then at Ochrida. All this is proved by firmans and berats accorded to them by numerous Sultans.

Those who take the scraps of liberty now-a-days octroyed to the rayah as evidences of a radical change in the maxims of Turkish rule, should bear in mind that far better terms were accorded by Turks to Christians five centuries ago. Those who put faith in Turkish

---

* In modern parlance, generals,—signification cognate with the German *Herzog* and Latin *dux*—hence also used for duke.

promises, should inquire how the liberties guaranteed to
such Christians as submitted to the first Sultans came to
be trampled under foot so soon as the Turks could call
themselves masters of the land.

Of the Bulgarian voivodes the most resolute were cut
off and the rest left to choose between emigration and
apostasy. In 1776 the autonomy of the Church was
destroyed, and in place of native bishops of one interest
with the people, Greeks were sent from Constantinople,
who plundered the peasants, denounced the chief men
to Turkish suspicion, set an example of social corruption,
and burnt all Slavonic books and MSS. whereon they
could lay their hands. The last schools and printing-
presses found shelter in the Danubian Principalities ;
when those lands came under Phanariote * government
nothing was left to the Bulgarians save some old convents in the recesses of their hills.

Few points are more remarkable in the history of
Ottoman rule than the mode in which Turks and
Greeks have played into each other's hands. The
Sultan could never have crushed the heart out of his
Christian subjects without the aid of a Christian middleman, and the Greek has used the brute force of his
Mahommedan employer to complement his own clever-
ness and guile. Under the later emperors Greek do-
minion was unknown in Slavonic and Rouman lands ;
whereas under Ottoman sultans, we find Greek prelates and Phanariote princes ruling the Rouman, the
Bulgarian, and the Serb. That nationality must be
of tough material which gave not way under this double
pressure.

The first break in the prison wall was made by the
revolution at the beginning of this century. " Free

---

* Phanariote : so called from the Phanar, a quarter of Constantinople where
the Greek Patriarch resides. The derivation of "Phanar" is variously assigned.

Greece, autonomous Serbia: may not Bulgaria have her turn?" Gradually the wealthier Bulgarians sent their sons for education no longer to Constantinople, but to Russia, Bohemia, France. In the country itself were founded native schools; and even in districts already half Hellenized the national spirit began to revive. Persons who used to write their own language in the Greek character learned late in life the Slavonic alphabet, and we have ourselves seen parents who spoke Bulgarian imperfectly anxiously providing that their children should know it well. It was the obstacle presented by a foreign hierarchy to these efforts at national development that brought the people to the resolution of freeing their Church from the control of the Phanar.

This temper was taken advantage of by the Roman Propagandists, and emissaries were sent all over Bulgaria, promising self-government and services in Slavonic, with no other condition than that a nominal recognition of the Patriarch should be exchanged for that of the Pope.* This condition cannot be called hard, and at its first start the Romanist Propaganda was a success. The number of converts has been hugely exaggerated, yet it doubtless included some persons of influence. But the principal bait to the adoption of Catholicism was the promise of sharing the protection of France; and when it became evident that this protection could not be unlimited, nor exempt its *protégés* from payment of taxes, the new-made Romanists recanted in troops.

* The contest between Constantinople and Rome for the ecclesiastical supremacy of Bulgaria dates as early as the ninth century, on the plea that the Danubian Provinces were anciently subject to the Archbishopric of Thessalonica, in the times when that archbishopric was immediately dependent on the Papal See. The Bulgarian czars seem to have deferred their choice between the Greek and Latin Churches until they obtained from Constantinople the recognition of a Patriarch of their own.

Then, too, their leaders became convinced that the
movement could have no other effect than to extend to
Bulgaria what had already broken the strength of
Bosnia and Albania, *i.e.*, a Latin sect, separated from
the other Christians, cowering under foreign protection, selling its assistance to the Turks. With these
views (we give their own version of the story), and
not from any religious sentiment or scruple, many
to whom the Propaganda owed its first encouragement
withdrew their aid and opposed it with all their
might.

But the indifference wherewith the common people
had talked of transferring ecclesiastical allegiance proved
to the thinkers in Bulgaria that the dangers of division might at any moment recur. For the second
time in their church history it was recognised that the
South Slavonians would remain in the Eastern Church
only on condition of ecclesiastical self-government. If
they are to have foreign bishops or a foreign head, it is
all one to them whether their Pope resides at Constantinople or Rome.

At this juncture deputies from Bulgaria made their
appearance in Constantinople. They came to demand
that in virtue of the Hatt-i-Humayoun, their national
patriarchate, formerly recognised by the Porte, should
be restored, or at least that their Church should be
declared autonomous, with native archbishop, bishops,
and synod, and an ecclesiastical seminary at Tirnova. In
short, they desired such a system of church government
as succeeds admirably in the Principality of Serbia. It
is years since the Bulgarians put in their claim, but the
Turk is in no hurry to remove a cause of quarrel between
his Christian subjects. With great subtlety he has tried
to improve the occasion by hinting to the Bulgarians
that they had better secede from the Eastern Church.

They have been told that by the treaty of Adrianople the Greek Patriarch is declared head of all the Orthodox communities in Turkey. "Be Catholic," says the Mahommedan judge, "or Protestants, or set up a sect of your own, and we will recognise you with pleasure; so long as you call yourselves 'Orthodox' we must know you only as Greeks."

But the Bulgarians avoided the snare. They replied that their demand affected no religious question, that they had no desire to separate themselves from the Orthodox communion. They were perfectly ready to yield the Greek Patriarch recognition as head of the Eastern Church; to be its *only* Patriarch he had never aspired. His predecessors had acknowledged a Patriarch of Bulgaria till within the last ninety years; he himself at the present moment recognised Patriarchs of Jerusalem and Antioch. Besides, the practical settlement of the business depends, not on the Patriarch, but on the Padishah. When the Bulgarian patriarchate was abolished it was by authority of the Sultan; to this day no prelate throughout the Ottoman Empire can exercise his functions without an imperial firman; and for such a firman a Bulgarian primate, already chosen by the people, was waiting in order to appoint his bishops, convoke his synod, and regulate internal affairs. Give him this, and the Greek Patriarch might defer his recognition so long as it suits his own convenience, while without a firman the recognition of the Greek Patriarch would be of no practical effect.

This statement places the Ottoman government in an attitude somewhat different from that which has been claimed for it; for it has been usually represented as striving vainly to reconcile Christians in a religious dispute, wherein it may mediate but not interfere.

No doubt, however, the Greek Patriarch might have done much to avoid an appeal to Mahommedan authority, and would have best consulted the interests of his own community by agreeing to accept the proffered recognition together with a fixed tribute.* But it must ever be remembered that in a post so important as that of the Constantinopolitan chair none but a pliant agent is tolerated by the Turk. Certain it is, that the Patriarch then in office behaved equally unworthily and unwisely. Three bishops (Hilarion, Accentios, and Paissios,) had declared themselves ready to resign their sees in Bulgaria unless confirmed therein by the choice of the people. They might have been used as mediators; on the contrary, they were seized and sent into exile. All such Bulgarians as did not accept the Patriarch's terms were anathematized and declared heretics.

By such measures the formidable wrath of a slow stubborn people has been thoroughly roused. The Patriarch who excommunicated them they have renounced; rather than receive his bishops, communities declare they will remain without any; should a Greek venture to impose himself upon them they resist him by every means in their power.

A series of scandals took place throughout the Provinces. Churches were closed, in order that the Greek liturgy might not be read therein. When the Greek

---

* Though some progress has lately been made towards a formal understanding between the Patriarch of Constantinople and the Bulgarian Church, recent confusions have prevented any real settlement. The Patriarch has declared his willingness to recognise the virtual independence of the Bulgarian Church, his own primacy, which has never been questioned, of course being retained. But he has limited the area to the territory north of the Balkan Mountains, which will be governed by an Exarch or Patriarch residing at Sophia. The Bulgarians contend that the independence should regard race, not territory; in which case a large portion of country between the southern slope of the Balkan Mountains and the Ægean Sea would be included within the rule of the Exarch of Bulgaria. Greek susceptibilities have as yet prevented this arrangement from being accepted at the Patriarchate.

bishops returned from their revenue-gathering progresses they found their palaces locked and were conducted beyond the city walls. If they entered a church to officiate, no Bulgarian priest would take part in the service; when they departed the floor was ostentatiously swept, as if to remove traces of impurity. In Sophia, when a new bishop was expected, men, women, and children filled the palace and blocked it up, till, unarmed as they were, they had to be expelled by Turkish soldiers. The bishop then dwelt in isolation, until, on occasion of a burial, he got hold of a Bulgarian priest and demanded why he did not come to see him. The priest answered that he must stand by his flock; that as it would not acknowledge the bishop neither could he. Thereupon the priest's beard was shorn, the fez of the dead man stuck on his head, and he was turned out into the streets as a warning and a sign. Again the unarmed citizens rose; shops were shut, houses evacuated, thousands of people prepared to leave Sophia. Their elders waited on the pasha and said, " Either the Greek bishop must go or *we.*" The pasha advised the prelate to withdraw, and as the authorities in Constantinople would not permit the people to elect a new one Sophia resolved to do without a bishop at all.*

At Nish, a town on the Serbian frontier, the bishops anticipated an inimical demonstration by accusing the elders of the Bulgarian community of a plot to join the Serbs. The elders were called before the pasha, and without a hearing, without being allowed to say farewell to their families or to send home for extra clothing, they were hurried into carriages and sent off into banishment. This occurred in the depth of winter, and when in the ensuing August we were hospitably received by

---

* For some further details see " Donau-Bulgarian und der Balkan." Kanitz, Leipzig, 1875.

the family of one of the exiles, they besought us to apply to some English consul to learn if their relatives were yet alive.

Meanwhile a variety of evils pressed on Bulgaria —outbreaks of haiduks, some political outlaws, some highwaymen—influx of Mahommedan Tartars from the Crimea, for whom the Bulgarians were forced to build houses and provide food—emigration of Bulgarians to Russia, succeeded by their destitute return—attempt of other Bulgarians to get off to Serbia, frustrated by the Turkish authorities—finally, a shoal of Bashi-bazouks turned loose among the villagers, on pretext of guarding the frontier from the Serbs.* In the summer of 1862 we were witnesses to this state of things. Another means resorted to for holding down the Bulgarian is the introduction of Mahommedan colonists, who replenish the declining Mussulman population, and are kept well supplied with arms, of which the Christian is deprived. Since the Tartars, Circassians have been introduced, and the idea has been adopted of planting them along the frontier of Serbia, so as to bar off the Bulgarians. The Tartars were only idle, whereas these new immigrants come thirsting to avenge their own sufferings on all who bear the Christian name. It is said, however, that the Circassian mountaineers do not thrive on the Bulgarian plains and are rapidly decreasing in number.

In Constantinople we heard a good deal of the Bulgarian question—the Greek side of it from the Patriarch and his secretary, the Slavonic side from the Bulgarian deputies. Each party supported its arguments in pamphlets swarming with protestations of loyalty to the Sultan, and taunting its antagonists as emissaries of

* The Bulgarian horrors of 1875 are the intense aggravation of a chronic condition. They could astonish no one personally acquainted with the interior of the country.

Russia. Russia in Turkey plays the part of "cat" in a careless household; being charged with the doing of all mischief by those who wish to exonerate themselves.

As to probably impartial judges, we appealed to the opinion of foreign residents; these, especially French, British, and American, gave their verdict for the Bulgarians. British consuls assured us they were astonished to find a population in Turkey so industrious, thrifty, moral, and clean. As for the Americans, in a quiet way they are the best friends the Bulgarians have. Their eminent scholar, Dr. Riggs, has rendered the Old Testament from ancient into modern Slavonic, and numerous school-books have been translated from the English; American schools are in the Bulgarian principal towns, and their books are sold by native colporteurs in several parts of the country.

During our own travels we saw proofs enough that the people are trying to improve, and we were especially struck with their eagerness for education. The mountain chains of the Balkan and the Rhodope divide Bulgaria into three sections—northern, central, and southern. Of the northern district, between the Balkan and the Danube, we cannot speak from eye-witness, as the Turks declared it too disturbed for travellers; but we say, on the authority of persons who have lived there, that those Bulgarians who grow up with the great waterway of commerce on one side of them and their natural mountain fortresses on the other are more independent and enterprising than their brethren on the inland plains. Here, too, the people maintain numerous schools, of which the best are at Tirnova and Shumla. Tirnova, the ancient capital, is the site proposed for an ecclesiastical seminary, and if possible for a printing press, both of which the jealousy of the Porte as yet denies.

Central Bulgaria is that which lies between the ranges of the Balkan and the Rhodope. Here we visited the schools of Adrianople, Philippopolis, Samakoff, Sophia, Nish,—all supported and managed by the Christian communities without pecuniary aid from the government or bishops. The school-houses, mostly of good size and airy, are, like everything in Bulgaria, clean. The school-books, gathered from various sources, are eked out with those of the American Board of Missions. To conciliate the Turks, Turkish is frequently taught to a scholar or two, and phrases complimentary to the Sultan have been framed into a sort of school hymn. True, the same tune has another set of words in honour of him who shall deliver the country from Turkish rule. One or other version is sung before the visitor, according as he is judged to be Christian or Turcophile. We had opportunities of hearing both.

At Philippopolis, Samakoff, and Sophia, there are girls' schools. That at Sophia was founded by a patriotic citizen.* In his own words : " When my wife died and left me but one son I resolved not to marry again, but to give all my money and attention to this school." He has brought a female teacher all the way from the Austrian border, for Slavonic trained schoolmistresses are hard to find in Turkey.

Southern Bulgaria lies, as we have already indicated, between the Rhodope and the frontiers of ancient Greece. Such schools as we there visited were smaller and poorer than elsewhere, but we did not see those of

---

* In 1877 we found a young relative of this patriotic merchant among the Bulgarian students at Agram in Croatia. Ten lads and four girls had been sent to the excellent schools in this town before the recent disasters in Bulgaria, and are still continuing their studies, in spite of the privations consequent on the cutting off of remittances from home. We were glad to be able to render them some timely help from a sum entrusted to us especially for Bulgarians. The young girl from Sophia told me that the schoolhouse built by Hadji Traiko had been seized by the Turks and turned into a barrack for soldiers.

Istib and other towns lying on the more northerly route between Salonica and Skopia. Those on the line of our journey we will notice as we proceed.

Throughout the places we have hitherto mentioned, the Greek Bishop contents himself with ignoring the Bulgarian school, or from time to time expelling an energetic teacher; but nearer the Græco-Slāv boundary we found Slavonic education positively impeded. In Vodena and Yenidjé a Greek school is founded, and the community must needs support it; in case poverty should not be sufficient to deter them from supporting also one of their own, every possible hindrance is thrown in the way.

One result of this anti-national policy is, that the Bulgarians, elsewhere so eager to learn, are in these districts listless and dull; another result is, that being alienated from their own clergy, they lend an ear to overtures from Rome. Some of them calculate on using Latin aid to get rid of the Patriarch, and then finding means to get rid of the Pope; others still fear that the yoke they know not may prove heavier than the yoke they know. In Monastir the Unionists * had a school, and at Yenidjé they were building a church.

Meanwhile, in the neighbourhood of Salonica, awakes a party which bethinks itself that Protestants acknowledge neither Pope nor Patriarch, and that the protection of England would do as well as that of France. The question is asked whether, supposing they became Protestants, England would take them under her wing. For answer they get an emphatic " No." Still they turn to the Protestant clergyman at Salonica, and beg that he will procure for them books and teachers in their own tongue, duly offering to pay for both.

* The name Unionist is given to communities which retain the Oriental rite while they acknowledge the supremacy of Rome.

CHAPTER VI.

" The fame Methodios acquired among his contemporaries, as well as from those
in after-times who saw his paintings, may be accepted as a proof that they possessed some touches of nature and truth."—Finlay's *Byzantine Empire*, vol. i.,
p. 266.

WE have now worked round to our starting-point, the
various-peopled city of Salonica. At no time were
the Bulgarians its masters, yet its name is identified with
the one incident in their obscure history which has left
a mark in the annals of civilisation. We allude to the
christianization first of Bulgaria and then of the whole
Slavonic race, through the medium of a translation of
the Scriptures in the dialect still called "Church" Slavonic. That dialect is generally considered to have been
the ancient written language of Bulgaria, and the translators were natives of Salonica.

In the ninth century Salonica formed part of the
Byzantine Empire, and its citizens are, without distinction, termed Greeks; but many Slavs had settled there,
their language was spoken in its streets, and long afterwards a Slavonic hero, named Doitschin, is celebrated in
the national songs as having delivered the city from the
exactions of a robber chief.*

* Even in Constantinople, and as early as the eighth century, the Slavic
element was sufficiently predominant for the Slavonian Niketas to fill the Patri-
archal Chair, and the Greeks tell an anecdote showing that he was by no means

G 2

At this period their lived in Salonica the brothers Cyril and Methodios. Cyril, the elder, was learned and studious; the younger, Methodios, enterprising and energetic. Both were inspired to make known the Gospel to the Slavonic population outside the walls, and while at home Cyril prepared himself by study and cultivation of the language, Methodios went forth as a missionary. The latter presented himself at the court of Boris, king of the Bulgarians, and, as the legend goes, caught the humour of the monarch by offering to paint the walls of a favourite hunting lodge. Boris came to examine the work, expecting to see wolves, bears, and regal huntsmen; instead, he beheld the picture of a Great Day of Judgment, like those still common among peoples where justice is dispensed by the monarch in person. On the throne sat a King, not like Boris, frowning in wild pomp; but majestic and mild. His courtiers stood around him, but they did not flaunt Bulgarian horsetails, nor flourish bloody weapons; they had soft waving hair, and gold circlets, and white wings dipped in rainbow hues. The approved servants were being received on the right hand, above them opened a golden gate; the condemned were dragged off on the left, and beneath them yawned a pit of fire. But the strangest part was, that among the honoured and accepted were to be seen many frail and shrinking forms, the weak, the defenceless, the sick, the blind, and even figures in vile raiment, while among the reprobated were more than one fierce warrior, not altogether unlike to Boris and his lords. The king called the artist to give him the interpretation of this

completely Hellenized. One day reading the Gospel of St. Matthew, he pronounced the name Ματθαῖον, instead of Ματθαῖον. One of his people whispered to him that the vowels of the diphthong were not to be separated. The prelate turned angrily round, and exclaimed, "My soul abhors diphthongs and triphthongs!" This story is remarked on by Mr. Finlay.

picture, and Methodios expounded it thus: "The great King is the God of the Christians. He made the earth, and for a while dwelt on it in the likeness of man; but as He took on Him a humble form, and was holy and truthful, wicked men hated Him, and He suffered of them all that the evil still inflict on the truthful and the good. At the Last Day He shall come again in His glorious majesty, and shall judge both the living and the dead. He knows the sufferings of the oppressed, who Himself was once suffering and poor; He knows the cruel and violent deeds of great men: such men ill-treated Him and crucified Him on a tree." Boris considered the judgment throne, the winged messengers, the golden light that played over the throne; he felt himself in the presence of power and glory, higher, other than his own. Then he considered the dress and countenances of the guilty and the grisly monsters that were carrying them away, and his conscience gave him an uneasy twinge as to his own mode of treating the weak and defenceless. He turned to Methodios and said, "Canst thou teach me how I and my subjects may escape being sentenced to the pit of fire?" Methodios answered, "Send to Constantinople, and pray the emperor that he give thee wise men who can instruct thee and show thee how to tame thy wild people." One year from this time King Boris and his nobles bowed their proud heads in Christian baptism, and to this day the Bulgarians attribute their conversion to the picture-sermon of Methodios. Therefore he is represented in their schools and churches with his painting in his hand.

Some time after the mission to Bulgaria there appeared in Constantinople a deputation of strange men speaking the Slavonic tongue. They came from the western Slavic peoples, who were then welding themselves into that great kingdom of Moravia which, but for the jealousy of the neighbouring Germans, might have saved eastern Europe from disunion and barbarism.* The words of this deputation are given by old Nestor, the monk of Kieff: "The Moravian princes, Rastislav, Sviatopolk, and Kotzel, sent to the Emperor Michael and said, 'Our land is baptized, but we have no teachers who can instruct us or translate for us the sacred books. We do not understand either the Greek or the Latin language; some teach us one thing, some another; therefore we do not understand the words of the Scriptures, neither their import. Send us teachers who may explain to us the Scriptures.' When the Emperor Michael heard this, he called together his philosophers, and told them the message of the Slavonic princes; and the philosophers said, 'There is at Thessalonica a man named Leon; he has two sons who both know the Slavonic language and are clever philosophers.' On hearing this, the Emperor sent to Thessalonica, to Leon, saying, 'Send to us thy sons Methodios and Constantine,' which hearing, Leon straightway sent them; and when they came to the Emperor he said to them, 'The Slavonic lands have sent unto me requesting teachers who may translate for them the Holy Scriptures.' And being persuaded by the Emperor, they went into the Slavonic land, to Rastislav, to Sviatopolk, and to Kotzel. Having arrived they began to compose a Slavonic alphabet, and translated the Gospels and the Acts of the Apostles, whereat the Slavonians rejoiced greatly, hearing the greatness of God in their own language. After which they translated the Psalter and other books." (Nestor's "Annals," original text edition of St. Petersburg, 1767, pp. 20-23.†) Well says the monk Chrabr, writing in

---

* For history of the great Moravian State see Palatzky's "History of Bohemia," German translation. And for a sketch of the same, and of part of its territories, see "Across the Carpathians." London: Macmillan & Co.

† For an account of the mission of Cyril and Methodios among the Western

the eleventh century, " Dost thou ask any of the Slavonic authors who invented your characters and who
translated the Books into your tongue ?   They all know,
and will answer, 'The holy philosopher Constantine,
called Cyril ; he and his brother Methodios invented our
characters and translated the Books into our language.'
But dost thou ask at what time this took place ? that
also do they know and will tell thee: 'In the days of
Michael the Greek Emperor, of Boris, the prince of the
Bulgarians, of Rastislav, prince of the Blatens,* in the
year of the creation of the world 6363 ' " (= 855 A.D.)

The strong presumption that the Salonican Apostles
were not by race Hellene, but Slavonic citizens of a
Byzantine city, rests less even on their perfect acquaintance with a tongue which the Greeks contemned as
barbarous, than on their carefulness to make their
mission a means of establishing the *Slavonic* language,
not, as Greeks would have made it, a means of extend-
ing *Greek*.

The work of Cyril and Methodios bears date 855, and
earlier than this it cannot be certain that the Slavonic
was a written tongue.   But that it was so is presumed, on the following grounds :—1st. Because unless
the language had attained a certain degree of development, Cyril could scarcely have made what he did—a
literal translation of part of the Scriptures—without
borrowing largely from the Greek ; nor could he
have rendered almost all the terms and epithets of the

Slāvs, see Count Krasinski's admirable work on the "Religious History of the
Sclavonic Nations." Shafarik gives his decision for the opinion urged by common
sense, that the greater part of this translation was prepared before Cyril and his
brother left Salonica. The dialects of the Slāvs north and south of the Danube
must at that time have been sufficiently alike for one written language to be
intelligible to both. The son and successor of Boris was himself the writer of
several books.

* " Slāvs on the Balaton, Blaten, or Platten-see," in the south-west of
Hungary.

original by Slavonic equivalents.* 2nd. Because the
alphabet in which the earliest Slavonic MSS. are
written bears trace of an existence prior to the introduction of Christianity, and would seem to have
been first cut on sticks in the Runic fashion. This
alphabet is called Glagolitic, from a letter named
Glagol, which signifies "word."

The so-called Cyrillic alphabet is supposed to have
been introduced as easier than the original character,
both for copyist to write and for foreigner to acquire.
Some of its signs are modified from the Glagolitic,
but those which Greek and Slavonic have in common
are simply taken from the Greek. Tradition calls its
inventor St. Cyril, and history proves that it was
brought into general use by his pupil Clement, first
bishop of Bulgaria. It is adopted by all the Slavonic
peoples belonging to the Eastern Church, and thus
again their version of the Scriptures points back to its
Bulgarian source.†

The Greek Christians of Salonica have always been
left the use of certain churches and monasteries. Hence
we looked for some testimonial to the memory of those
missionaries whom their communion has to thank that
at the present day it is represented in the councils of
Europe by the Slavonic power of Russia. But no chapel,
no monument, not even a house or a shrine, is pointed
out as connected with Cyril and Methodios; and the
monks whom we questioned on the subject would not

---

* Unlike the translations of the Scriptures in German, French, English, &c.,
wherein theological terms are borrowed wholesale from Greek and Latin, in the
Slavonic they are mostly rendered by equivalents. Thus the word " theology "
is translated *bogoslovie;* orthodox, *pravoslav,* &c.

† There was long debate between Slavic scholars as to the relative antiquity
of the Glagolitic and Cyrillic alphabets, and it has been but lately decided that
the former is the oldest. To recommend it to the court of Rome, it was said to
have been invented by St. Jerome; and now, to recommend it to the Slavs of the
Oriental communion, the fact is insisted on that its origin dates from a period
before the split between the Eastern and Western Churches.

know or hear anything about them. In fact, that
Pope who in 1016 interdicted the Slavonic alphabet, and
branded as a heretic the very missionary whom his wiser
predecessor had consecrated archbishop,* did not bear
more emphatic testimony to the national character of the
ministry of Methodios than do these Greeks of the nine-
teenth century to the national character of the translation
of Cyril.

It is to the possession of a liturgy and Scriptures in
their own tongue that the Slavonic churches owe it, that
they never have been utterly denationalised by foreign
influence, whether proceeding from Constantinople or
Rome. Nay, the common possession of these Scriptures
and liturgy has proved a link between Slavonic peoples,
even when long divided as adherents of Latin or Greek.
In 1862 occurred the thousandth anniversary of the
Salonican Apostles; it was celebrated by more than
eighty millions of Slavonic Christians, without distinction of sect or denomination, from Prague to the Pacific,
from the Baltic to Salonica.

* To obtain the Pope's permission for the establishment of a Slavonic ritual
Methodios made two journeys to Rome, and was there consecrated Archbishop of
Pannonia and Moravia, with full powers to carry out his plans. Even during
his lifetime, however, this authority was qualified, and after his death the Council
of Salona (1016) went so far as to brand the Slavonic missionaries as heretics
and the Slavonic alphabet as an invention of the devil. It is no small proof of
national tenacity that from that day to this the native liturgy should have maintained its ground in a part of Roman Catholic Dalmatia, and, so far from being
likely to relinquish it now, the Croatians are taking measures to substitute it for
Latin throughout their churches. In Bohemia the Slavonic Bible has held its
ground, through struggles that form a long and important chapter in religious
history.

CHAPTER VII.

OUR visit to Salonica happened in June, when silk merchants were scouring the country, taking up all decent horses, and over-paying the Turkish guards. The pasha, with so many buyourdís (passports) on his hands, neglected to send ours till late on the evening before we started; moreover he gave our escort no instructions to behave properly, and took no pains to secure us good steeds. Consequently the guards showed themselves generally disaffected, and refused obedience to various directions; the horses brought were so miserable that we had to send them away, and at the last moment sit down to wait for others. We did not get off till long after sunrise; and let no one attempt to ride over the plain of Salonica in the sun.

The first stage was Yenidjé, a town near the site of ancient Pella, about nine hours from Salonica and as many from Vodena. The whole way thither passes over the plain, which is for the most part desert, and here and there marked with hitherto unexplained tumuli. Through it runs the new road "Imperial," a rascally performance in the fullest sense of the term. In the first place it is badly made, and full of ruts; in summer it is as hard as stone, and in winter a Slough of Despond; furthermore, it was made by fraud. The pasha raised an extra tax from the country people, on plea that all

their work on the road would be paid for, but having
once got the money he put it in his own pocket, and
made the road by forced labour.   Families upon families
were ruined by the double process.

The road Imperial crosses the Vardar, and to this end
a bridge is in process of erection.   Considering when it
was begun, one might have expected it to have been
finished long ago ; but this did not suit the private views
of the workmen.   They began at each end, and worked
till near the middle ; then, where the stream runs
deepest, they stopped, and bridged over the chasm by
planks removable at pleasure.   When a traveller appeared
these planks were taken up until he paid what the workmen required, and then they were put down for him to
pass over.   At length the pasha made an end of this
system of black-mail ; nevertheless, when we traversed
the bridge it was in a very imperfect state.

On the other side of the river stands a large new khan
with several separate cells.   Here we took shelter for
our mid-day meal, and the great heat kept us within
doors till well on in the afternoon.   Even then we could
not help envying the buffaloes that lay cooling in the
shallow river—their heads and humps alone visible above
water, and their muzzles just sufficiently approached to
enhance felicity by companionship.   These huge beasts
are the only creatures on the plain of the Vardar that do
not show signs of ill-treatment ; slow and stubborn in
disposition, they are too strong to be bullied and too
useful to be neglected.   The eye, turning from their
repose, falls on the trains of patient horses carrying iron
from Cardiff and cotton from Manchester to the markets
of inland towns.

It was sunset when we reached the slightly elevated
field which marks the site of ancient Pella.   A large
cistern lies between the rising ground and the road, on

the other side of which is a khan with trees. The sight of carved stones in the walls of this khan attracted the British consul at Salonica, and he obtained permission to dig for further remains. His workmen had just begun, and we found the hole excavated by them at the foot of a rude fragment of Turkish wall. Leaving our horses, we descended into it, and carried off a sherd of ancient pottery.

From the site of Pella it is scarcely two hours to Yenidjé, for which place we had been provided with a letter to a principal Bulgarian. We sent it on by one of the zaptiés, and desired him to meet us outside the town, and conduct us to our quarters for the night. No one showing, we were obliged to follow the other zaptié to the khan, whence his fellow issued and deliberately stated that he had left the letter with the Bulgarian and had desired him to meet us; then, lazily giving some insufficient directions as to the whereabouts of the house, he returned to his rest. His comrade, gruffly murmuring, led us about and around Yenidjé, now stumbling over ill-paved alleys, now stooping under the boughs of enormous planes. The night had fallen, and after nine hours' ride in the heat the chills struck us through and through.

At last we gained the door of a court which proved to be our hoped-for *konak.** Here the master of the house received us, and explained in consternation that he had been to meet us, but that we had missed him by entering by another gate. This he spoke in Greek, but the mistress welcomed us with the Slavonic " Dobro doshlé."† The room to which we were conducted was

---

* A Turkish word used hereabouts to express either the residence of a governor or one's night-quarters. It is one of those that has passed into use among the Slāvs: even in Croatia, *konatchiti* signifies " to pass the night."

† " Dobro doshlé " (f. pl.), lit. " You are welcome." To which greeting the response is " Bolié vas nashli," " Better we have found you."

upstairs, large and well-carpeted—one side all windows, mostly unglazed. We seated ourselves on the divan, waiting for our luggage, and here happened the greatest breach of respect we ever met with in Turkey. Our principal guard entered the room, threw himself down on the opposite end of the divan, and roared out "Voda" (water). We instantly rose and left the chamber, and on being followed to see what was amiss we pointed without a word to the zaptié on the divan. He dared not remain, and the master of the house was diffidently following him out of the room, when we called the latter back, requested him to be seated, and bade the woman shut the door, leaving the Turk in the dark outside.

The luggage had missed the road; it seemed ages before it came, and again ages till our beds were put up, our tea made, and chicken and rice ready. Overtired, our sleep was not refreshing. But the worst part was yet to come. Next morning the horses did not appear, and we saw with dismay the cool hours shortening while messenger after messenger went to summon them.

Then came one of the zaptiés to inform us that, before proceeding, the kiradgees wished to be paid for their last day's work. Perceiving that the zaptié himself supported their requirement, we immediately exclaimed, "Surely these kiradgees are Turks!" It proved but too true, and now we knew what we had to expect. The message being interpreted, meant that the kiradgees wanted to turn back. We answered, "If they turn back here, we do not give them a single piastre. The zaptiés must go instantly with the dragoman, show our buyourdí to the mudir of Yenidjé, and demand horses in place of these." When the kiradgees heard this they asked only for half their pay. We required obedience, and would listen to no terms. Next it was alleged that one of the horses was ill. "Then begone all of you, with your horses; as we

have said, we will get fresh ones." More than once the
dragoman actually left the court to go to the mudir, and
was each time called back by promises of obedience.
At length, all excuses being exhausted, they began to
bungle over and misload the luggage. We saw that
our poor dragoman, unsupported by the zaptiés, could do
nothing, while his not wearing the European dress
further detracted from his influence.

The sun always getting higher and higher—yet we
would not go without a word with the master of the
house; so when luggage and Turks were at last packed
off we called in the Bulgarian for a talk. He gave
us not much fresh intelligence, but confirmation of
what we had heard from the most trustworthy sources
at Salonica.

Yenidjé numbered about 6000 houses, half Bulgarian,
half Turks; the Mussulmans being all Osmanlis. The
Christians here, as in the country around, are Slavonic,
the only Greeks being the bishop and the schoolmaster.
The principal men speak Greek, for commercial purposes, but none of the women know it. As for the
Papal movement, at that time two Bulgarian United
priests celebrated a Slavonic service in a room—but a
new church was being built. Converts once numbered
fifty to sixty families, then not more than thirty-five;
their number having declined because they were deceived as to exemption from paying the taxes. They
would, however, increase again should the new church
turn out exactly like those to which they are accustomed,
for "they would then be persuaded that the Pope *does not
want to latinise them*—only to supersede the Patriarch."
Aware of this, the Greek bishop was doing his utmost to
prevent the completion of the building; and should
this be impossible, he hoped to obtain a mandate for-
bidding the Roman Catholics to imitate the Orthodox

style, decoration, and service. Some Bulgarians regard
the Unionists as deceivers, but our informant was
evidently not quite decided as to his opinion of them.
For himself, he felt an objection to do anything that
would be considered a desertion of his father's faith,
but at the same time entertained reasonable doubt that
any real blame could attach to a person for substituting
in his prayers the name of the Pope, whom he did not
know, for that of the Patriarch, whom he could not
bear. "What we want," said he, "is, protection, and
some help to start with. We are not rich enough to
build a second school, and since the bishop forces us
to keep up the Greek one all we now ask is that his
teacher should also know Bulgarian. But if we had
the protection of some foreign power we could get on,
and if a school with a Bulgarian teacher were once
founded it is to it that we would send our children.
Should we agree to go over to the Romanists, they
promise us both church services and school teaching
in our own tongue; and though we would rather get
these benefits in some other manner, it is better to get
them thus than not at all."

From Yenidjé we had but six hours to Vodena, but
starting late, the first part of the ride was, as yesterday,
in the burning sun. We halted at the khan of the
little village of St. Georgio, inhabited by Bulgarians,
but having a Greek school. This khan has no separate
room, but the heat was too great to remain out of
doors, so we had to dine in the stable, on a sort of
platform raised round the poles that support the roof.

By the time we again started a cloud had come over
the sun, and the last three hours of this day's ride
proved delicious. We reached the Karasmak (the
ancient Lydias), its banks dotted with grazing herds;
and this boundary passed over, every step brought us

nearer to the glen of Vodena, where the weary level of
the treeless plain melts into mountain shadow, bowery
verdure, and overflowing streams. It was evening
when we entered the glen ; in the mulberry gardens
that fringe the road the nightingales were singing
their serenade, while a light breeze shook the scarlet
bells of pomegranate bushes in full bloom.

Presently we came on a meeting of waters over-
shaded by mighty planes, and there halted to take in
the scene. We found ourselves at the foot of a precipice wherewith the upper glen suddenly breaks off
from the mountains on either side. Over this precipice
breaks the river, not in one sheet, but in five large cascades, while countless little watercourses flash out from
the green on the height, and run races in the valley
below—a glorious confusion of verdure and foam.
Above, on the rock, at the head of the cascades—its
glittering minarets seeming to rise besprayed out of
the river — stands Vodena, the Bulgarian "city of
waters," once the Macedonian Edessa.

In Vodena we were most fortunate in being accom-
modated in the house of a Swiss silk merchant. The
family was absent, but, unlike our hosts of Salonica,
had left its furniture behind. The manager of the
factory, a Bulgarian, educated in Vienna, had been
indicated to us as a person of intelligence ; and besides
the introduction from his master, we brought him a
letter from a Bulgarian friend ; hence he received us
with great cordiality. We were soon at supper in a
large airy room, comfortably furnished, and having but
one fault, *i.e.,* two of its sides were glass windows, and
this, during the sunny hours, made it like a hot-house.

At Vodena, fearing fresh carelessness in the orders
given for our journey, we sent to desire the mudir
would come to see us, and he duly appeared—the fattest,

most stolid, most uncouth Turk we ever beheld. With
him we tried to arrange our route to Castoria, but this
turned out to be beset with obstacles. The authority
of the mudir of Vodena, as subordinate of the pasha of
Salonica, went no farther than Ostrovo, *i.e.*, about three
hours distance, and at that station there were no officials
and no horses. Then the mudir insisted that between
Ostrovo and Castoria the way was infested by robbers,
and that he did not know, and no one could tell him,
whether we should find anything like a road between
Castoria and Naum on the lake of Ochrida. Altogether
we were obliged to come back to the plan we ought to
have adopted from the first, and decide to go straight
to Monastir. On this, after another endless series of
conferences, a bargain was struck with some Bulgarian
kiradgees. With Turkish carriers we would have no
more to do.

So much time had been taken up by these affairs that
we stayed a second day at Vodena in order to see
something of the place. When the heat was past, our
obliging and intelligent host came to take us a walk
round the town. The character of Vodena is most
peculiar, the river running alongside of the street; it
might be called a miniature Venice, but for the difference between still canal water and rushing mountain
streams. Straight out of the water rise the handsome
houses of the wealthier citizens. Among them many
are merchants, a few Swiss, and some Bulgarians.
The lower story in these houses is stone, the upper,
wood, and the great fashion here is to paint the walls
white, picked out with blue. The lounge of the town is
a grove on the river, over which plane trees throw their
shade. Here we saw a group of Mussulmans seated in
circle, holding grave and earnest converse. Our host
told us that many councils are held there, and that

at present the Turks are alarmed in prospect of a
regular income-tax, for hitherto they have succeeded
(as the consul at Salonica told us) in paying one piastre
where the rayah paid twelve. Besides being engaged in
a little row with the mudir, which it requires some organisation to prolong, they are busy consulting together
on means to neutralise the effect of the new system;
and as the valuation of property will be performed by
Mahommedan agents, what through national partialities,
what through bribes, they have every prospect of getting
off as before.

We were next taken to see the place on the rock where
materials were hauled up to build the school. Such is
the steepness of the bank whereon the city stands that
it cost less to wind up the stones with a windlass to the
site of the building, than to bring them thither by road.
From this spot the view is lovely, and as we exclaimed
at the beauty of the landscape a Bulgarian muttered,
" Aye, a good land; and it is *Turkish.* The pig always
gets into the best garden." We were now invited to
the garden of a neighbouring house, where we could sit
down and enjoy the view at our ease. A carpet was
spread on the brink of the cliff, and thence, with the
scarlet pomegranate blossoms for our foreground, we
looked down on a scene of beauty which has few
equals. On each side of Vodena the mountains widen,
and through gradual descents of glen and valley subside
into the Vardar plain. The plain in its purple distance
melts into the glittering sea, and on the rising ground
on the farther side of the gulf the light falls on the
white walls of Salonica. Such is the view right before
us; but turn to the left and behold another picture:
from the cascades and mulberry groves of Vodena rises
a low range of wooded hills; above this a higher range
and a higher, till all culminate in the Mount Olympus,

whose broad snowy brow now shines golden in the setting sun. On scenes like these one must gaze and gaze till they are painted on the memory—every hue and line and shade—so that, in after times, among dull street walls and duller walls of drawing-rooms, one may have but to shut one's eyes and call back the living picture. For the sake of thus bearing away the views from Vodena we would have thought no price too dear save that which we paid for it. Sitting in the garden after sunset we both caught the fever.

Had we known what was the matter with us next morning, when we felt so aching and so heavy, we certainly should not have started, even after all the bother of getting the kiradgees to come. As it was, of course they came late, and were of more than Bulgarian stolidity, so that again, for the third time, we had to ride in the sun.

For some distance from Vodena the scenery is of the same enchanting character. You follow the river up a green luxuriant glen, from the head of which it falls in a cascade. Look back, the view is exquisite. On this road we came to a species of toll-bar, and saw foot passengers stopped by Albanians. To our surprise no demand was made on ourselves, our guides calling out that we travelled with buyourdí, and explaining that the toll was only meant for the "poor." Afterwards, for three hours, you descend abruptly on the Lake of Ostrovo. If not so bleak, this little lake would be pretty; its waters are picturesquely broken by a small island, with a mosque. The story is, that this mosque once stood in the centre of the village, and that the waters have submerged all round. But since last year they have taken the turn, and disgorged a strip of bare beach in place of all they swept away. The village of Ostrovo is miserable in the extreme, the dwelling-houses

ruinous, and all of wood; the khan, where we halted for
mid-day, is scarcely in a better condition.

Because of the steepness of both sides of the lake the
zaptiés on this station are not mounted. Those who
accompanied us changed every half-hour at the little
"bothies" which serve them for stations. It is only on
seeing these rural guard-houses that one recognises the
mode in which this road is guarded or infested by its
Albanian police.

After mounting to some height on the other side of
the lake, we came to the khan of Gornischevo, where we
were to spend the night. Great was our consternation
to find it so very bad, that, but for the cutting cold of
the high land whereon it stands, we should have preferred sleeping in our tent. This was, however, not to
be dared, so we had to instal ourselves upstairs in a tiny
room, with mud walls and floor, no glass in windows,
and some difficulty in fastening the door. It may be
imagined that, if it had been possible, we would have
left this place of penance by next morning at daybreak;
but, alas! it was not possible, and we found our only
course was to lie still and tide over the fever fit.

At first the kiradgees were impatient, the guards
unruly, and the villagers, as usual when one comes with
Turks, declared they had nothing to sell. Our obstinacy
conquered theirs, for we were too ill to be driven away.
The guards we let go; the kiradgees were satisfied by
promises to pay their expenses while we remained. The
villagers, seeing the Turks depart and being spoken to in
their own language, brought forth milk, fowls, and food
for the horses, and finally negotiated for a Bulgarian
spelling-book. But at the end of the first day we were
no better. Then the objection to say "die" yielded
to the fear of dying in reality, and dying in this
detestable khan; we despatched a note to the consul

at Monastir, to whom we had already forwarded our
letters of introduction, and asked him to be so kind as, if
possible, to send some sort of a carriage to fetch us. There
is not, in Turkey, one out of a hundred places where
such a request could be complied with ; nor, perhaps, one
other place in the world where such a reception would
await sick travellers as we met with in Mr. and Mrs.
Charles Calvert's house at Monastir.

CHAPTER VIII.

THE ANCIENT BULGARIAN CAPITAL AND THE MODERN TURKISH TOWN.

"Samuel, King of Bulgaria, at the end of the tenth century, established the central administration of his dominions at Achrida. The site was well adapted for rapid communication with his Sclavonian subjects in Macedonia, who furnished his armies with their best recruits. To Achrida, therefore, he transferred the seat of the Bulgarian patriarchate. As a military position, also, Achrida had many advantages; it commanded an important point in the Via Egnatia, the great commercial road connecting the Adriatic with Bulgaria, as well as with Thessalonica and Constantinople, and afforded many facilities for enabling Samuel to choose his points of attack on the Byzantine towns of Macedonia, Hellas, Dyrrachium, and Nicopolis. Here, therefore, Samuel established the capital of the Bulgaro-Sclavonian kingdom he founded."—FINLAY'S *History of the Byzantine and Greek Empires*, vol. i., p. 438.

"To talk with Turks, no men seem better to understand everything, or more fit to rule; to witness their real practice, no men so inapt for authority; all that is debased and debasing, ruinous and disloyal. . . . Those who have chatted with the elegant Turkish agent over a bottle of claret at the hotel, or held agreeable discourse with him in a carpeted kiosk on the shores of the Bosphorus, may find it hard to bring themselves to imagine how the burning houses and violated women of Damascus, the desolated villages and butchered peasants of Syria and Anseyreeyah, can be anyhow the work of a government headed by men so intelligent, so amicable, and, above all, so polite."—PALGRAVE'S *Central and Eastern Arabia*, vol. i. p. 299.

DURING the fortnight we spent at Monastir our strength was not sufficiently re-established to allow of any lengthened expedition, and a ride or two to the neighbouring convents, with a visit to the schools in the town, were all that we could manage in the cool hours of the day. So far as our own pleasure was concerned, the loss of an excursion to the Albanian lake country proved a disappointment; for we had looked forward

CATHEDRAL OF OCHRIDA.

to enjoyment from the beauty of the scenery. On the other hand, our principal aim being to see those parts of Turkey least familiar to Europeans, we were consoled for missing the Albanian lakes by the knowledge that they had been well described in the travels of Mr. Lear. We heard too that another description was in progress from the pen and pencil of an accomplished lady.*

But even these considerations availed little to make up for foregoing Ochrida, not only a scene of unusual beauty, but to us a spot of unusual interest, as the " hundred-bridged city " of ancient Bulgaria. Here, towards the end of the tenth century, Samuel, czar of the Bulgarians, established the capital of a really formidable monarchy, in defiance of the then Byzantine emperor, himself the representative of a Slavonian line. We will not go into the story of those campaigns which at length won for Basil II. the grim title of " slayer of the Bulgarians," but we cannot refrain from telling a quaint love-tale, of which the heroine is Samuel's daughter, and the hero one of the early Serbian kings. We dwell on this legend the rather because it turns on an incident when Bulgaria, in one of its moments of strength, meets the slowly-growing power of its western sister-state, Serbia, with whose history we shall soon have to do. The subject of dispute between them, viz., the cities on the Adriatic, illustrates a point to which we must afterwards refer—that the first kinglets of southern Serbia were also rulers of the northern Albanians, and that the same state which comprehended Montenegro stretched to Alessio and Elbassan.†

---

* See " Through Macedonia to the Albanian Lakes," by Mrs. Walker.

† The early rulers of Serbia are properly called *zupan*, but the " chronicler of Dioclea " speaks of them in this chronicle as " kings," *reges*. Almost to the present day the hereditary pasha of Scutari, in Albania, was descended from a renegade branch of the old Serbian princes of Zeta.

Czar Samuel had resolved to extend his realm to the sea, so he began by taking Durazzo from its Byzantine garrison; but not content herewith he pushed forward to Dulcigno, a town belonging to the young Serbian king Vladimir. In the war that ensued Vladimir was driven to the mountains, where his warriors suffered greatly, and he then resolved to purchase peace for his people by resigning his own person to the enemy. " The Good Shepherd giveth his life for the sheep ; " thus spake the King, according to the old chronicle, and for this among other reasons he is revered as a saint. Samuel led his captive to Prespa, a town not far from Ochrida, where he had a strong castle and kept his treasures ; it was also at that time the residence of his family, among others of his daughter Kosara, a damsel fair, pitiful, and devout.

The pious Vladimir, praying in his dungeon, was comforted by the vision of an angel promising him speedy deliverance ; the pious Kosara, praying in the palace, was bidden by an angel to visit the prison, and humble herself by washing the captives' feet. " In the process of this her good work, she came on Vladimir, and was struck with his noble looks, his dignity, his calmness ; she spoke to him, and was equally astonished with his wisdom and piety ; then hearing that he was of royal rank, and filled with pity for his misfortunes, she felt her heart move towards him, and bade him farewell, bowing herself before him. Resolved to free the noble captive, she hastened to the Czar her father, threw herself at his feet, and besought him, saying, ' My lord and father, I know that thou art thinking to provide me with a husband, as is the custom at my years; therefore I beseech thee of thy goodness give me thy captive the Serbian Vladimir, or know that, rather than wed any other than he, I will die.' The Czar, who deeply loved his daughter, and knew that Vladimir was a king, her equal, rejoiced at her saying and resolved to fulfil her petition. He sent for Vladimir, and after he had been bathed and dressed in royal apparel, he was brought before the Czar, who looked on him favourably, and before all his great men received him with a kiss and gave him to his daughter. After the marriage had been celebrated right royally, Samuel restored Vladimir to his kingdom, and gave him, besides his patrimonial lands, Durazzo and the district thereof. Further, the Czar sent messengers to tell Dragomir, the uncle of Vladimir, that he need no longer remain hidden in the mountain, but might return to his territory of Trebigne, call his people together again, and inhabit the land. Which all took place."

With this glance at the old Bulgarian days we will now return to the present Turkish days, wherein Ochrida has become a place of far less importance than the military station, Monastir. This town is beautifully situated at the extremity of a great plain, flanked by a majestic range of mountains, amid which the snow-clad crest of Peristeri attains a height of 7,500 feet. Besides its Greek name, Monastir has a Slāvic one, *i.e.*, Bitolia (from an older form, Butel), while the Turks uniting both, call the town Toli Monastir.

This variety of appellation is answered to by a variety of population almost as great as that of Salonica, though of somewhat different ingredients. The Jews are numerous, but do not outweigh the other races ; the Mahommedans are Osmanli ; the Slāvs, of whom but few live in the town, people its environs and all the country around ; the Greeks, who people neither town nor country, contrive to have their interests and language represented by the wealthy and crafty Tzintzars. The story of this race, so called by their Slavonic neighbours,

is very curious. It forms part of that which calls itself
Rouman, and inhabits Wallachia, Moldavia, with a portion of Transylvania: without doubt, too, it once was
numerous in Thessaly and Macedonia. At present it is
represented south of the Danube by mercantile communities in Turkish towns, villagers in eastern Serbia, and
shepherds on the Pindus and the Balkan. To this day
the greater part of these speak their own language,
which some call a barbarian dialect Latinized, others a
Latin dialect barbarized. Of late years, however, Greek
schools have been introduced among them, and the Hel-
lenes have been clever enough to persuade them that they
were originally Macedonian Greeks, romanized during
the Empire; hence they identify themselves with Greek
ambitions and antipathies, and make common cause with
the Phanariote bishop in his determination to keep down
the Slavonic element. The sly, grinding, and servile
character of the Tzintzars in Turkey detracts from the
respect one would otherwise feel for their industry and
shrewdness; while the kindliness and honesty of the
oppressed Bulgarian conciliates sympathy, even when, as
here, his intelligence is at the lowest ebb. At that time
the only Bulgarian school belonged to Unionists, and
was superintended by a priest from Brittany, assisted by
a native schoolmaster.

The Mahommedans of Monastir and in the country
about it and Ochrida are said to be more numerous than
the Christians. Wherever this is the case the state of
the disarmed and disfranchised rayah is most pitiable,
and open murder occurs frequently and unpunished.
We will relate two instances which we had at first hand.

A lady with her husband and friend were spending
Sunday at a village near Ochrida. Looking on the
lovely and peaceful scene they said to each other,
" Surely here at least violence has not entered in." But

at that very moment, in the grove below, among the
group of Christians who had been enjoying its shade,
one lay dead, another maimed. The murderer was one
of the Mahommedan zaptiés or rural police. This man had
a grudge at the Christian elder, who had caused him to
be reprimanded for a gross offence. He had been sentenced to a short imprisonment for burglary, but at the
end of forty days was not only liberated, but received
back into his former office, and thus let loose on the
community he had offended—excited by revenge and
armed. Forthwith repairing to a spot where the aged
Christian was at dinner with his friends, he discharged
his pistol at him, and hit, not the intended victim, but a
young man sitting by his side. Three other zaptiés
were present, yet none of them moved to stop the
assassin. A young unarmed Bulgarian, a friend of the
murdered man, raised his hand to arrest the murderer,
and he was at once struck down by a blow which severed
an artery and left him a cripple for life. The cowardly
assassin afterwards made off to the woods, but except for
the accidental presence of an European consul in the
town, he need not have troubled himself even thus far.
The mudir was dead drunk, and when forced to appear
was scarcely able to give the order that the other zaptiés
should pursue their colleague. They went just far
enough to fancy they were not watched, but were seen
to hold a parley with the murderer, who afterwards disappeared in the woods, the zaptiés returning to say that
further search was useless.

Another case of the same kind happened shortly afterwards. A Bulgarian, one of the most prosperous men
in Ochrida, had a sum of money borrowed from him by
a Turk who did not repay it, so at length he made
interest with the mudir to get his debtor put into prison.
At the end of a few days, however, he let him out, only

fixing a future time for payment; but this indulgence
was vain; for the son of the Turk resolved that his
father's imprisonment by a rayah should be bloodily
avenged. He watched a moment when the merchant
was taking his siesta under a tree, and then crept up to
him and discharged a gun into his body. A few weeks
later the merchant died of the wound; yet the murderer
remained at large.*

In this manner murders are committed every day, and
so long as the victims are rayahs the authorities take no
notice; but even if they did the conviction of the assassin
is hopeless, for a Christian cannot give evidence in criminal cases. It may be asked, why do the Christians
not resist? In the first place, they are not, like the
Mahommedans, armed; secondly, the injury of a Mahommedan by a Christian, even in self-defence or the
defence of another, is rigorously punished in Mussulman
courts.

A terrible instance of this deserves record. A late
grand vizier, travelling through the provinces by way
of doing justice and reforming abuses, stopped in his
progress at Monastir. He found before the tribunal the
case of two boys, a Christian and a Mussulman, who had
been fighting, and were both hurt. The Christian
remained long and severely ill, the Mussulman died;
thereupon the grand vizier ordered the execution of
the Christian boy. Now, it may not be known that in

---

* Since writing the above, we have found these and other stories related at
length in "Through Macedonia to the Albanian Lakes," by Mrs. Walker, sister of
the Rev. Charles Curtis, British chaplain at Constantinople. She also says:—
"The Christians of Ochrida complain bitterly of the murders of their co-religionists which have taken place in that neighbourhood within the last three
years. No less than thirty lives have been thus sacrificed, but in no single
instance have the assassins been brought to justice" (p. 211). An American
missionary told us (1863) that near Eski Sagra, in Bulgaria, where he was
stationed, from seventy to one hundred Christians were killed annually by
Mussulmans without inquiry being made.

Turkey capital sentences are rare. A criminal will be ordered to receive a number of lashes, under the half of which he dies, or he is assigned a term of imprisonment in a loathsome den, wherein he is certain to perish ; but he is not *sentenced* to die. Hence the sentence of death pronounced on this Christian caused great and painful sensation. He had only struck in self-defence, while defending a friend from the molestation of Mussulmans ; moreover, he had been himself wounded. It was felt that if in the face of all these extenuating circumstances the Christian lad were to suffer capital punishment, and that too on the sentence of the highest functionary of the central government, it was equivalent to a declaration that any Christian who might defend himself against the blows of a Mussulman should be punishable with the utmost rigour of the law. For this reason a petition for pardon was thrown into the vizier's carriage, and the consuls endeavoured to procure a revision of the sentence. But the very inference deprecated by the Christians was that which the vizier intended them to draw. Accordingly the consular remonstrance was disregarded, the petitioning citizens were punished and exiled, and the vizier himself (a europeanized Turk, who speaks French to perfection), although on the point of departure from Monastir, delayed his journey to witness the execution, and kept his carriage waiting at the door until he saw the Christian die.

No wonder the Bulgarian feels that, so long as the Turk rules the country, resistance to abuse of power is vain ; the Christians of the Serbian principality, however, who have enjoyed at least one generation of freedom, already meet injustice very differently, and an instance illustrating their higher spirit occurred while we were at Monastir.

A Serb merchant, trading in wine, had the ill-luck to fall in love and marry out of his own country, and his wife, a Turkish subject, could not bear to be separated from her family. Hence he passed much of his time near Monastir. The man was supposed to be rich, and a scheme was entered into—and that among the highest personages—to get a sum of money out of him. Accordingly they trumped up an accusation, and got some creature to swear that six months before, on the bombardment of Belgrade, he and the Serb had agreed to seize booty together and to divide it. A share in the plunder was what he claimed. The falsehood of the charge was transparent, but it served as an excuse to put the merchant in prison, and so soon as he was there he received the message, "Only pay so much, and you shall be let out." He answered, "I owe nothing, and will pay nothing." The affair came to the ears of the consuls and some representations were made. Fearing he should escape, the authorities sent to the man, offering him liberation for half the sum originally proposed. He refused as steadily as before. Again representations were made, and at this juncture the Commissioner Subi Bey arrived. This commissioner must visit the prisons, and ask every prisoner the cause of his detention. The case of the Serb having attracted consular notice could not be shelved, and his mouth would not easily be stopped. Yet once more an attempt was made on him, and he was offered his liberty on the payment of only 100 piastres. It was then that the Turks found out they had to do with a man who was accustomed to take no less than justice. The answer was the same : "Do your worst. I will not pay a single para." Under the circumstances there was nothing for it but to try the merchant as fast as possible and to release him on bail. If he took the advice of his friends, he made the best of his way back to Serbia before the commissioner left Monastir.

In this last story we have alluded to a " commissioner," and will therefore explain his visit and functions. From time to time, and frequently at the instance of some European ambassador, the Turkish government despatches a so-called " commissioner " to perambulate the provinces, and root out and punish local abuse. If any further testimony were needful as to the corruption of Turkish officials, the results of one such commissioner's investigations would furnish all the evidence required. When we were at Monastir scarcely a day passed without some maladministrations coming to light, and so far as we heard, Subi Bey lacked neither energy to punish nor shrewdness to detect. But there is little use in ruining wretched subordinates while pashas and their secretaries escape ; so a most unpleasant impression was made on those who heard that another commissioner in the western provinces, having presumed to arrest a high official, had forthwith been recalled. It was much feared that this example would not strengthen the hands nor sharpen the sight of Subi Bey.

One day a mudir entered the consulate. He was an honest, jovial-looking personage, and his face beamed with satisfaction in relating how triumphantly his examination had been passed. In a tone of decent regret he added, however, that of all those examined at the same time none had come out with clean hands but he. Nor did even this unique mudir pretend to have been acquitted of more than dishonesty and injustice ; his mudirlik was in sad disorder, the local Mussulmans despising the law, Albanian brigands infesting the road. But these things were no fault of his, and encouraged by the commissioner's approbation, he had

even ventured to tell him so, declaring himself power-
less to effect improvement unless his authority were
supported by better agents than the local zaptiés.
The commissioner had of course promised him that
all should be done as he wished; a body of regular
troops should execute his orders, and he himself be
raised to the rank of kaimakam. " If God will," ended
the mudir.

Unfortunately his case is no solitary one. Supposing
a new Turkish governor to come to his post, rapacious
and cruel, all those who await him there will be ready
to abet his plunder on condition of sharing his spoils.
But let him be an honest man, with a desire to do justly
and restore order, and he finds that all the traditions of
his predecessors, all his own myrmidons, are against him;
while the central government rarely puts him in a position to be independent of the local Mussulmans, who will
only support him on condition of being suffered to prolong their corrupt régime. Nor, alas, is it only Mussulmans who thrive on abuses and strengthen wicked
hands. We have already alluded to the miserable circumstance that in Roumelia Greek bishops are amongst the
most decried hangers-on of the most decried governors;
and hatred of race or greed of gain is ever sure to
keep numerous rayah agents at a powerful Mussulman's beck and call. Such Christians, being the worst
specimens of their own community, are of course still
more reckless and base than their Mahommedan fellow-
workers; consequently those travellers whose experience
lies mainly in official circles are apt to affirm, and that
with truth, that they found the Christians worse than
the Turks. But these parasite Christians in Turkey are
regarded by their honester brethren with horror as
great as we can feel for them; and bitterly do the better
sort complain that the material oppression of the Turkish

system is a lesser evil than its demoralising action. Only those among the rayahs who are servile and unscrupulous can make their way to power; lawful demands are disregarded, outspokenness and independence of spirit crushed out; while prizes are held out to cupidity and treachery, and the scum of society is raised to the top.

At Monastir we strove to collect information as to ways and means of travelling between Macedonia and the southern frontier of the Serbian Principality. The lamentable plight wherein we had appeared before our kind hosts made us ashamed to tell them that we had purposed, after leaving Monastir, to visit all the places of interest in so wild a district as Old Serbia; on the other hand, we could not make up our minds quite to surrender this cherished plan. By way of compromise, we resolved on going straight from Monastir to Belgrade, seeing the battle-field of Kóssovo, and such other famous spots as could be taken en route. This, at the time, really seemed the utmost our scarcely restored strength could attempt, and even for this it was deemed necessary to ascertain that the road could be traversed in a carriage. Our furthest point on Turkish ground was to be the town of Novi Bazaar, and the way between Bitolia and this station is one of the regular tracks of inland commerce, therefore we had counted on being able to hear all about it at Monastir. But herein we were disappointed; for after asking all sorts of people, nothing but contradictory statements could be obtained, and we had to fall back on the strangers in the land. The consul and his wife could answer for having made their way *tant bien que mal* with a carriage as far as Vélesa. Then Hahn's book testified that he had taken a carriage between Vélesa and the town of Príshtina on the field of Kóssovo. But beyond Príshtina to the Serbian frontier

went no man's ken, and one might have supposed that
Novi Bazaar lay at the other end of the empire, instead
of within a distance of about seventy hours. At last a
Polish officer in the Turkish service, happening to pass
through Monastir, declared that he had ridden over the
whole road and knew that it was traversed by *cannon*,
and thereupon some one remembered that talikas conveying the officials' harems must sometimes pass that
way. On this collected evidence our bargain was made
for a sort of covered waggon drawn by two stout horses,
which, when necessary, were to be assisted by oxen.
Some Tzintzar kiradgees undertook the luggage, and the
consul allowed an intelligent young Albanian trained in
his service to accompany us as cavass.

CHAPTER IX.

" *King.*—Son Marko, may God slay thee! Thou shalt have neither monument nor posterity; and ere thy spirit leaves thy body the Turkish Sultan thou shalt serve.

" *Czar.*—Friend Marko, may God help thee! Bright be thy face in the Senate ; sharp thy sword in the battle. Never shall hero surpass thee. And thy name shall be remembered so long as sun and moon endure.

" Thus they spake, and thus 'tis come to pass."—*Old Serbian Ballad: "Marko's Judgment."*

NOTWITHSTANDING all the comfort and kindness experienced during our stay at Monastir, it was no unwelcome change from a modern Turkish town to that atmosphere of poetry and romance which surrounds the mediæval sites of Serbian power. The site in question is the Castle of Marko Kralïevitch, *i.e.*, of the king's son Marko; it overlooks the town of Prilip, and is one of the rare feudal remains of any size to be found in this part of Turkey.

Even as Scādār, or Scodra, is common ground to Serbians and Albanians, so is Prilip, or Perlepé, common ground to Bulgarians and Serbs. The population of the town and district of Prilip is Bulgarian, but the presence of Marko Kralïevitch's castle connects the whole place and neighbourhood with Old Serbian memories and myths. Who Marko was, and how his name is interwoven with the web of historical legend, forms a story of no common interest; but one so long that, if we begin with it here, we shall afterwards be in no humour to climb a hill and see his tower. Therefore, with our reader's permission, we will do the castle first, our point of departure being that small monastery which stands at the foot of a three-horned rock, some hundred yards distant from Prilip.

Perhaps the monks might have been pleased to show us the ruin and tell us all manner of legends; at least so they usually did when we approached them through a Slavonic medium; but we had left the dragoman at home, and one of the party addressed the caloyers most affably in *Turkish.* Then all was over; the Bulgarians stiffened into wooden stupidity, and left us to make our way to the castle with no better cicerone than the guard. One attempt to mollify them we did make, but unsuccessfully, not being strong in Bulgarian, so began, " We would see Marko———," but then stopped short to recollect the next word. The monk shrugged his shoulders, with a smile, as if to say, "All your wilfulness cannot achieve *that,*" and then answered, " God forgive us ! Marko has been dead these 400 years." So he has; and yet, if all tales be true, this is no reason why we should not see him, if only we could wait until the anniversary of his festival or " slava," and hide ourselves in a certain little chapel where some of his family lie entombed. At midnight the doors burst open and in rides Marko, fully armed, and mounted on his favourite charger—that famous steed Sharatz.*

Left to make our own way to the ruin, we climbed thither straight up from the monastery, but soon found that in this, as in other cases, the longest way round is the shortest way there. An easier road, apparently the ancient approach, leads round the lower part of the hill, and had we followed it we should have avoided clambering over blank slabs of rock, whereon the gentle-

* Sharatz—literally " the variegated ; " probably " piebald."

men's boots slid as on ice. At length we gained an
open space, said to have been the old *place d'armes,*
whence the horns of the rock branch upward right and
left. The best view of the highest of these eminences
is to be obtained from one of the lower, which we
therefore ascended, and thereon found a group of
enormous stones poised against each other, and in
appearance not unlike rocking-stones; however, they
would not rock.

Near the top of the hill is a ruined tower, but the
path thither was barred by a lean grey form which
stopped the narrowest part of the way, and seemed
jealously to watch our meditated ascent. So steadily
did it stand, that we had time to draw nearer and see
what it was—a mountain goat, last sentinel in the feudal
hold.

And now, reaching the higher brow of rock, we found
it covered with walls, but without a single roofed
chamber; so that though one enclosure is commonly
called "the powder magazine," and another "the
lady's weaving-room," they might as well pass for
sheep-pens. On the highest crag poises another of the
giant stones, so surrounded below by masonry that
under it there runs a little corridor. On the top of this
block stand the remnants of a cell, called by the country
people "Marko's Kiosk," wherein Bulgarian legends
describe him as seated, and viewing from afar all who
approach his castle, either as guests or foes. On the
kiosk walls are still to be found the traces of rude
frescoes, horses and dogs—not that we saw them, but
we had heard of them beforehand—and a zaptié who
clambered up the big stone, which we could not, exclaimed at the wondrous drawings he found. Immediately below this perch one finds the enclosure of a lower
chamber, to which the approach is over a slab of rock,

so steep and smooth as to explain the necessity of the
foot-rests therein hewn; some of these are in form
like a horse's shoe; and it would be deemed hyper-
critical to question that they were made by Sharatz.
From this point, looking over the fortified hill, the town
below and the plain beyond, the landscape is picturesque, and might be pretty but from the scarcity of
trees. Though less curious, it has some likeness to the
view from Castle Blagaï in the Herzegovina.

Returning to Prilip by the proper road, we saw
several graves cut in the rock, and passed by the walls
of a small church. It seems that at the back of the
hill there is a ruined chapel, containing some paintings
and tombs, and on a high-peaked separate eminence stands
a monastery, from whence the view is said to be fine.
Dilapidated as Marko's Castle is, it has evidently been a
place of larger dimensions than any mere watch-tower
or Albanian kula. It recalls, not the hold of a robber
chief, but the residence of a feudal potentate, and as
such belongs to the date when careers like those of the
King's Son and his compeers were possible in Turkey.
Hence the sight of it gives local colour to that story of
Kralïevitch Marko, whereon we will now enter without
further delay.

With some writers it is as inevitable to draw parallels
as with some speakers to make puns; but surely a bad
parallel is even more vexatious than a bad pun. We
begin with this remark, in order somewhat to excuse
the irritation wherewith one cannot but reflect on those
writers on the character of the King's Son Marko, who
have called him the Serbian "Roi Arthur." No doubt
Marko resembles Arthur in so far that he is the hero
of a wide cycle of legend; but in no one of them does
he occupy the position of a Roi; and the character
of Arthur as chief of a circle of paladins, as champion

of a falling cause, as perfect knight and Christian king, is realised, not in Marko, but in Lāzar, the last of the Serbian czars. Indeed, with one exception, the ballads about Marko belong to a phase later in date, lower and feebler in tone, than the highest strains of Serbian minstrelsy ; and these lower-pitched songs group themselves around the Kralïevitch, just because he in his own person is typical of a lower period, because his class of achievements began when that of the heroes of the czardom was closed.

These legends convey to us the only extant picture of manners in Serbia during that dark period after the Mussulman had succeeded in overthrowing Christian rule, yet had not thoroughly substituted his own. At this time the policy of the Sultans exhibited, what some persons are pleased to term, an unprecedented regard for the feelings and rights of the vanquished ; in other words, these rights and feelings were regarded until the conquerer had established himself in the country and could tread the vanquished down. Until in one way or another every noted Christian could be got rid of, it was necessary to begin by soothing and flattering such prominent aristocrats as would agree to do the Sultan homage ; and during this interval the said aristocrats found themselves following the Grand Turk in his Asiatic campaigns and serving him against the Latin abroad, while yet at home they attempted to protect their countrymen from the lawlessness of Moslem spoilers.

Of these Slavonic nobles, in their eminently false and eventually untenable position, Marko Kralïevitch furnishes us the type. It is because of this his typical character that there is interest in examining into the functions and qualities attributed to the King's Son by

popular song, for thus we may form some idea how the
Serbian people looked on the leaders left to them during
the first three centuries that followed the Moslem invasion. Over this whole transition period Marko's life
is supposed to extend. He lives 300 years, and during
this long career his character undergoes all the phases of
a gradual degradation, such as undoubtedly showed themselves in the class he personifies, as it passed from its
prime to its fall.

Marko begins life as one among the chosen circle of
youths educated by the Serbian Czar Dushan to be the
future ruling class in that empire which he hoped to
leave more extended and more civilised. In spite of his
high birth and warlike tastes, the Kralïevitch is studious
and turns his studies to account. An archpriest instructs
him in writing, and in reading books both clerical and
lay ; during the Czar's last campaign young Marko
appears as his secretary and as the depositary of his
testament.

Such Marko's spring-time ; but the premature death
of his master leaves his half-tame spirit to run wild in
the mazes of the troubled times. He is well-intentioned,
kindly, and dauntless, but devoid of settled purpose ; he
lacks the moral strength that can steadily sacrifice small
aims to great ones, and subordinate egotism to an ideal :
he is too haughty to yield place to an equal, and ends
by falling under his inferiors. Marko becomes a Turkish
vassal.

This is the first step downward ; but for some time its
pernicious consequences appear not in their full extent.
Marko is still a champion to whom the Christian looks
for protection, and whom the Mussulman flatters and
fears : songs tell of his exploits in camp, castle, and
court. A change for the worse comes on slowly, but
surely. The King's Son is insulted by the Turks, and

though he takes signal vengeance on the individual, his
equal comradeship with them is at an end. He retires
more and more from political scenes; his achievements
become those of a slayer of monsters, or mere feats of
strength, such as excite the wonder of the hunter and
the hind. They grow, too, ever more mythical in
character, till at length, merging into the lingering
myths of heathenism, local legends of Marko can hardly
be distinguished from those properly belonging to the
ancient wood-gods.

Deeper and deeper Marko sinks into the forest, till
his bond-sister, the Vila, or mountain-nymph, tells him
he must die. The last we see of him—once knight in a
Christian court, and long the pride of the Padishah's
armies—is lying outstretched on his mantle, close to a
mountain spring, his cap drawn over his eyes, dying like
a worn-out haïduk—robber-outlaw. Yes, a haïduk;
300 years after Serbia's warrior nobles consented to do
homage to the Mussulman the last trace of independent
Serbians seemed to die out in the mountain forests as
haïduks.

Marko leaves neither monument nor successor. The
class to which he belonged sank into unknown, un-
honoured graves; the Turk they had helped to establish
in Europe suffered no Christian to continue in the position
held by Serbian nobles; the Slavonic race in the empire
of the Sultan came to be represented only by rayahs or
by renegades.

Such is the story of Marko; nor less significant than
the incidents of his career are the virtues and vices
assigned to him by the popular song. This Serbian
King's Son is never represented as an oppressor of the
lower classes; on the contrary, we find in him the
people's champion, defending them against outrages
perpetrated by the Turk. Again, we find Marko sung

by the peasants as manfully drubbing every Turk with
whom he comes into antagonism; nor dares the Grand
Seignor himself contradict him, even when he slays a
vizier. "Of any Turk," so says the Sultan, "I could
make another vizier; but where could I find another
Marko?" Moreover, at least in his earlier days, Marko
"fears naught save God and the truth," and judges
righteously even to his own hindrance. Dutiful he
shows himself to both parents—to a worthless father and
to a mother noble as a Roman or Spartan, or, better said,
as a *Christian* matron. Finally, Marko is hospitable
and bountiful; he is the friend of the unfortunate, of
little children, of dumb animals; and he is true to his
creed; for, although a vassal of the Sultan, he never
forsakes the Orthodox faith.*

Doubtless the picture has its shady shade. Marko is
rough in manners, and a hard drinker; nay, he bursts
into passion so sudden and violent as almost to equal
the Scandinavian Berserk.† Though a true friend, he
is relentless to those who affront him, even to women;
and his outrageous treatment of one lady who mingled
the refusal of his hand with a jibe, must be set off

---

* In Bosnia a blind minstrel was one day heard reciting a poem about Marko
to a street audience of Orthodox, Latins, and Mussulmans, all equally interested
in the Slavonic champion. The minstrel being himself a Latin, chose to represent his hero as belonging to the Western Church, when instantly one of the
Mahommedans present interrupted him with a blow, exclaiming, "How darest
thou make out Marko a Latin, when during 400 years we have never been able
to make him out a Mussulman?"

† In one song a Serbian noble is represented as cautioning his attendants not
to press too obsequiously to welcome Marko, not to kiss his mantle, or try to
relieve him of his sabre, lest Marko, being in an ill-humour or excited with wine,
should push his horse past them and ride them down. This instance has been
cited to prove how mercilessly Serbian nobles must have treated their attendants.
Surely it rather indicates the reverse. The noble in question would scarcely have
thought it necessary to warn his servants against incurring treatment to which
they were accustomed from his own hands or those of most of his guests. No
doubt the times were rough enough; but Marko's violence is always instanced as
exceptional. The very word for "oppression" used in the Serbian songs is a
Turkish word.

against his disinterested championship of numerous damsels in need.

Other peculiarities of temperament are curiously characteristic of the still primitive race to which he belonged. For instance, although he asks more than one lady in marriage, and saves more than one lady from offence, the rough Serbian hero is never represented as performing his exploits under the influence of *la belle passion*. On the other hand, of all those questionable gallantries, deemed so excusable by Romance minstrels, Marko is guiltless by look, act, or word.

Another strongly marked trait is his rooted antipathy to the Osmanli, an antipathy perpetuated to this day among those renegade Serbian nobles — the Bosniac Mussulmans. Bitterly hating the Asiatic, Marko absolutely loathes the African. Taken captive by a Moorish king, he represents as worse than all the weariness of his prison the love-making of the Moorish princess. When at last the promise of freedom bribes him to flee with her, he only bears with her till she attempts to embrace him with her black arms, and then in a frenzy of disgust draws his sabre and strikes off her head. The graceless deed is humbly repented of; churches and monasteries are raised to atone for it; but still, when Marko confesses it to his mother, he half excuses himself by describing his sensations : " Oh, mother ! when I saw her close to me, all black, and her white teeth shining ! "

More excusable and more dignified is the last evidence of hatred to the Mussulmans given when Marko's death-hour is come. He shivers his lance that the Turk may not use it ; he slays his horse that the Turk may not force it to carry wood and water in its old age ; he breaks his sword into four pieces that it may not be used by the Mahommedan, and Christendom curse him as one who has put a weapon into the enemy's hand; he even desires that his grave may be concealed, lest the Turk should rejoice over his fall. Nay, the Serbian peasant believes that Marko's thorough detestation of the Mussulman, whom he himself detests so thoroughly, will yet find a more practical expression. "When the times shall be fulfilled the Kralïevitch will arise out of the cave where he is sleeping, and valorously lead the Serbians to drive the intruder from their fatherland."

So much for Marko's typical character; and long it was commonly supposed that he had no existence in any other. But some years ago a diligent numismatic collector brought to the Museum of Belgrade some coins found in Northern Macedonia, with the superscription "Marko Krāl." To no other person in Serbian history could this name possibly belong, so inquiries were set on foot, old records consulted, and the discovery made that Marko Kralïevitch actually reigned at Prilip, and had had an historical career.

He was found to be really, as tradition had reported, the son of the historic Kral Vukashine, one of the governors appointed by Czar Dūshan. Vukashine's territory extended from Macedonia to the Adriatic, and thus had for its two principal fortresses, on the west Scādār, on the east Prilip. At the sudden death of Dūshan, the regency of the empire and the care of his young son passed to the Kral, as to the second person in the realm; and he, to retain the power in his own hands, treacherously murdered his ward.

Marko took no part in this crime, nor did he even share the fruit of it, separating himself from his father and continuing faithful to the old royal line. But when both the young prince and the wicked Kral were dead, and the Serbian people met to choose a new czar, Marko considered himself a candidate whose claims ought to distance every other, and he could not forgive the election in his stead of Lāzar Grebliánovitch, Count of Sirmium. It would seem that in his disappointment he gave way to a burst of menace ; for Lāzar, usually so mild, called on the assembled nobles to support him in reducing Marko, and finally deprived him of his fief. Landless and exasperate, Marko sought the camp of the Turks and offered his sword to the Sultan,—apparently for those campaigns in Asia wherein, Mahommedan warring against Mahommedan, adventurers from Christendom cared not on which side they fought, so that they earned booty and renown.

It is said that the Sultan at one time gave Marko the nominal investiture of " Castoria and the Argolide " (?) but afterwards, when Amurath marched on Serbia, the heir of Vukashine resumed possession of his own Castle of Prilip. Hence, whereas the Serbians know Marko only as Kralïevitch, or King's Son, the Bulgarians of Prilip call him " Marko Krāl."

That Marko fought for the Turkish Sultan in many a campaign is doubtless, but that he ever marched against his native country remains at least wholly uncertain. Indeed it appears impossible that he should have been in the habit of serving against any people of his own communion, when we read of his consternation at being summoned to fight the Orthodox Prince of the Roumans. Loyal to his suzerain, Marko Kralïevitch came into the field ; but when he saw men of his own faith arrayed in battle against Mahommedans, and himself on the Infidels' side, horror took possession of his soul. " Oh, God ! " cried he, " do thou this day destroy all those who fight against Christendom, and foremost Marko." Then, throwing himself upon the spears of the Christians, or, as some say, plunging into a morass, he met the doom he felt he had deserved.

Of this repentant death, the feeling, if not the facts, has been truthfully preserved in popular poetry. Taken in conjunction with Marko's life-long antipathy to the Turks, his proud bearing towards them, and his championship of the oppressed among his own countrymen —all these extenuating circumstances have contributed, in the eyes of the Serbian peasantry, to throw a veil over the one stain on the shield of their favourite hero, namely, that he served the Sultan. They cannot deny it, they would not palliate it, but they regard it less as a crime than as a calamity; indeed they set it down to the effect of a curse hurled against the Kralïevitch by his own father, when by one of his righteous judgments he prevented him from becoming Czar.

Unfortunately modern literati, emulous of the *naseweis* school of modern Germany, have showed themselves determined not to let the errors of the "peasants' hero" lie thus reverently enveloped in mist. On the stage of the little theatre of Belgrade, an author ventured to exhibit Marko Kralïevitch, not in his traditional character—rescuing the oppressed, and performing marvellous exploits—but in a situation wherein tradition and history have alike forborne to exhibit him : arrayed on the side of the Turks in a battle between them and the Serbs.

The announcement of an historical piece had, as usual, drawn to the little playhouse numerous spectators of the poorer class, and the entrance of each traditional hero was welcomed with delight. But when Marko, the well-beloved Marko, presented himself in so odious a character, a sudden chill fell on the audience : to enthusiasm succeeded (not even the expected hoots and hisses, but) a gloomy, restless silence; the silence of those who are at once puzzled and pained.

It appeared however as if, to the end of the scene,

the people hoped that Marko would do something to atone for his false position; but at last he quitted the stage without a redeeming act or word. Then one simple heart could bear it no longer; and bursting out, almost with a sob, a peasant's voice cried, "Marko is *not* a traitor."

CHAPTER X

THE distance from Monastir to Prilip is estimated at about six hours, and six very long hours it took us to jog over the rough and dusty plain that separates the two towns.

On the outskirts of Monastir we passed a church lately built by the Bulgarians for themselves, but in which, as we have since heard, the bishop insists on performing service in Greek. However, half-way between Monastir and Prilip one crosses the stream of the Tzerna Rïeka (Black River), and at every step on the other side the Greco-Tzintzar element becomes weaker, and the Bulgarians have got more and more the upper hand, both in church and school.

The spurs of the Babuna range, surmounted by the ruin of Marko Krāl's Castle, become visible some distance from Prilip, and a prospect of getting to hills and a river makes one quite impatient to arrive at the journey's end.

Prilip is a town of from 6,000 to 7,000 inhabitants, and forms the seat of a large yearly fair: hence it is one of the most prosperous places in southern Bulgaria, and boasts a very tolerable bazaar. On occasion of this fair the peasantry from the neighbourhood crowd hither, and are said to be well worth seeing. In one district the women are remarkably tall and stout, strong, thrifty, and industrious. It seems they are not allowed to marry until the age of thirty years, and that for two reasons : first, in order that their parents, who had the labour of bringing them up, may be rewarded for their services ; and secondly, that they themselves may not be encumbered early in life with large families. ˙A similar practice ˙ prevails in some of the country districts in Serbia, men marrying young, and choosing housewives in the full *force de l'âge.* This arrangement struck us as somewhat queer, and as unlikely to be agreeable to the woman, being conceived on the principle of getting the greatest possible amount of work out of her ; but the men justify it by its results, and say that domestic comfort, social morality, and fine physical development prevail in the districts where it is followed. In the towns, both of Serbia and Bulgaria, the women follow the Oriental fashion of marrying and fading extremely young.

A letter from the British consul at Monastir procured us hospitable entertainment at the house of a rich Bulgarian merchant, where two rooms were given up to our use. The inner chamber was large, well stocked with cushions and carpets, and so cleanly that, although we prepared our beds on the divan instead of on our iron bedsteads, no disturbance of rest ensued. The merchant and his family trade in tobacco, which grows in abundance on the Prilip plain, and one of the brothers conducts the business of the house with Vienna. Unluckily he was from home, but his Viennese proclivities were represented by a musical clock, which strikes up tunes every quarter of an hour. We had been warned that we should find this article in our bedrooms, and that its performances would be fatal to sleep ; but it seems our good-natured hosts had found out that it disturbed their former visitors, for just as we were vainly composing

ourselves to rest, a daughter of the house demanded
entrance, clambered up on the divan, and stopped the
clock.

The civilised importer of the musical timepiece, and
the grave and portly master of the house, are both
members of a family of five brothers, who with their
wives and children eat at one table and live in houses
opening on one court, within the protection of one high
wall. These family associations, or zadroogas, are general throughout Bulgaria, and have certainly tended to
sustain the Christians under the lawless régime of the
Turk. Besides securing to every household the presence
of a number of men to protect the women from intruders,
they ensure widows and orphans a maintenance and
security in the bosom of their own kindred. Where
land is to be cultivated, they enable a family to do its
own work without hiring strangers, and they provide a
sphere for younger sons without sending them out to
service. Thus, too, family intercourse is kept free from
the dread of spies; old ties, old memories and customs
can be fostered, and foreign innovations can be with-
stood. Above all, natural affections find their due satisfaction; young women are preserved from temptation
and young men are certain of a comfortable and well-
regulated home. The Bulgarians may thank their united
family life if they have preserved at once their nationality and their purity of manners while living under the
yoke of strangers, and often side by side with people the
most depraved.

Of course, however, the use of these family societies
being mainly to defend and conserve, they become
unnecessary when danger is past; neither can they
co-exist with the movable relations and individual
enterprise of modern society.

There are three Christian schools in Prilip, one for

the Tzintzar merchants who choose their children to
learn Greek, the other two for the Bulgarians, who
bring together 400 scholars, and manage them their
own way. The Bulgarian books come from various
places—Philippopolis, Pesth, Vienna, Belgrade; some
are translated from the Serb reading-books, some from
those of the Americans. The principal schoolmaster
was a Serbian, and told us the children could read his
language as well as their own. They showed us very
fair writing, and seemed to know their way on the
map. We asked if they could sing, and were at first
told "No;" but presently a big boy was produced who
was being trained as a priest, and he began to intone a
psalm. We soon regretted having provoked his performance, for it proved at once dismal and monotonous,
and was strongly sounded through the nose.

Not observing the usual picture of Cyril and Methodios we asked after it, and in the course of some
incidental explanation we found that the children were
well acquainted with the history of the national
apostles. Nor did they omit to apply its teaching,
for they coupled with the memory of the translators
of the Slavonic Bible the name of a patriotic citizen
of Prilip, who had been principally active in founding
their own school.

Prilip was one of the places where some years ago
the Greek clergy held their burning of Slavonic works;
believing therefore that a present of books would be ac-
ceptable, we gave some to our hosts, to the schoolmaster,
and to the best scholars. There was great anxiety
for histories of Serbia, and scarcely were we returned
to our quarters when a Bulgarian pope called on us,
and requested that we should give a book also to him.
We begged his acceptance of a New Testament, and
seeing that it was in the common language of the

people, he forthwith began reading it aloud. Another
student in a humble line of literature was found in the
little nephew of our host, who opened one of our
spelling-books and began to read from thence an edify-
ing description of the "Domestic Cat." The little girls
collected eagerly to hear him, so we took the book and
gave it to one of them, telling the boy that he would
obtain access to it by offering to read it to his sisters.
When the mother heard this she called to the other
women, and they all blessed us heartily for letting the
men know that women too should learn from books. The
housefathers, thus challenged, declared that they did
wish for a female school, and had room and money for it,
but how to obtain a teacher they could not tell.

Conversation over the books induced a certain degree
of cordiality; but as our letter of recommendation to our
entertainers was not from one of their own people, they
showed us little confidence, and eluded questions as to
the state of the country. Having heard all we wanted
from other sources, this was of less importance ; but unluckily we found them equally unwilling to tell us any
stories of Marko Kralïevitch, though Prilip, being his
own patrimony, is said to produce a plentiful crop.
Afterwards we obtained a book of popular poems, and
therein found some Bulgarian tales respecting the
famous Krāl, but they proved very inferior to the Serbian
legends—long-winded, trivial, and full of Turkish words.
As a grotesque specimen of a quasi-religious story, we
will here give a Bulgarian song, which so far as we
know has not hitherto been translated. It is called—

THE GRUDGING OLD WOMAN.

When St. Peter received his summons to enter into
the Paradise of God, his old mother followed at his heels
—a wicked mother, a sinful soul. And she called after

him, "Stop, my son; wait for me, that I may enter
with thee; for I also would see Paradise." Then St.
Peter turned him about, and answered: "Begone, thou
sinful mother; it is not so easy to enter Paradise; the
gates of Paradise are closed, but open stand the gates of
Hell. Hast thou forgotten thy conduct while we both
were yet in the world? Thou wert rich; yes, my
mother, a rich woman, with much substance, and flocks
and herds more than enough [*lit.* over thy head]. But
the mighty devil had power over thee, and kept thee
from giving anything for God's sake to the poor. One
day two beggars came to thee; they came to thee, and
played before thee—from morning till evening did they
play before thee; and yet, mother, thy heart did not
melt to them, thou didst not take pity upon them. Thou
didst bring forth a crust of bread, grown stale by three
weeks' keeping; thou didst bring forth a flaxen girdle,
and this thou gavest them as alms; and even as thou
gavest it thou didst turn away, and cry out crossly,
'Ah, God! golden God! hast thou given me flocks
and herds that my substance be eaten by strangers
and foreigners, by the German and the dumb Turk?*
What is left for my own children?' Alas, mother!
sinful soul! those beggars were not beggars; they were
two of God's angels: one of them was St. Elias and the
other St. Nicholas.

"Of another sin I will convince thee. Thou didst
accept the office of godmother—of godmother to little
children—and thou frequentedst the christening feasts;
but thou wentest to the christening for the eating and
the drinking: to the children thou gavest no gift; not

---

* "Dumb" is an epithet applied by Slavonic peoples to all who do not speak
their language; more particularly to the German, whom they call by no other
name than *nemac*, the dumb. The word *Slav* is probably derived from *slovo*, word,
and signifies those who can understand each other's speech.

a shirt, nor baby-linen, nor stockings, nor a little cap.
Naked, barefooted, these children are standing to accuse
thee before the Lord. How wilt thou answer to the
Lord?

"Yet again I will convince thee. Thou, mother,
wert a landlady, and thou didst pour out the glowing
wine. Travellers came to thee, poor travellers, and
asked of thee, 'How dost thou sell?' And, mother, thou
didst swear to them, 'May God or the devil receive my
soul, as I give full measure for full payment.' Then
what didst thou pour out to them but one hundred
drachms of wine mixed with three hundred of pure
water? Oh mother! sinful soul! full payment thou
tookest, short measure thou gavest. Wait, mother,
while I condemn thee. The mighty devil had power
over thee, and from thy poor neighbour thou didst
borrow flour; pure flour didst thou borrow, and didst
render again half flour, half ash-dust."

And now St. Peter and his mother came nigh to the
Paradise of God; St. Peter walking first, after him the
sinful soul. They had to pass the Bridge of Thread,*
and over it the saint passed safely; but when the sinful
soul would follow him, and had got to the middle of the
bridge, in the midst it broke under her, and she sank
down to the lowest Hell.

St. Peter became chief of the archangels, and prayed
constantly to the Lord. Three years he begged and
prayed—three years and three days: "Alas, Lord!
golden God! grant me a pardon for my mother, for my
mother's sinful soul!"

But he was answered: "Don't ask for that, St. Peter;
thou mayst not beg pardon for thy mother; thy mother
has many sins on her soul."

---

* Evidently an idea borrowed from the Mahommedans; as we have said, the
legend is full of Turkish words.

Still St. Peter prayed on for three years and three days; and at the end of three years and three days the Lord said to him: "Cease now, St. Peter, for thou hast obtained pardon for thy mother's soul. Get thee to the sea-shore, and twist thee a slender rope, and lower it to the bottom of Hell. There may thy mother catch it, and be hauled up to the light of day. But, besides thy mother, there are seventy other souls; let them take hold of her skirts and her sleeves, that they too may be drawn out of Hell."

Off went St. Peter—off went he hastily to the sea-shore; and he tore off half his skirt, and he tore off his flaxen girdle, and of these he twisted a long slender rope, and lowered it to the pit of Hell. Alas! the little rope proved too short! But St. Peter wore a red feather; this too he tore off, and added it to the length of the rope.

And now St. Peter cried aloud: "Catch hold, sinful old mother! I have obtained a pardon for thy soul. And you seventy other souls, do you hear? You are to lay hold of my mother's skirt—of her skirt and of her sleeves—and you too shall be drawn up into the light of day."

But behold the old woman was *grudging*, even as she had been while yet in the white world. She called out to the seventy other souls: "Begone, you dogs! begone, you swine! what right have you to be saved with St. Peter's mother? I myself suckled St. Peter: I sang the lullaby of St. Peter: ye did not suckle him; ye did not sing his lullaby."

The Lord heard the old woman's words; suddenly the rope brake, and down she fell to the lowest pit. Alas, mother! sinful soul! thy place in Hell has been fully earned.

*　　*　　*　　*　　*　　*

From Prilip to Vélesa is a journey of eleven to twelve hours, too far for one day without travelling through the heat ; we therefore started from the former place after dinner, and resolved to sleep in the Vezir khan, at the foot of the Babūna Pass.

The entrance to this pass begins about two hours from Prilip, but we had been led to believe the distance shorter ; and had been warned that after entering the hills we must not attempt to sit in the carriage. We therefore concluded that it was not worth while to get into the carriage at all, and started on horseback at once ; but we found, to our cost, that this was a mistake. Crossing the plain the heat was perfectly sickening ; and when succeeded by the chill of the ravine produced sensations which caused us to anticipate a revival of all the horrors of Gornischevo. We were yet to continue for a few days the disagreeable part of our journey, so called in contradistinction to the agreeable part which followed. Certainly it is a difficult thing to know at what time of year to travel in Bulgaria. In winter the cold in the plains is terrible, in summer the heat ; in spring, roads are all but impassable, while the mountain regions are exposed to the swelling of streams; finally, autumn is the unhealthy season, when most places become almost uninhabitable from fever.

Leaving Prilip by the road to Vélesa, one has on the left the Prilipska Řieka, Marko Krāl's castle, and the range of Babūna hills. Here and there we perceived some small ruins, but heard that they are not old, only kulas, which, till lately, were tenanted by the haïduks. Instead of the haïduks, their next of kin, the zaptiés now hold a kula on the highest point of the pass ; here one pauses to rest after scrambling up the vile Turkish road on one side of the ravine, and before scrambling down the vile Turkish road on the other.

The descent is certainly all but dangerous. Our poor beasts slipped most distressingly, and crossed and re-crossed in search of footing, that is to say in search of some spot of earth which the Turks have not attempted to pave. The attention necessary to get safely to the bottom was the more grudgingly bestowed on our part, because, after the bare ugliness of the Macedonian side of the Babūna, we wanted thoroughly to enjoy the wooded valley on which we had come among these recesses of the hills. Truly picturesque are the peaked summits of its steep green sides, whereon the little village of Czenitza lies in the midst of a patch of golden field.

Our mid-day halt on the morrow was at the Khan of Vranofzé, where we obtained access to a cool dark corner set apart for the drying of curd. There we found a victim to Bulgarian notions of hospitality, *i.e.*, a relative of the family in whose house we were to lodge at Vélesa, who had ridden out thus far in the scorching heat to meet us. It was cooler when we resumed our road, but a particularly rough bit of ground occurring shortly before we arrived at Vélesa the carriage lurched violently, and one of the horses sprained its foot. Nevertheless, when we begged to be set down at our quarters by the back door, which was easy of access, our remonstrances were disregarded, and we were mercilessly dragged up a steep street to the front. Thus ended for the second time (the first happened in the course of a journey between Constantinople and Belgrade) our attempt to traverse the interior of Turkey in a coach. The luckless harems, that cannot help themselves, may possibly be transported part of the way in talikas; and Consul Hahn, being resolved to make the experiment in the interest of his projected railway, succeeded in taking a light vehicle with good horses the whole distance from Belgrade to Salonica.

Vélesa lies on the banks of the Vardar, which at this distance from its mouth forms already a powerful stream, and is made use of by wood-merchants to float rafts down to the Ægean. The banks of the river are steep and high; and the town, climbing them on both sides, seems to contain a fair number of good houses. Indeed its situation affords such facilities for trade as made it even in early times a place of importance and comparative civilisation.

Vélesa is a thoroughly Bulgarian town; out of 4,000 houses only 1,000 were divided between Turks and Tzintzars, while the other 3,000 were Christian Slāvs. Under such circumstances the Bulgarians of Vélesa were able, till long after the Turkish conquest, to continue as the guardians of a certain amount of national learning. A store of valuable MSS. was said to be hidden in one of their monasteries; and for a short time it would appear that their city possessed a Bulgarian printing-press. All this adds evidence to the fact, which a nearer acquaintance with the Christians in Turkey in Europe is ever revealing to the traveller, namely, that the earliest times of Turkish oppression were not in all respects the worst, and that for the Bulgarians the cruellest trial of patience occurred within the last ninety years. Till the end of the last century the Slavonic patriarchates were not abolished; and while they remained, the conditions on which the Slavonic Christians parted with their national liberty did not appear to be altogether ignored.

The books stored at Vélesa escaped destruction during more than 400 years of subjection to the Ottoman; it was his Christian middleman, the Greek bishop, who ordered the bonfire that consumed them on the market-place; and it is said that this took place only thirty years ago. Hence, so long as the Porte continues to refuse to Bulgarian communities their native pastors, and to force on them a foreign clergy, its Slavonic subjects cannot but believe that it is even more disposed to trample on their liberties than it was in the first era of its rule.

Five or six years ago the Bulgarian movement gained strength sufficient in Vélesa to menace serious disturbances; at last, in the words of the people themselves, " The authorities saw that Bulgarians never could be made into Greeks and never would agree with Greeks, so we got some of the consuls to take our part in order to keep the country quiet. Since then we have been suffered to hold service in our own language and to set up our own schools."

The Bulgarians at Vélesa are certainly of a sturdy stock, as is shown by the following incident which has lately been communicated to us by letter. The deputy of the Greek bishop being on a tour to collect revenue, came to Vélesa, held service in the church, and began to read in Greek. The people instantly interrupted him, ordering him to read Slavonic. He replied that he did not understand it. "Then," said they, " we have some one who does;" and thereupon the service was performed in Slavonic as they desired. But besides being stubborn in the assertion of their rights, these people are really anxious for the spread of education, and to our knowledge have sent forth at least one active disciple of progress, Hadji Traïko, to whom we have already alluded as patron of the girl's school at Sophia.

Of course, such Bulgarians at Vélesa as have traffic with the south speak Greek, just as those who trade north of the Danube acquire German. The merchant in whose house we lodged spoke Greek fluently, but his wife and family did not know a word. European

travellers who do not know Slavonic, or even know about
it, are often deceived as to the extent to which Turkish
and Greek are spoken in the interior of Turkey in
Europe; inasmuch as in a Slavonic city they are frequently quartered with one of the very few citizens
acquainted with either of these tongues.

The house in which we lodged at Vélesa was that of
a rich merchant. It was furnished in the European
style, and its master wore a phase of Frankish dress very
common in Turkish towns, viz., loose white trousers, a
black coat, and small red fez. He had had just converse
enough with the world to rub the crust off that solid and
shrewd intelligence which characterizes the Bulgarian
mind, and which needs only the prospect that honest
pains will be compensated to develop into as sturdy and
practical a national character as any south of the cliffs
of Dover. So long, however, as the Bulgarians live
under an Oriental despotism they will scarcely get rid
of their present defects, a sulky timidity and want of
openness.

The master of the school at Vélesa is a priest, reputed
among his own people for learning. We had a private
letter for him, so he came to see us, and told us a good
deal about the Bulgarian movement. Both he and our
host declared that the state of the country was much the
same as that which we have already alluded to in the
neighbourhood of Prilip, Monastir, and Salonica. Christians are frequently murdered by Mahommedans, who
thus pay off debts and get rid of any one whom they think
in their way; highway robberies are constant. None of
these vexations can be put an end to until the Turkish
governors take to punishing Mussulmans with rigid and
summary justice; this, however, they will not do, inasmuch as their rule depends for support on the interest
which the Mussulman element has in perpetuating it.

The raising of the taxes in the new method was also
bitterly complained of. When they were raised in kind,
things seemed so bad that they could not be imagined
worse; but now that the peasant is compelled to pay in
money, while he remains without means of bringing his
produce to market, the oppression is intolerably greater.
As the government of the Porte must have money, taxes
are now taken from Mussulmans as well as Christians,
although not in the same proportion. But the Mussulmans being lazy are thus completely ruined, and those
who were landed proprietors in the neighbourhood are
trying to sell their tchifliks, but trying in vain. No one
is willing to buy them, partly because few are rich
enough, and partly because Christians, if they improved
the land, would run a risk of having it taken back from
them. These grievances relating to the sale of land are
almost identical with those we heard of in Bosnia.

In all the principal rooms of the house at Vélesa the
side that looked on the river was entirely given up to
windows, and windows without shutters, while in these
countries Venetian blinds are yet unknown. The glare
was terrible, the heat that of a forcing-house; all day
long we felt ourselves, as it were, melting in the sun.
By the time of evening coolness the schools were closed,
so we did not see them, and had to take the word of our
informants that the Tzintzar school contains thirty to
forty pupils, and the two Bulgarian schools 500 between
them. There is also a curious little Bulgarian monastery, which is said to be worth seeing.

But what we could not do ourselves in ascertaining
the state of education at Vélesa, was to some extent
supplied by our dragoman, who opened the store of books
he had received from the Missionary at Salonica, and
announced that he was prepared to sell. Immediately
purchasers flocked to claim them, and especially pounced

upon the Old Testaments—of which the few books already translated into modern Bulgarian were bound together in volumes, costing half-a-crown a-piece. All our store was sold at Vélesa, and the priest was quite cross with us because we had not brought a larger supply. Some of the elder men slowly counted up the number of the prophetic books, and asked, somewhat suspiciously, why the *whole* Testament was not there. Our explanation appeared necessary to satisfy them that there was no intention of suppressing certain writers.

At Prilip—where the historical associations of Marco Krāl's Castle connect the town with the history of Serbia—the schoolmaster came from Serbia, and much interest was shown to possess Serbian histories. In Vélesa, where the historical associations are entirely Bulgarian, and only those of a seat of learning, the Serbian works of history and popular poetry were not asked for, and Bulgarian religious books were the thing desired. Apropos of this we may remark, that the Bulgarian's mode of cultivating his language necessarily differs from that of the Serbian. The written language now cultivated in Serbia is taken from the mouth of the shepherd and mountaineer, its root vocabulary is that of the national songs, and its pronunciation is borrowed from the minstrel warriors of Herzegovina and Montenegro. With the Bulgarians, on the contrary, the language of the common people has degenerated into a corrupt and frightful patois, full of foreign words, Greek, Turkish, and mongrel, with hurried enunciation and snarling accent. In short, if anything can excuse the Greeks for their inability to comprehend that the Bulgarian objects to part with his mother-tongue, it is the excuse suggested by one's ears on hearing Bulgarian spoken after Greek. On the other

hand, the Bulgarians regard the Slavonic of Cyril
and Methodios as their own ancient language, and
are inclined to make use of it (as the Greeks of
Athens make use of ancient Greek) for a model
whereon to reform their modern tongue. Should
they ever succeed in resuscitating this glorious old
language, with its organ tones and rich depth of expression, they will do an unparalleled service to the
whole Slavonic world, and their national life will find
its expression in one of the noblest channels of human
speech.

The editor of a Bulgarian newspaper aspired to make
it equally readable by Serbians, Croats, and Bulgarians.
Practically he succeeded, and he told us that the old
Slavonic furnished him with words and forms intelligible
to all southern Slāvs.

In the meantime, next to the patois of the Bulgarians,
the Serbian spoken by the mongrel population of Belgrade may perhaps take rank as the least musical and
dignified of all Iugo-Slāvic dialects ; while the pure
Serbian, wherein Montenegrine pleaders advocate their
own cases before the judgment-seat of Cetigne, is
the most pleasing to the ear for its distinctness and
harmony. A master in the gymnasium of Belgrade
told us that among the scholars were a few from the
mountains on the southern frontier, and that when they
and the other boys were repeating the same lesson their
intonation and style were as different as the declama-
tion of orators and the chattering of apes.

Among the books we disposed of at Vélesa the translation of the Bulgarian Old Testament is due to the
exertions of the American, Dr. Riggs ; while the translation of the Bulgarian New Testament was undertaken
for a Protestant society by John Neophytos, the present
abbot of Rilo, a monastery in the Rhodope, about four

days' journey north-east of Vélesa.* As we did not visit the convent of Vélesa itself, and we did visit the convent of Rilo, we will go back a summer and pass over a chain of mountains to describe the largest of the Bulgarian monasteries, and that wherein the national element has most successfully held its ground.

* Through Istib, Karatova, and Kustendil.

CHAPTER XI.

THE traveller on the high road between Stamboul and Belgrade journeys for many a weary day along the sultry and feverish Thracian plain, nor until he approaches the town of Philippopolis does he espy in the west the boundary of the Rhodope, on the north the distant range of the Balkan. A day later he has gained the hills, and supposing him still to keep to the post-road he will cross the Balkan by its most westerly and most famous pass, the Kapu Derbend, or Gate of Trajan.

But we, though on the way to Belgrade, did not at this point keep to the straight line, for we wanted to visit an old Bulgarian monastery, said to lie in a gorge of the Rhodope, at the foot of its highest mountain, Rilo; so we struck into the hills, crossed the pass called Kis Derbend, between the Rhodope and the Balkan, made our first stage at the mineral waters of Bania, and our second at the little town of Samakoff.

The upland plain wherein Samakoff lies is crossed by the bridle roads from Bulgaria, Macedonia, Albania, and Thrace. Hence it forms a point of meeting, not, as might be expected, for commercial travellers, but for highwaymen escaping from one pashalik to another; for which purpose the Turkish authorities take care to allow an interval between each crime and the pursuit.

We came to Samakoff provided with a letter to one

of its wealthiest Christian inhabitants, who received us hospitably, and conducted us to a chamber surrounded by a broad divan. In arranging the cushions to form our beds we lighted on a pair of loaded pistols. Of course we covered them up again and said nothing, but their concealment testified to what we had been told already, *i.e.*, that although to pacify a revolt it was nominally conceded that every Bulgarian may have the means of defending his women from Mussulman intruders, yet while Mussulmans swagger about in belts full of pistols, the Christian, if he have arms, must take care that they be not seen.

Samakoff was the first place west of Constantinople where we found Greek not even understood, but this did not constitute the people barbarians. On the contrary, they had two nice schools—one for boys, one for girls; large airy edifices, built of wood, and gaily painted, after the fashion of the country. Over the doors was an inscription to the effect that they had been erected by the elders of the community without a farthing of help from any one; the emphasis being a reflection on the late Greek bishop and existing Turkish government. We visited these schools—examined the work, the maps and the copy-books, heard the children sing hymns and read, and rewarded the best scholar in each with a copy of the Bulgarian New Testament.

Another object of interest at Samakoff is the convent of Bulgarian nuns, which we came to visit under the following auspices. We were scarcely settled in our chamber before it was entered by a sweet-looking young woman, dressed in a black mantle and a quaint coif. To our amazement she accosted us in German. She told us that she was an Austrian Slāv, and had come from Vienna with her mother, who was servant to a German physician; on her mother's death the old doctor advised her to seek protection as a nun. She said the community at Samakoff was of the order of St. John of Rilo, and acknowledged as spiritual superior the abbot of the monastery of that name. It was formed by a number of elderly women, each of whom took a young woman to live with her, wait on her, and after death become her heir. The nuns supported themselves by their own spinning and weaving, and of their earnings have built them a church: they do not attempt outward benevolence, but on the other hand pride themselves on receiving help from none. To beg a livelihood they hold as degrading as we do ourselves. The works of merit constituting sainthood seem in their estimation to be five: diligence, obedience, abstinence from meat, wearing black garments, and making a pilgrimage to Jerusalem. This journey to Jerusalem is the event of each still life, and lends it its redeeming spice of expectation, retrospect, adventure, poetry. The nuns have not their goods in common; some are comparatively rich, others poor; some are assisted by their relatives towards defraying the expense of the expedition, others have to pay all from their savings. When the money is in hand two set out, and walk till they fall-in with one of those parties of pilgrims constantly passing to Jerusalem from Bulgaria. They cross the sea to Joppa, journey thence to the Holy City, and are received into a monastery, where they may remain a whole year, to join in all the feasts and festivals. On their return home they bring away with them a holy picture, a marvellous concoction of scarlet and gold, depicting all the Holy Places, all the holy persons, and the devil, distinguished by horns and a tail—as is not unnecessary among so many grim forms.

Primed with this information, we set out to visit the nunnery, and having hopped from one to another of the

big stones which act as bridges to the muddy river-
street, we entered a gate and found ourselves in a clean
and dry inclosure in front of a neat little church. Behind
it lay the gardens of the nuns with their little dwellings,
containing two rooms—a tiny kitchen and divan-encircled
parlour. Here we paid a succession of visits, first to the
principal mother of the community, then to a very old
and saintly mother possessed of a famous picture of Jerusalem, and beloved among the younger nuns for her endless stories of adventures by the way; finally, to the
special mother of our guide, who caused her dear child
to show us various little treasures and to bring out her
best Sunday mantle. Then came evening service, which
we attended, and in the dusk of the church the young
nun whispered to us with sparkling eyes how the sisters
prayed for the success of the brave Montenegrīnes, and
that God would give all Christians a good courage and a
united heart. "The great Christian Powers," said she
—"is it true that they are leaving that little band to
fight alone? Of the people here I say nothing, they
deserve what they suffer, for they have not the hearts of
men. But the Montenegrīnes are the soldiers of the
Cross. No nation in all Christendom has battled with
the Infidels as they."

We wished to have taken the nun with us next day to
the monastery as an interpreter, but it was thought more
discreet for her to stay at home, so we gave her at parting a Bulgarian Testament and she gave us each a rosary
of plaited silk, marked here and there with large mother-
of-pearl beads—a gift involving the sacrifice of some
thirty piastres from the fund she was storing for her
journey to the Holy Grave.

This day there had been rain, so the glorious sun of
the morrow rose on an earth refreshed and green; men
and horses had enjoyed a rest, and now set forth with

glad spirits and bounding tread. Our shining-armed
cavalcade was clattering and gay: eight well-mounted
Mahommedan zaptiés—two of whom were cavasses of the
pasha of Philippopolis—our dragoman, and an Ionian,
deputed by the British consul to give us the benefit of
one Christian sword in case we should be attacked in
the mountains by the first cousins of our Mussulman
guards. The Bulgarian driver of the waggon wherein
we had come over the hot plain could not leave his
horses even for a pilgrimage, but the boy was allowed
to go, and on his nimble feet soon had the advantage of
us all.

But all our enjoyment would have been marred had
we ourselves been left to ride the sorry steeds furnished
us by the mudir at Samakoff. Luckily a bakshish
induced our guards to change with us, and we could not
but laugh at the superstition current respecting horses
"accustomed to carry a lady" when we felt these high-
mettled animals treading proudly and gently under the
unwonted side-saddle, the flowing skirt, and fluttering
veil. A well-trained Turkish horse is delightful for a
journey, being used to walk both for travel and parade.
Hour after hour he bears you evenly, lightly, over the
rough track, and when you enter the town he rears his
head and marches with a procession step, representative
of your dignity and his own.

But something more than fine walking became necessary when we left the plain for the pathless glen, and
began to dispute with the torrents their rocky passage
down the mountain side. When at length we reached
the head of the pass we came to a bit of rough highland,
where a halt was called, and the guard showed us the
graves of a party of robbers here run to earth and killed.
"Until quite lately," said he, "this was the worst glen
in all the hills, but the new pasha of Sophia has lately

put some robbers to death and caused their heads to be
stuck on poles: that will stop it for this summer." Soon
after they called our attention to the hollow sound of the
earth beneath the horses' feet, and explained that it was
caused "by prodigious wild boars, which lived underground and undermined all that part of the hill."

And now came a descent almost impracticable for
horses, and yet so cutting to the human foot that we
remained mounted far longer than was safe. The stiff
stair led down to a basin, receptacle of waters from all
the neighbouring mountain streams. One of the zaptiés
pointed out to us a clear pebbly spot where the water
escaped by an underground passage. This little tarn of
the Balkan,* with its grey stones and solemn fir-trees, is
one of those scenes which would repay an artist for the
journey from England, only to carry it home in his
portfolio. We sat down on its beach, and could have
sat there till now, but the sun was sinking, and the
road, ostensibly six hours, was very certain to take ten.
The first sight on remounting was a view over beech
forests opening on a grassy vale, at the extremity of
which rose an outline of grey walls. "Here," quoth
the guards, "is the boundary of the domain conceded
by old sultans to the great monastery of Rilo." Scarcely
had we crossed the frontier when we were met by the
convent guard, dressed in white linen tunics and scarlet
girdles, and commanded by a man in the garb of an
Albanian, who, however, styled himself a Serb, meaning,
doubtless, that he belonged to the Serbian creed. The
array of armed men on horse and foot lent sound and
colour to the long dark wood that followed, and once
below, the passage through the narrow valley became
every moment more beautiful. Exceptionally beautiful

---

* The Turkish name Balkan, though usually limited to the northern chain, or
Hæmus, is in this part of Turkey given to all mountain ranges.

BULGARIAN MONASTERY OF RILO.

indeed, for the mountain scenery between the north of
Albania and the Danube is usually rather wild than picturesque. Amphitheatres of hills, covered with wood,
to which the blending of beech and oak with fir gives
in the distance a bluish green; few sudden elevations,
few rocky precipices—such is its character, answering
exactly to its Slavonic name, "Plánina," that is to say,
"forest mountain." Doubtless single scenes show extraordinary loveliness, and the gorge of Rilo is of this
number. The hills terminate in horned crags of the
most picturesque abruptness, of the most fantastic form.
From these the wood sweeps down in masses, which
break into groups and tufts on the park-like meadows
which fringe the valley stream. On one side a large
building lies to the right, which we took for the monastery, but which proved to be a house set apart for
pilgrims, who crowd hither on certain days. To arrive
at the convent itself the whole length of the valley must
be traversed. The mountains draw nearer and nearer—
they seem once more about to close—when, serried in
their angle, rise the rugged towers and swelling domes.
Outside the gate, in stately row, stand long-gowned,
long-veiled, long-bearded caloyers, who gravely salute
and sign to us to enter. As we pass through the portal
out ring the bells—Christian bells. Who knows what it
is to hear their voices in a Mussulman land? not in
the city, nor in the villages of the plain, where they are
forbidden, and where at any rate they would jar with a
thousand conflicting sounds, but in the wild hiding of
the Balkan, breaking on the stillness of convent air.

We were so thoroughly tired out by our long day's
scramble, that we scarcely received more than a general
sense of peace and beauty as we passed through the court
and into the galleries of the monastery. They led us to
a chamber painted in bright colours, and furnished with

low well-carpeted divans. Here we remained, and had our supper served—as much chicken, fruit, and sweetmeat as the hungriest could wish, besides rice and clotted cream and a huge glass jar of excellent wine. We found also a little cupboard in the wall wherein a bottle of wine and sweetmeats were placed in store for private refection. But that night we wanted nothing but sleep.

Next morning we were invited to an interview with the abbot in his chamber of audience, and found him with two or three venerable monks, one of whom, with a long white beard, we had the night before mistaken for the superior. The real superior is not more than middle-aged, small and spare, with a refined intellectual countenance unusual among Bulgarians, who are generally large and ponderous men, with a wise expression rather than a clever one. But John Neophytos is no common person. His name stands on the title-page of the modern Bulgarian New Testament, and his knowledge of his own language, both ancient and modern, together with his zeal to educate and benefit his people, caused him to accept the offer of a Protestant society to undertake the translation. He has a store of the sacred books in his convent, and finding we had several with us he exhorted us to turn our journey to account by dispersing them abroad among the people. He told us that the American missionaries in Constantinople, who are translating the Scriptures, keep up a correspondence with him, and that two of them had that year been to visit him. Then were shown us the curious old documents which mark the early history of the convent. An inscription on the tower in the court states it to have existed under the mighty Czar Stephan Dūshan, who united Serbia and Bulgaria in his realm. But the earliest chrysobul is of the end of the fourteenth century, and from a personage who styles himself John Shishman, Faithful Czar and

Autocrat of all the Bulgarians and Greeks, *i.e.*, of the Greeks in Bulgaria.

The next documents are Turkish firmans, such as many of the richer monasteries were able to buy from the first Sultans. The monastery of Rilo, in virtue of its privileges, stands (like our Abbey of Westminster) under no bishop, and hence has been able to maintain its exclusively Bulgarian character. It consists of 150 monks, each of whom has a pupil, who becomes his heir. In all, the personnel of the convent amounts to 400 souls. Women are excluded, and it is even said that no one of them may dwell on convent land. This does not, however, extend to visitors, nor to the female relatives of pilgrims. The revenues of the convent depend partly on its mountain pasturage, partly on the gifts of pilgrims. Within the last century it has been benefited by the liberality of its northern co-religionists, and the monks have been allowed to gather funds for their new church by begging journeys through Russia, Serbia, Austria, &c.

The acquaintance which the superior showed with the history of his country and with the present needs of his countrymen, his services in the matter of the translation, —all struck us as strangely contradictory of a report we had heard at Constantinople, that the Greek Patriarch did not appoint native bishops to Bulgarian eparchies because there were no natives sufficiently educated. We afterwards heard that John Neophytos had been pointed out and demanded as bishop by his countrymen, but that the only effect of thus recognising his talents was for the jealous Phanariotes to banish him to this secluded abbey of the Balkan. As it is, he has a lithographic apparatus in the convent, and spoke of setting up a printing-press. Though, under the eye of jealous prelates, the light must be carefully hid under a bushel, there can be little doubt that the influence of such an abbot on the young

students in the monastery of Rilo, will send them
forth on their begging journeys able to sow as well as
glean.

One remark of the abbot's struck us especially. We
told him that the first Slavonic monastery we had ever
seen was that of Cetigne in Montenegro. His brow grew
dark, and after a moment's hesitation he said, "It is
reported that that monastery is now given up to the
Mussulmans and burnt." We asked him where he had
read it? "In a transcript from the *Journal de Constantinople.*" "Is that all?" cried we. "Then do not
distress yourself; that journal has burnt Cetigne and
killed the whole population of Montenegro already two
or three times over."

"But," asked the abbot, "do you believe the great
powers of Europe will sit still and allow that monastery
to be burnt?" "We trust and believe not. France
will do her best to save it." "France," said he, "perhaps; but England!" Feeling heartily ashamed of
ourselves, we answered that the want of interest displayed by England in the Slavonic Christians arose in
great part from her ignorance respecting them—that one
really never heard their name.

"I have understood so," he replied. "The Americans
have told me as much. It is, however, a pity that so
great a country, whose children are free to travel where
they please, and publish what they please, should remain
in such profound ignorance of the *Christians* in a country
where she is on such intimate terms with the *Turks.*
For the rest," he added, changing his tone, "what have
I to do with these matters? I live here as a mouse in a
hole, and our Bulgarian people are quiet. Do you please
to go over the monastery?"

The monastery is well worth going over, but first let
us pause in its open gallery, and feast our eyes on the

rich mass of wood that rises precipitately behind the towers in the court. The hill serves the convent at once for wall and screen.

The church standing in the court is new, the former one having been burnt to its foundations. The restoration took place in 1839, with money in great part gathered from alms. The building is in the form of a Greek cross, with domes, and has cloisters painted both within and without. The interior is supported on columns, and has a beautiful iconastasis of gilded wood, achieved by the Tzintzar carvers who do all that sort of work in Turkey. A Christ's head was pointed out to us as painted by a native of Samakoff who had studied at Moscow. It showed the softened Byzantine type of the modern Russian school.

Strange worshippers were in the temple—shepherds from the Balkan, talking a barbarous dialect of Latin and calling themselves "Romans," while they live as savages. These people herd flocks, and when the men are absent the women defend the huts, and like the female Albanians, are noted for their accurate shooting. Their wild mode of life was illustrated by their remarks on ourselves; for, seeing that we were foreigners and accompanied by a Turkish guard, they took it for granted that we had not come hither of our own free will, and pointing at us asked, "From what country have they been *robbed ?* "

But for such monasteries as that of Rilo these shepherds would be shut out from any form of worship, but here they assemble at certain times to confess and take the sacrament. How far these people are edified by services in a language which they understand not is perhaps an open question, but we were witnesses of the instruction which in such instances may be conveyed by sacred pictures. A fresco of the birth of Christ is painted on the wall of the church. The older of such frescoes are grisly icons, respecting which it may at least be said that those who bow down to them are *not* worshipping " the likeness of anything in heaven or earth ;" but the modern pictures are more life-like, and this one was a genuine Oriental scene. One of the shepherd-pilgrims caught sight of it, and shouted out in rapture, " See, there is the birth of the Christ." The women crowded round him, and he pointed out to them the Babe, the mother, the star, the shepherds, the ox, the ass—explaining as he went on.

We afterwards attended evening service, at one part of which the monks took of their caps, and remained for some time bare-headed, their long locks flowing down their backs. The singing was good as to voices, but monotonous and nasal-intoned. It seemed to us to differ somewhat from what we had heard in Greek churches ; but not to have improved as far as the Serbian psalmody, in which Western influence has counteracted the idea, apparently prevalent in the East as in Scotland, that there is something saintly in music through the nose.

The most interesting part of the Rilo monastery is the old tower containing the original church. The times wherein the latter was built reveal themselves by its position high up in the wall, which has no window or lower opening, except one overhanging the doorway through which to pour stones or boiling oil on the assailants of the gate. This is not the chapel of St. John of Rilo, who lived and died a hermit, worshipping in caves and hollow trees ; it is not even the place of his interment, which lies at some distance on the hill. It is said to have been built at a very early date to defend the monastery from robbers, and was doubtless afterwards useful during the worst days of Mussulman fanaticism, when the life of a monk must have demanded a brave man. At the foot of the tower is a cell, wherein insane persons are confined, and whence they are brought into the church during service by way of being exorcised. The monk asked us if such persons were found in our country. We answered "Yes; but instead of cells we lodge them in large and airy dwellings, and instead of the priest they are brought to the doctor." "And do they recover?" "They do sometimes, but alas! not always." "Strange!" cried he; "that is just the way with ours."

The last place to be visited is the mortuary chapel, wherein we perceived numerous skulls on the altar. We were told that to have a skull placed there is a compliment to the departed, for which the relatives are willing to pay. Also that here, as in the Greek parts of Turkey, the dead are disinterred in order to judge by the state of their bodies whether their souls are in heaven or hell.

In recompense for our liberal entertainment at the convent we could get permission to leave nothing next morning save a donation, ostensibly for the church. On the other hand, we carried away some curiously carved wooden spoons, the portrait of old King Shishman, taken from a contemporary document, and a brand new history of St. John of Rilo, depicting his eccentricities, miracles, and burial.

CHAPTER XII.

HAVING got to Vélesa, the thing was to get away again. The horse which had sprained its foot was not seriously injured, but could not be used again for some time, and the driver wanted us to wait at Vélesa while he rode back to Monastir to get another. But this was not to be thought of; so we paid him his bakshish, and gave him a letter of explanation to the consul at Monastir, while another letter of the same tenor was sent by the Turkish post.

Being rid of the coach, how were we to proceed? On horseback? But the road to Skopia passed over a broiling plain; besides, we felt too weak and ill to ride throughout a whole day. In a talika drawn by buffaloes, after the fashion of the country? But buffaloes walk three times as slow as the slowest horses, and can only journey during the few hours of cool. In this dilemma, our dragoman came to us with a suggestion from the master of the house, which, as he expounded it, sounded strange enough. " Listen," said he, "that I may explain to you how the Turks convey their women from place to place, and themselves travel when they are sick, for hereabouts no one goes in coaches. There is a little chamber, with a door and windows, made of wood, and fastened on poles; horses go between these poles, before and behind, to carry the chamber, and men walk, two on

each side, to steady it. The Turks call this a taktaravān."* In other words, there was nothing for it
but to travel in a litter, and, as it proved, a very rude
one. Its sides were not padded, it contained no seats,
and yet was not long enough to lie flat in. It was,
moreover, too narrow for us to sit comfortably side by
side, and in any other position one or other ran the risk
of bursting open the door. The supporting poles were
fastened to each side of the wooden saddles of the horses,
but in the rudest fashion, with ill-tied knots which constantly slipped, so that now the equilibrium of the
" piccola camera " was overthrown on one side and now
on the other. The few men who attended on the litter
paid very little attention to its balance; and but for our
cavass, whose love of fault-finding and ordering about
him stood us on this occasion in good stead, we should
have been upset many times. The heat of the sun,
beating on a low, dark lid, we avoided by nailing some
sheets over the roof so as to form a white drapery. Of
course it is vain to attempt to see country traversed
in such a fashion, so the landscape through which we
passed between Vélesa and Skopia may remain unde-
scribed.

Our mid-day halt was in the Kaplan khan, and while
there we became sensible that the weather was under-
going a change : the kiradgees predicted that on the
morrow there would be a thunderstorm. We started
again in the taktaravān, but ordered our horses to be
saddled and led by its side. Soon, the heat abating
and the day drawing near to its close, we began to fear
being late in Skopia, and lost all patience with the slow
motion of the litter. We got out, and found ourselves
on a desert-looking plain bounded by low hills ; over-

* We spell this as the pronunciation—possibly the mispronunciation—struck
our ears.

head a grey sky lit up with a lurid sunset; the castle of
Skopia in the distance. A sense of unwonted coolness
was scarcely more refreshing than that of freedom to our
cramped limbs. Usually we were very sparing of our
horses, fearful of knocking them up by fast travelling,
but the neighbourhood of their night's quarters and the
comparatively easy ground now gave us an excuse for
the gallop wherein we longed to indulge; so off we set,
and arrived at the end of that day's journey in better
spirits and far less wearied than we had felt or fancied
ourselves when starting from Vélesa.

From the little window of the taktaraván we had
looked out for the village of Taor, identified by Hahn
with Tauresium, birthplace of the Emperor Justinian.
After we arrived at Skopia, and were comfortably
ensconced in the clean house of a Tzintzar merchant, we
got out our books, and read up all such lore as we could
find regarding the emperor and his cradle. The Goths,
who from beginning to end have stood godfathers to
so many Slavonic achievements and personages, were
long set down as the country folk of Justinian, and his
native name was derived from a Gothic word. Luckily,
philology has lent its aid to the refutation of this error.
"Upravda" is no longer forced into "aufrichtig," but
allowed to be the genuine Slavonic equivalent of
Justinian. Even the name of the emperor's father,
Istok, is now assigned to its real origin. It is a curious
coincidence that the famous Byzantine emperor of
Slavonic extraction should also be the emperor famous
for compiling a code of laws, for in the early history of
every Slavonic people the kingly lawgiver is a person
of higher repute even than the war-leader or conqueror.
Whether it be the Bohemian Krok, Queen Libussa,
the Polish Cracus, the Slovakian Svatoplūk, the Serbian
Dūshan, or, nearer our own day, Peter the Great of

Russia, and St. Peter the bishop-chief of Montenegro ; the warlike character is the subordinate, while that of the remodeller, the legislator, is the aspect under which the Slavonic hero is most admired.*

Justinian showed his regard for his native village by causing it to be defended by a square wall and four towers—a style of fortification termed a "tetrapyrgon ; " he also built or restored towns and villages throughout the district, and especially the chief city Skopia. To it, when rebuilt and beautified, he gave the name Justinianea Prima, and made it the seat of the archbishop of Illyria. So it remained until Samuel, king of Bulgaria, established his residence at Ochrida, and removed the archiepiscopal seat thither, when it would appear that the name of Justinianea Prima, being identified with the see, was transferred from Skopia to the new capital. Procopius says that it would be hard to describe the churches, the magnificent houses, the pillared halls, the market-places, and fountains, wherewith Skopia was adorned in its Justinianea Prima days; it was also well supplied with water by an aqueduct ; and altogether its prosperity was so firmly established that it long continued one of the finest and most opulent cities in that part of the world. Under the Serbian czardom it flourished, under the name of Skoplïe, as a free city with a great yearly fair, and specimens of its coins may be seen in the museum of Belgrade. In 1347 Skoplïe became the scene of that great Serbian *sabor*, or parliament, wherein Stephan Dūshan was proclaimed by the title of Czar, and promulgated the code that bears his name.

---

* As regards the present prince of Montenegro, Mr. Stillman gives the following testimony : " I have myself heard Turkish functionaries in Albania praise his justice and trustworthiness in terms which recalled Haroun-al-Raschid, while in any dispute in which Turk and Christian are engaged near the frontier, and in which the Turk believes he is in the right, the disputants go to a Montenegrin judge in preference to a Turkish one."—*Herzegovina.* W. J. STILLMAN. Longmans. 1877.

Here, too, the metropolitan of Serbia was raised to the rank of independent patriarch.

As the last czar of Serbia made his stand against the Turks on the field of Kóssovo, north of Skopia, this town was one of the first prizes of the conquerors; nay, some traditions say that it became peaceably subject to them as part of the inheritance of Marko Kralïevitch. In the very year of the battle of Kóssovo certain it is that Sultan Bajazet sent Turkish colonists to Skopia, so that it must have fallen directly under Turkish rule long before other parts of the Serbian realm. The withering influence told on it surely, but at first slowly; the early colonists built handsome mosques; in 1686 a traveller describes it as still a flourishing city; and even in the last century Ragusan and Venetian merchants frequented it, and have left their names written on the pillars of the principal khan. But now Ragusa is no longer free, and Skopia is a decaying and wretched place, its inhabitants sickening under the unhealthy exhalations of undrained marshes. A still more melancholy fate has overtaken Novo Berdo, a town two days' journey north of Skopia, whose coins we also saw in Belgrade. In Serbian days, Novo Berdo was celebrated for its rich silver mines, and was called the Mother of Cities; Major Zach, who visited it in 1858, found only sixteen houses, of which one was Christian, and fifteen Mahommedan. The Mussulmans, who are descended from Asiatic colonists, say that the city used to contain 6,000 houses; this, however, is only half the number insisted on by the Christians. One source of decay is to be traced in the neighbourhood of a certain castle, now a ruin, but till lately the residence of an hereditary governor. Such governors were lawless Albanian chieftains, who, during the disorders of Turkish rule, exchanged their hills for the pillage of flourishing Serbian cities, and finally themselves perished in revolts against the Sultan's government.

At Skopia we found our quarters prepared for us in the house of a Tzintzar merchant, who lived in the most agreeable part of the town, *i.e.*, on the banks of the river Vardar. Our host was a grumbling old man, who astonished our servants by the extreme parsimony which, in spite of considerable riches, he practised in his own diet. The day we left, a younger man and a pretty-looking young woman in rich costume entered the garden, and we heard that it was a family festival. They seemed ready enough to enter into conversation, but the presence of the cross housefather tied our tongues.

The proverbial unhealthiness of Skopia led us to fear taking the fever while we remained there; but this time the change of weather saved us, though our cavass was unwell, and wore a livid hue during the whole time of our stay. To run no risk, we had intended remaining only one day, and then to journey through the pass of Katchanik to the monastery of Gratchanitza and the town of Príshtina, on the plain of Kóssovo. But the kaimakam of Skopia sent to urge our remaining two days, since by that time he could provide us with a carriage wherein we could travel the whole way to Gratchanitza. To this arrangement we agreed, and resolved to devote our second evening to a visit to the castle.

The citadel of Skopia stands on a low platform of rocks, which must have been fortified from a remote period. We were told that, properly speaking, we ought not to have been suffered to pass within the castle gate on horseback, but that we had been permitted to do so, lest, not understanding the custom, we might be offended by a request to dismount. Within

the fort we found a few poor-looking Turkish artillery-
men, and the whole place looked deserted and melancholy. The kaimakam used to reside in it, but his
seraï (palace) was lately burnt down, so at present he
lives in the town, while the blackened walls of his
deserted dwelling by no means add to the trimness of
the citadel.

Mounting by means of a stair in the wall to one part
of the crenulated battlements, we enjoyed a singular
though not a pretty view over the treeless level and
low-topped hills.

On the north-east the plain of Skopia is bounded by a
low chain of mountains, called by the Turks Kara Dagh,
or Black Mountain, and by the Slavonians "Bulgarian Tzerna Gora." The zaptiés said that these hills
were inhabited partly by Albanians and partly by Bulgarians. Northward lie the collateral ranges of the
Shaar Plánina (ancient Scardus). In these are the
sources of the River Vardar, which flows through the
plain of Skopia. Part of the plain is planted with rice-
fields, and the eastern half is occupied by a marshy lake,
whose surface Hahn estimates at "an hour" in length,
the same in breadth. It could easily be drained, but
not being so, leaves Skopia a prey to pestilential fevers.
From our position on the citadel we could trace the
two highways, or rather high tracks, which traverse
Skopia. That by which we were travelling leads from
Macedonia to old Serbia and Bosnia; another, running
from east to west, crosses a pass in the Shaar Plánina
to Prizren, and unites Thrace and Northern Bulgaria
with Albania and the Adriatic.

The only building of any beauty that struck our eye
was a mosque with a particularly handsome minaret.
The guide said it was "four hundred years old"—meaning that it was as old as a mosque hereabouts could be,

for four hundred years is the term roughly assigned to Mahommedan occupation of the Slavonic lands. To say that any building is "four hundred years old," implies that it was built by the first conquerors; to say that it is "*more* than four hundred years old" is a significant mode of referring it to Christian times. "Now-a-days," added the zaptié, "they build no fine mosques, nothing but wretched little white-washed things."

Next day our visit was to the Slavonic school, our host assuring us that the Greeks had none. In this direction, then, we had traced the Græco-Tzintzar influence to its vanishing point. Whereas at Monastir the Tzintzars have schools, and contrive to withhold them from the Bulgarians, at Prilip they have but one school, while the Bulgarians have two; at Vélesa, their one school is much smaller than those of the Slāvs, but at Skopia they have no school at all. Skopia is, indeed, the point where the Bulgarian element meets the Serbian, and in Serbian districts neither Rouman nor Greek can ever assert himself to the exclusion of the Slāv. It would appear that the historical pride and expectation of one day resuming empire, which gives the Greek so positive a power of self-assertion in face of the Bulgarian, meets its match in the historical pride and definite ambition of the Serb. The Tzintzar merchants at Skopia are its most wealthy citizens, but the Christian schoolmaster was a Serb, and in his sanctum we found pictures of the ancient Serbian kings and of the heroes who had flourished in those days when Skopia was the seat of a Serbian sabor.

There were three Slavonic schools in Skopia: two contained 60 scholars between them, and another, which was larger, held 100. The Christians had built a large church, apparently unmolested, for which liberty they

were possibly indebted to the circumstance that Skopia was
at one time a consular station.   In districts between this
and Nish there are places where the Christians, having
received the Sultan's firman permitting them to build a
church, have seen it twice thrown down by the neighbouring Mussulmans, and only succeeded in keeping it
after the expense and labour necessary to rear it a third
time.   If any such story were connected with the
church of Skopia we should probably have heard it; but
we did not even hear complaints of the Greek bishop.
At the time of our visit he was absent, and probably
his substitute read the service in whatever language the
people pleased.

While we were in the school at Skopia, there arrived
a merchant who was anxious to see us, because, as he
said, he had heard of us the year before in Bosna Seraï.
He traded with that city, and told us that he had been
taking thither cotton from Seres and tobacco from
Prilip.   He further related that his father was a Mon-
tenegrîne, banished from the mountains for breaking
the laws; that he himself had made money as a travelling merchant, and settled in Skopia.   Appealing to
his experience of different parts of the country, we
asked him whether he considered that Bosnian or
Albanian Mussulmans behaved the better to the rayah.
He said that the most cruel, rapacious, and lawless
Mussulmans in Turkey were the Albanians at Ipek,
Diakova, Prisren, Prishtina, and the Mahommedans
near Prilip.   The Bosnian Mussulmans are very oppressive, but after all it is "only because they are
Mussulmans; they speak the same language as ourselves," whereas Albanians and Osmanlis, "not speaking our language," would be enemies, whether Mus-
sulmans or no.   We asked him if he had found the
Albanians faithful to their engagements when they

promised protection and peace. That he admitted. "If the fiercest Arnaout give his word of ' Bessa '—peace— to the poorest rayah, he will keep it; the Bosnians have no such talisman, and scarce think a promise to the Christian sacred."

CHAPTER XIII.

ON the evening before we left Skopia, sounds of rumbling and crashing, as of a cart upset at the door, announced the carriage promised by the kaïmakam. We went down for an inspection, and found the horses tolerable, the driver an Arab. The vehicle was, we were assured, the best in the country, and had conveyed the harem of a rich official between Skopia and Salonica. Hence it deserves to be described. A little cart on four wheels, without springs or seats; four poles support its canopy, and from the canopy depend curtains: the curtains are cut in strips, and devoid of buttons or strings, so that they keep out neither sun nor rain, but when the wind blows they stream outward like banners or flap the faces of the inside passengers.

For the use of this family coach for two days we had been told that the due price would be at most 200 piastres; the proprietor, who accompanied it, demanded 700. We left the arrangement to be discussed, but were surprised when, after long debate, the figure did not come down. It was the old story: the proprietor was a Mahommedan, and the zaptiés had a finger in the pie. We had to send our cavass to the governor with this message: "Two days ago the kaïmakam induced us to wait here on promise of a coach. The coach has come, but the owner requires a price which every one assures us is exorbitant. We are willing to pay the usual price, *i.e.*, 200 piastres; he asks 700. What is to done?"

It was now late, so the chances were that the kaï-makam would be retired in his harem, and the subordinates refuse to attend to business. The cavass requested that he might take with him, by way of credentials, the buyourdi. But the buyourdi was with the kaïmakam already, and we had nothing left but the firman. The eyes of the cavass sparkled when we told him what it was; he seized it eagerly from our hands and made off. In about half an hour he returned in great excitement. The kaïmakam was gone home for the night, and the subordinates were enjoying *kef;* but at the sight of the firman the uzbashi had waked up at once, turned on the proprietor of the carriage like a tiger, and told him we were only too good to allow him anything for its use. He then sent us the message to give what we chose; "200 piastres was more than the tariff, but even if we did not choose to pay at all it would be made up out of the government money." It was not a little to the surprise of the driver, and, we fear, a good deal to the disappointment of our attendants, that we abode by our former bargain. Now that it was known we had a firman, the difficulty was to get along quietly or pay honestly for what we used.

Next morning we left Skopia; late, of course, but yesterday's thunder-shower had broken up the weather, so that the sun was no longer to be feared. The riding-horses were fresh, and we rode briskly forward, our coach following with streamers flying like a mediæval *carroccio.* Its intended use was to give us shelter in case of showers, but it creaked so frightfully that we fled out of hearing, and were generally too far off to get back before the rain.

A short distance outside the town we passed the ruins of Justinian's Aqueduct, and left the road for a nearer view. This aqueduct used to conduct water from a distance of about two and a half hours, supplying Skopia from a stream in the Kara Dagh: near the town there occurs a depression in the ground, which had to be traversed by the building whereof the ruins remain. There is still standing a double row of about 120 arches, all in the round style; between these larger arches come small ones, of which some are round and others pointed.

From one arch now pours a stream of water. Under the shade of another we descried a tiny garden of melons and pumpkins, and therein, seated and smoking, a white-turbaned Turk. Strange! to find thus in juxtaposition the witnesses of two conquering races : the Roman who builded, the Ottoman who destroys.

Pursuing our way, we in due time reached those hills which bound the feverish plain of Skopia. To get from thence to the green upland field of Kóssovo one must traverse the Pass of Katchanik, a long, narrow defile, through which flows the river Lepenaé.

To render this pass traversable for cannon, a road has been made by the Turkish government, but not without considerable difficulty. In one place the passage is bored through a rock; in others, lack of earth on the side of the bank renders it necessary to support the path by a sort of wooden scaffolding or shelf. The sight of such a piece of workmanship in the backwoods of Turkey in Europe not a little edified the travellers Zach and Hahn, and they gave it a bountiful meed of praise; however, on nearer inspection one of them perceived that part of the wood used in construction was green. Not long after, this traveller met with the engineer under whom the road was made, and told us that he had remarked to him on the detected blemish,

adding, "Your road is very well now, but in a year or
two it will be thoroughly unsafe." The engineer, a
European renegade in the Turkish service, shrugged
his shoulders, and answered, "I know that as well as
you." Five years after this conversation took place
we passed over the road to Katchanik, and it *had* become
thoroughly unsafe; the bridges were full of holes, the
scaffolding over the ravines was nearly worn through.

The Pass of Katchanik is peopled by Albanians.
Now the Albanians are great favourites of Austria, for
in case of her ever getting hold of these regions she
must, like the Porte, make use of these cut-throats to
keep down the Bulgarians and Serbs. Accordingly, it
appears that the observant and far-sighted Austrian consul Hahn gladly came to the conclusion—if indeed he
was not actually told—that the work of the road of Katchanik, having been done by the inhabitants of neighbouring villages, must have been done by Arnaouts. This,
if certain, would be a notable fact. Call the Albanians
ruffians, robbers, what you will, see, with a little drill-
ing, how useful they can be. But the consul's fellow-
traveller was of opinion that the matter admitted of a
different explanation. He said to us—

"Although Arnaouts hold the Pass of Katchanik, it
is not likely that the Turkish governor, having a road
to make, would seek the labourers in their glens; the
adjacent plain of Skopia and other neighbouring districts are inhabited by industrious Christian Bulgarians;
and here—let who will state to the contrary—it is
most probable, and according to all precedent, that the
workmen would chiefly be sought and found." Of
course it is not for us to decide which of these opinions
was correct, and possibly the truth rests between them;
but in support of the latter we may quote the testimony
of the Albanians themselves, of whom two, in the

capacity of zaptiés, accompanied us through the defile.
Indeed they seemed highly entertained at the idea of the
Sultan asking Mussulmans to work when rayahs were to
be had close by.

In the course of the ride these zaptiés told us some
traits of their local countrymen, which, if less promising
in a utilitarian point of view, were more in accordance
with the nature of the Skipetār. For instance, at one
point we stopped to look at the view, and our cavass
told the zaptié that we thought the place beautiful.
With a hard laugh he cried, "Beautiful? yes, indeed, a
beautiful place for robbers!" He then explained that
hereabouts a band of forty thieves had a fierce battle
with a former kaïmakam of Skopia, who had been
obliged to march against them in full force, and in
reward for defeating them was made a pasha. Only two
days ago six robbers had been captured on the very spot
where we stood. At another point the zaptié bade the
cavass attract our attention to a house perched near
the top of a wooded hill. In front of it a space was
cleared for an Indian-corn field and some haycocks, and
from its position the inhabitants could survey the approaches on every side. "There," said the zaptié, "is
a specimen of the houses hereabouts. They stand alone,
and in strong positions, like so many kulas."* In these
glens there are no villages, and more than three Albanian houses seldom stand together. We were not near
enough to observe how this place was built; such Albanian kulas as we afterwards saw served for the residence of several brothers with their families, and were
defensible, by shooting through loopholes, against any
attack but a surprise. Presently we passed two women.
"Look at them," cried the zaptié; "they are women

---

* *Kula*, or tower, is a Turkish name applied in these countries to all small
forts or fortified houses, and even to the stations of the rural police.

worth looking at, for well do they know how to handle a gun." We asked, "Are they Mahommedans?" "Assuredly." "But they do not wear the yashmak?" "Not they, indeed; they have never worn it; and wherefore should they? they are fiercer and more unapproachable than the men." After these descriptions of the tenants of the Pass of Katchanik we no longer wondered that it is given in the Serbian songs as the scene of Marko's famous encounter with Mūssa, the bandit Arnaout.

We have already noticed that Sultan Amurath, or, as he is called hereabouts, the "Turkish Czar Murad," when leading his army to Kóssovo, is believed to have halted at Skopia, and hence an opinion has generally prevailed that he must have traversed the Pass of Katchanik. On this hypothesis, and not being personally acquainted with the ground, some Serbs of the Principality have wasted much good indignation on their own Czar Lāzar, for not having fallen on the Moslem host while entangled in the defile; others have even accused Marko Kralïevitch of traitorously holding the passage for the foe. But according to Turkish sources the Sultan went from Kustendil to Karatova, where he lay for some time encamped. From thence the army passed through the Moravitza valley, and near the village of Dolnia Chukarka a mound is shown as marking the spot where Sultan Murad's tent was pitched when he encamped on the way to Kóssovo. The only natural obstacle to the advance of the Turks by this route would be the necessity of crossing the river Morava, which they did cross, if their own records may be believed. It would have been almost impossible to transport a large army through the long and narrow Pass of Katchanik, even if uninterrupted by the Serbians, who had the Albanians on their side.*

* The famous Albanian hero, George Kastrioti, called by the Turks Scander-

We once held an interesting conversation on this subject with a Serbian officer, comparing our respective notes on the country with passages from " Hahn's Travels " and Hammer's " History of the Ottoman Empire." He was of opinion that if the Turks really followed this route, and debouched on the plain at Grachanitza, and not at Katchanik, the position wherein they were awaited by the Serbians, behind the rivers Lab and Sitnitza, admitted of explanation, and would in all probability be justified by future investigators of the question and of the ground.

A fight did take place at Katchanik, and our zaptié failed not to mention it. It occurred three centuries later than the great battle of Kóssovo, and in it the Turks drove back an outpost of the Austrian army, which at that time was encamped on the neighbouring plains. This was preparatory to the retreat of the Imperial army, which abandoned to the vengeance of the enemy those Christian inhabitants of the country whom Imperial promises had induced to join the campaign.

The scenery of Katchanik is hardly grand enough to require a particular description, but, like wooded river defiles in general, it is wild and picturesque. Near its mouth the way is closed by a singular bar of rock, reaching from the top of the bank to the brink of the stream. Hard by, the ruins of a bridge show that at one time this obstacle was avoided by crossing the river ; now the road passes right through it by means of a tunnel, which an inscription at its entrance ascribes to a pasha of Skopia, 1794. On the other side of this tunnel

---

beg, was present at the battle of Kóssovo. (*See* Hahn.) He is said to have dissuaded Czar Lázar from surprising the Turks at night, remarking, with characteristic Albanian boastfulness, that daylight was wanted in order that they might be utterly destroyed ; in the darkness too many would escape. He himself survived the battle, to conduct the heroic defence of his own country.

one arrives at the best place for taking a last look at the pass, and at this point the view is striking.

As you proceed the precipitous banks abate, and the river Neredimka flowing towards you joins its stream to that of the Lepenitz. Low in the angle of their junction stands the ruined castle of Katchanik; the so-called town occupies the left bank of the Neredimka, and lies to your right as you issue from the ravine.

Outside the walls of Katchanik we found the chief citizens drawn up in a line to meet us—Albanians all, but showing by their dress that they lived on the borders of a Serb district; for the fustanella was exchanged for a simple short white tunic, and no dangling sleeves descended from the vest of crimson embroidered with gold. The chief man came into the middle of the road to welcome us, and then led the way through the town; say, rather, he sprang from point to point of the rubbish heaped where a town may have been.

On one hand lay the ruins of a large building; they said it was once a seraï (palace); the houses looked as if they could not stand a day longer, the streets were deserted, the shop-boards all but bare of goods, and tenanted instead by solitary and often sleeping forms. Much as we had seen of Turkish villages, still Katchanik was something startling; here, too, appeared that worst of all signs, namely, that the place was not only in a bad state, but in a state that grows worse every day. Some explanation was wanted, but it was not wanting long; in reply to our first question as to the population, we heard that the town consisted of seventy Mahommedan houses, " not one rayah among them all ! "

Having traversed the street, we halted before a gate, and the Albanian shouted his order that it should be set open; then, taking our horses by the bridle, he pulled them into a large court, with dwellings at the further

end, and stopped before a very low house. Here we
dismounted, and were conducted through the kitchen
into a room where we took our places on the divan and
were served with coffee. The Arnaout, standing before
us, and speaking in Albanian, desired our cavass to tell
us that this was his house, and this the room where, in
passing through Katchanik, all pashas, Begs, and consuls, invariably spent the night. Further, we were to
be informed that he himself was a great Beg, and that
under his roof we need fear no ill.

As we knew it had been debated at Skopia whether
the Mussulmans at Katchanik could be induced to
receive us at all, we acknowledged his hospitality in a
phrase as elaborate as our knowledge of Greek would
afford, and by the length of the cavass's translation into
Albanian it seemed not to have lost anything in its
passage. The Beg looked pleased, and again assured us
that we need "fear nothing;" but as μή φοβῆσθε was
repeated again and again, we could not help interrupting
to ask why it occurred to him that we were likely to be
afraid. A longer experience of Arnaoutluk accustomed
us to be told "not to fear," and moreover taught us not
to take it for granted that we were sure to be safe.

So long as the master of the house was present,
politeness deterred us from an examination of our
apartment, but when he was gone we began to congra-
tulate ourselves on its being so much better than the
dilapidated outside led us to expect. Though extremely
low, it was not small, and its windows had panes, of
which some were filled with glass. The rest were covered
with paper, and the excessive stuffiness of the atmosphere,
added to the discovery that the windows would not open,
at last reduced us to make an incision in one of these
paper panes. All rooms in Turkey have a certain family
resemblance, which renders a description unnecessary to

those who have seen any of them; but, as the coldness
of the climate in the northern provinces occasions some
divergence from the best known models, we will herewith
describe our Arnaout room at Katchanik, even at the
risk of telling some people what they already know.
The ceiling was carved, and both it and the plaster walls
were painted in the gayest hues. In this instance the
execution was rough and tasteless, but in richer houses
it is often artistic. Unfortunately, the beautiful wood-
work harbours insects, so that chambers literally "ceiled
with cedar, and painted with vermilion," are often infested by innumerable plagues. In many rooms, we have
already mentioned that two sides are entirely taken up
by windows; but in mountain regions like Katchanik,
where the climate is chilly and society unsettled, the
apertures of dwelling-houses are small and few and
overhung by the roof. Immediately within the windows
is the divan, covered with cushions, and in front of the
divan comes a raised part of the floor, usually of wood
and carpeted, where it is ill-mannered to tread in shoes.
Between the raised floor and the door intervenes a lower
gradation, uncarpeted, and often of bare ground; this is
subdivided into a standing-place for servants, a cupboard,
and a stove. The cupboards are very convenient, even
the space between their doors being provided with little
cells; the stove, which in form is like a beehive and
usually painted green and white, is on the outside pressed
full of round holes, wherein we more than once baked
apples for supper. There is also a fence of rails round
the stove, on which garments can be hung to dry. Pegs
abound in various parts of the room, and under the ceiling
runs a high shelf, on which china dishes or other treasures
may be displayed.

Such is the usual dwelling-room of a Mussulman
house in this part of Turkey in Europe. As for the

kiosk, it is the very poetry of a chamber, giving you
at once a large open fireplace and large open windows,
a comfortable sofa and the full enjoyment of the air.
Unluckily, in rooms as well as in garments, the poor
Turks are surrendering, for imitations of Europe, the
few characteristics which they would do well to retain.
On the other hand, they retain, even in good houses, certain blemishes in domestic arrangement, which cannot be
sufficiently stigmatised. First, the plan of sleeping in
rooms where they also sit and eat, and by day hiding
away their bedclothes in cupboards ; secondly, the har-
bourage of unnamable insects, which infest alike furniture, carpets, and clothes ; thirdly, the toleration of
accumulated filth under windows, under divans, in short,
everywhere. This latter grievance is connected with a
total absence of ways and means for removing impurities
to a distance from dwellings. Certainly much of our
own experience would go to prove that in their habits
the Turks are dirty, and respecting the degree of cleanliness which results from ceremonial washings we confess ourselves unable to give a report. On this head,
too, the accounts we received from others were absolutely contradictory. For instance, one resident would
assure us that no adoption of Frankish fashion can make
the Turk disregard his religious cleansing, while another
had Turkish acquaintances who, being just europeanised
enough to wear boots instead of slippers, limited their
nether ablutions to besprinkling their *chaussure*. Again,
we have been told by persons who professed to speak
from experience, that Turks wash their hands and faces
but very rarely change their linen ; and in direct con-
tradiction to this statement, we have been told that
they change their linen every day. So far as our own
observation is concerned, we must say that the Ottoman soldiers and officials, the Greeks, men, women, and

children, and the Albanians of all clans and creeds, seemed to us heinously unclean.

Of their Slavonic neighbours, the least cleanly are the Montenegrínes, who, however, are ashamed of it, excusing themselves from the fact that during a great part of the year their villages are ill supplied with water. On the other hand the Bulgarians are more cleanly than any people between them and the Dutch, and orderly and careful to boot. The Danubian Serbians are less dirty than Germans; they love fresh air, and let it well through their houses; though not as yet tidy, they are particularly anxious to become so, inasmuch as they regard "shiftlessness" as one of the attributes of the Turk. Their brethren of race, the Mussulman gentlemen of Bosnia, cultivate snowy linen and beautifully clean houses, and so do the Bosniac Christians as far as their poverty will permit. Indeed an appreciation of cleanliness is one of those points in which the Slavonic Christians differ in character from their southern co-religionists the Greeks, with whom they are so often confused.

Soon after we were settled in our room at Katchanik there came a message from the women of the Bey's family. They wished to visit us, and to this end, requested that we would send our men servants out of the house. Of course we agreed; and thereupon the Bey, having first seen our attendants to a safe distance, liberated his female relatives and himself withdrew. In a moment our room was full of Arnaout women, and we were reciprocally scanning one another—on our side with disappointment and disgust. For in Turkey, as elsewhere, it is usual for ladies, when paying a call, to be arrayed in their best, and we had expected to see some fine specimens of Albanian costume; instead of which these dames showed themselves in all the shabbiness of

N 2

Albanian *deshabille*. One of the maids spoke a few words
of Slavonic, so we asked her whether her mistress had
not anything better to put on; and thereupon it appeared that the poor creatures had not dared to sport
their best clothes for fear of exciting our cupidity. The
maid, anxious for her lady's honour, began to describe her
parure of ducats, when her mistress snubbed her, fiercely
snapping out, " Who talks of ducats ? Hold your tongue."
Failing the subject of dress (on which in such interviews
we frequently relied), and the Slavonic words between us
being few, we sought to amuse them with the pictures in
a Bulgarian spelling-book. At this juncture the party
was joined by a boy about twelve years old. To our
surprise and the immense admiration of the rest of the
audience, he knew all the Slavonic letters and read the
alphabet aloud; he seemed, indeed, a quick enough child;
but like every lad we saw in a harem, his manner to
his female associates was not unlike that of a young
turkey-cock among his silly troop of hens.

While all were thus intent suddenly a cry was raised,
and the whole party bundled out, throwing their dirty
wraps over their dirty and ugly faces, tumbling over one
another, and in their haste leaving their slippers behind.
The cause was explained next moment when our cavass
entered bringing in the soup; but after all this fuss we
happened to leave our room unexpectedly, and found
two or three women in the kitchen while the dragoman
was cooking. " Ah, ha !" said he; " they are not so
particular as they would have you believe. When they
want the kitchen they don't mind me."

Next morning before starting we made the discovery
that the " great Bey " of Katchanik, like more than one
Bey in Bosnia, was the proprietor of a khan, and only as
such consented to offer distinguished guests the superior
accommodation of his own house. He sent in his demand

for so many piastres with no greater scruple than the most ordinary khangee.

Quitting Katchanik, *en route* for the monastery of Gratchanitza, we had to cross the river Neredimka; for this purpose, and in order to get safe out of the street, we mounted our horses and rode on during the next two hours. The way skirting the bank of the Lepenic traverses steep and broken ground, and it was to our surprise that the carriage rejoined us uninjured.

The hills that form the western wall of the Pass of Katchanik here meet the eastern extremity of the Shaar Plánina, and their point of junction is the pyramidal mountain, Liubatern, which rises to 6,400 feet. The zaptié who rode before us pointed to the cloud-veiled summit, and called out, "Look up there! Near the peak of that great mountain lies a lake whose shores are of snow; from that lake comes this river, but truly, it makes many twinings and twirlings on the hill-side before it gets down here."

We have never been so fortunate as to hear this assertion either confirmed or contradicted on competent authority, nor did we ever meet any one who had ascended the peak of Liubatern.

And now the unwinding of the mountain ranges showed us the great upland plain of Kóssovo, stretching to Mitrovic at the northern extremity, a distance of fourteen hours as the rider goes. It lies on an average 1,700 feet above the level of the sea, and forms the watershed of the Ægean and the Danube.*

* The whole surface was doubtless once a lake, and part of it still remains a marsh, while of the four rivers that drain it, two—the Lepenic and the Neredimka—fall into the Vardar (Axius); and two—the Lab and the Sitnitza—are carried through the Ibar and Morava into the Danube. The country people say that the Neredimka sends water both to the Black Sea and the White, meaning by the latter the Mediterranean. What they imply is, that while its principal stream falls into the Lepenic, a portion of its water contributes to feed a mill-brook which loses itself in the bog of Sasli, the source of the river Sitnitza.

CHAPTER XIV.

THE BATTLE-FIELD OF KÓSSOVO.[*]

"Cursed be Vuk Brancovic, for he betrayed the Czar on Kóssovo. But the name of Milosh shall be remembered by the Serbian people as long as the world and Kóssovo endure."—*Serbian Ballad.*

"Never let me hear that brave blood has been shed in vain; it sends a roaring voice down through all time."—*Saying of Sir Walter Scott.*

THE morning on which we entered Kóssovo was chequered by those alternations of cloud and gleam which usually herald a showery day. The wind blew fresh from the snow-wreaths on Liubatern, and swung aloft the boughs of the oak-copse, showing bright little lawns and dewy pastures, to which the grazing horses and cattle pushed their way through brushwood and fern: we felt that we had exchanged the yellow plains of the East for the green mountains and watered valleys of Europe. Unhappily, the verdure and the breeze are all that now testify of Europe on the field of Kóssovo. Old chronicles tell that at the time when a Turkish army first appeared on it the country was well cultivated and peopled with villages; roads and bridges were the especial care of the ruler; the Serbian parliament generally held its meetings in the neighbourhood; and the adjacent

---

[*] The name *Kóssovo Polié* has always been rendered by the Germans *Amselfeld*, i.e., field of the blackbirds. Serbian etymologists now incline to derive the word not from *kos*, merula, but from *kositi*, to mow. Of the battle there are differing accounts; we have followed those most generally accepted both by Mahommedans and Christians, and which form the text of the principal national songs. Later ballads ascribe almost every engagement between Turks and Serbians to the battle of Kóssovo, and thus abound in contradictory details.

cities of Skopia, Novo Berdo, and Prizren, had great
yearly marts, which formed the rendezvous of foreign
merchants. Yes, in those days Kóssovo belonged to
Europe—to a society, though rude, of activity and progress ; but it was conquered to be a pasture-ground for
Turkish horses, on just such a showery morning as this,
some five hundred years ago.

The large plain of Kóssovo, situated in a mountainous
region, and lying as it were before the doors of Danubian
Serbia, Bosnia, and Albania, has in all ages been marked
by its position as a battle-field, and it is still pointed
out as the spot where combat may once more decide the
fate of the surrounding lands. The earliest battle of
Kóssovo of which there is a record, was fought between
old Stephen Némania and the Byzantine governor of the
adjacent castle of Svétchani, and it delivered the Serbs
of this district from the last claims of Byzantine suze-
rainty. Again, it was on Kóssovo that the Turks first
appeared as invaders of Serbia, and were on that occasion
beaten and driven away ; while in 1448 there was a
celebrated combat, wherein the Hungarian general, John
Hunyady, fought the Turks for three days running, in
vain hope of recovering the land. But the great battle
of Kóssovo was that wherein the last Czar of Serbia met
the Moslem invaders of his country ; and so fresh remains
its memory that to this day it is scarcely possible for a
traveller to converse for more than a few minutes with a
genuine Serbian without hearing the name of Kóssovo.
After five centuries, the lessons taught by the defeat
are constantly applied ; the loss of the country is an
ever-rankling thorn. We have ourselves been present
when Serbians quarrelling were quieted by the remonstrance, " What, will ye strive among yourselves like
your fathers before the battle of Kóssovo ?" and we
have heard a Serbian peasant answer, when praised for

bringing in a large load of wood, " Ay, but it is time we
Serbians should gather in our wood from the field of
Kóssovo." As for any one who has been much in Serbia,
and has studied the national traditions and songs, he will
at last come to feel almost as if he had been at the battle
of Kóssovo himself, so minutely is every detail enume-
rated, so vividly are the motives and actions realised, so
deep the lines, so strong the colours, in which the principal characters are drawn.

It was on " fair St. Vitus's day," June 15, 1389, that
the Turkish and vassal hosts, led by the Ottoman Sultan
Amurath, engaged the combined forces of the Serbs,
Bosniacs, and Albanians, which were drawn up on the
field of Kóssovo to repel further invasion of their land.
The relative numbers of the combatants are very variously stated, each party raising that of its adversary to
not less than 300,000, and declaring that itself was out-
numbered as one to three.

The pride of the Serbs was their heavy-armed cavalry ;
and Turkish histories relate that on the evening before
the battle it was debated among the Ottoman leaders
whether it would not be advisable to try and frighten
the enemy's horses by placing a row of camels before
the Turkish line.   Bajazet, eldest son of Amurath, objected to employ stratagem, inasmuch as it showed dis-
trust of God.   The grand vizier deemed it unnecessary,
because, when he last opened the Koran, he had lighted
on a promise of victory.   Beglerbeg Timour Tash settled
the question by declaring that the camels were more
likely to run away from the Serb cavalry than the Serb
cavalry from the camels.   Another difficulty perplexed
the Turks.   All night long the wind blew strong from
the Christian camp and towards theirs; the leaders were
uneasy, lest, during the combat, it should blow the dust
into their men's eyes.   Sultan Amurath spent the night

in gloomy foreboding that this battle was his last ; he had recourse to prayer, and just before sunrise a light rain fell, laying the dust and wind. When the shower ceased and the sun shone out it was the signal for the armies to engage.

Meanwhile, in the camp of the Serbs counsel was darkened by domestic quarrels. Czar Lāzar had two sons-in-law ; the one, Vūk Brankovic, was the greatest and best-born vlasteline in Serbia, the other, Milosh Obilic, was her bravest and most chivalrous warrior. The Czar loved Milosh, and trusted him as his own soul. Vūk was moved to jealousy at the sight of a man who owed his position to his sword preferred before himself; accidentally the jealousy of the brothers-in-law was brought to a point by a dispute between their wives. The quarrel had to be settled by a duel, in which Milosh unhorsed his antagonist, but forbore to follow up his advantage, and generously offered to make friends. But Vūk was envious, and envy does not forgive. It is said the Turkish Sultan had already been trying to weaken the resistance of Serbia by tampering with some of Lāzar's nobles, and had offered the crown to any one who would assist him to overthrow the Czar; it is said that Vūk Brankovic accepted the offer, and engaged to desert during the impending battle. Certain it is, that towards the end of the engagement he did lead his men from the field, and afterwards he applied to Amurath for the crown; hence to this day the popular voice of Serbia curses him as a traitor. But the Turkish chroniclers know nothing of Vūk's treachery, and in default of evidence, modern historians of Serbia are fain to suppose that he was no more than a mean sluggish character, who left the field because he deemed the battle lost. It is possible that he and Milosh mutually suspected each other of having listened to propositions from Amurath,

and Vūk was too glad to undermine the credit of his
rival by accusing him to the Czar. But Lāzar, true to
his noble nature, was slow to believe evil; he would
tolerate no private malignity, act on no private suspicion.
If a doubt rested on the fidelity of Milosh he should be
given the opportunity of justifying himself publicly;
the accusation should be accompanied with a recognition
of his former services and with a token of the gratitude
of his prince.

On the evening before the battle the Czar sat at table
with his vlastela. At his right hand was placed old Iūg
Bogdan, vicegerent of Macedonia, and after him his nine
sons—the brave brethren of the Czarine Militza. On
the Czar's left was Vūk Brankovic, and after him all
the other vlastela. Opposite the Czar sat Milosh
Obilic, and on either side of him his bond-brothers,
Ivan Kosanchic and Milan of Toplitz. Every Serb
between the Danube and the Adriatic is as familiar
with the names of all here mentioned as with those of
his own brothers.

After supper, began the usual ceremony of proposing
toasts; wine was poured, and the Czar, taking from his
cupbearer a costly golden goblet, thus addressed the
assembled voivodes:—

"To whom of you all, my lords, shall I drink this
cup to-night? If the claim be age, I must drink to
the aged Iūg Bogdan; if rank, to Vūk Brankovic; if
affection, to my brothers-in-law, my nine brothers, the
Iugovics; if beauty, I drink to Ivan Kosanchic; if
height, to Milan of Toplitz; but if valour, then to
Milosh. And to none will I drink to-night save unto
thee, Milosh Obilic. Health to thee true! health to
thee, traitor! Once thou wert true: traitor at last.
To-morrow on Kóssovo thou wilt betray me—wilt
desert me for the Turkish Sultan. Yet here's to thy

health! And now do thou drink : drink out my wine, keep the cup as my gift."

To his light feet springs Milosh Obilic, and bows him before the Czar to the earth :—

"Thanks to thee!" cries he, "glorious Prince Lāzar! thanks to thee for thy toast—for thy toast and for thy gift—but no thanks to thee for thy words. Traitor I am not, was not, will never be. Rather, on the field of Kóssovo will I perish in defence of my faith. Traitor is he who sits at thy knee, under thy skirt—sipping the cool wine. The false, the accursed Vūk Brankovic. Enough. To-morrow is fair St. Vitus's day, and on the battle-field we shall see who is true and who is traitor. As for me, so help me God! my hand shall slay the Turkish Sultan, my foot shall stand upon his neck."

We next see Milosh in consultation with his bond-brother, Ivan Kosanchic. In the words of the song, he says to him :—

> " Oh, my brother, Ivan Kosanchic,
> Hast thou spied out the Turkish host ?
> Have the Moslems many warriors ?
> Are we strong enough to fight them ?
> Are we strong enough to beat them ?"

> And thus answers Ivan Kosanchic :
> " Oh, my brother, Milosh Obilic !
> I have spied out the Turkish army,
> And truly it is a mighty host.
> If we all were turned to salt
> We could not salt one Turkish meal.
> Full fifteen days I go around them
> And find no limit nor end of numbers.
> For wide-spread is the host, yet dense ;
> Horse pressed on horse, hero on hero,
> Lances a forest, banners as clouds,
> And tents whitening the earth like snow.
> Should a storm-shower rain from heaven
> Not a drop could reach the earth,
> All would fall on steeds and warriors."
> •   •   •   •   •   •
> The Sultan camps on Mazgit plain,
> And holds the rivers Lab and Sitnitza.

Yet again asks Milosh Obilic,
" Oh, Ivan, tell me truly
Where stands the tent of Sultan Murad ?
For to our Prince I have vowed a vow
That I will slay the Turkish Sultan
And set my foot upon his neck.''

" Milosh, my brother, art thou mad ?
Dost thou ask where Murad's tent stands ?
In the centre of the camp,
Hemmed in by the thickest squadrons.
If thou hadst a falcon's plumes
And couldst swoop on it from heaven,
Verily thy wings would not
Avail to bring thee out alive."

Then doth Milosh thus adjure him :
" Swear to me, bond-brother Ivan
(Thou who, not my brother born,
Hast to me a brother been),
That what thou hast told to me,
Thou wilt not tell to our Prince,
Lest it weigh down his heart with care,
And spread a panic through the host."

Next morning, the morning of the battle, Milosh had disappeared from the Serbian camp. Was he gone to fulfil his wild vow? or, as suspicion again hinted, had he indeed deserted to the enemy? Vūk Brankovic pressed the latter interpretation; Czar Lāzar was sore at heart; for, on what errand soever, Milosh was *gone.*

His arm, his word, his example, all were needed, and all were absent; the division of the army which he was to have commanded missed its leader and murmured. At this juncture in came spies, bringing such accounts of the mighty force of the Turks, that even now, at the eleventh hour, many of the Serb lords counselled negotiations. But this Czar Lāzar could not brook; in a few noble words he spoke courage to his troops and arrayed them for battle. But first the whole army confessed and took the sacrament. The Serbian Czar, in that priestly character still upheld by the Czar of

Russia, solemnly absolved them from their sins, and declared, that in fulfilling their allegiance to the Cross and to him they died as martyrs for their faith and fatherland.

Before the host the banner of the Cross was carried by the Czarine's eldest brother, brave Bosko Iugovic. Says the old song: "His chestnut steed is trapped with glittering gold, but o'er himself the great Cross banner flings its flowing folds, hiding him to the saddle. Above the banner shines the golden globe, out of the globe the golden crosses rise; down from the crosses golden tassels hang, and strike on Bosko's shoulder as he rides." True is the poetic instinct which thus represents the Christian standard-bearer: covered with the flag, his personality is lost in his office, and not he, but the Cross-banner alone, fills the eye.

We now return to the account of the Turkish historian. The battle raged and the left wing of the Ottomans had begun to give way, when Bajazet, surnamed "the Lightning," flew to its aid, crushing before him the heads of the foes with his iron mace. "Already streams of blood had dyed the diamond sword-blades to hyacinth, and the mirror-bright steel of the spear to ruby; already, by the multitude of heads struck off and of turbans rolling hither and thither, the battle-field was made to resemble a bed of many-coloured tulips; when, as a bird of prey rising from carcases, there raised himself from the heaps of slain a noble Serb." Milosh Obilic—for it was he—forced aside the crowd of myrmidons that surrounded the Sultan, shouting out that he had a secret to tell; Amurath signed that he should be allowed to approach. The Serb fell down before him, as if to kiss his feet, seized his foot, dragged him to the ground, and plunged a dagger into his body. The Sultan was mortally wounded : a thousand swords were drawn on the assassin ; but he, strong of arm and light of foot, shook them off, struck them aside, and three times, by prodigious leaps, rid himself of the pursuing crowd. Almost he had reached the river's brink, almost he had regained his trusty steed, when a fourth time the multitude closed on him, overbore him, cut him down.

Some versions of the story say that he was killed at once, but most assert that he was brought back wounded and fainting to the Sultan's tent, and there kept till the end of the battle, when he was executed with other prisoners to glut the eyes of the dying Turk.

The hand of Milosh, who slew an Ottoman Sultan, was long preserved at the tomb of Amurath, near Broussa ; and from his daring act dated the practice that strangers admitted to the presence of the Padishah must give their weapons in charge to his attendants, and even allow their hands to be held.

The deed of Milosh being thus related by his enemies, one fears not to give the version of his countrymen. Indeed this differs only so far as to make him appear before the Sultan with twelve companions, gain access to his tent in guise of a deserter, and take his life before the battle began. On both sides the deed is noticed as one of heroism ; and even in our own day it deserves honour as an instance of self-devotion. Milosh, rendered desperate by calumny, resolved to show his patriotism by a desperate service ; he beheld in Amurath an Infidel, a barbarian, and the invader of his country ; but he used craft only to the point necessary to gain access to his victim, and he paid the price of blood with his own.

Meanwhile the combat raged on. Amurath, though dying, was still able to give orders, and Bajazet inspired his hosts with new fury by calling on them to avenge their Sultan. The tide of battle turned against the Serbs; and at this juncture Vūk Brankovic, who commanded the reserve, marched off the field without striking a blow. His brave men, 12,000 in number, believed they were only shifting their position, but their involuntary desertion decided the fate of the day. They were among the best troops of the army—the trusted, vaunted cuirassiers.

Still, however, the Bosniacs fought well, and the centre led by the gallant Czar bore all before it. But at length the Czar's horse broke down and he had to exchange it for another. For the moment he vanished from the view of his men, and the sight of his well-known dappled charger led from the front spread the report that he had fallen. The Christian ranks broke; and when Lāzar, remounted, strove with voice and example to rally them, he was borne along by the panic-stricken crowd; his horse stumbled and fell in a trench, he was surrounded and taken.

The Turkish Sultan lay in his death struggle when the Serbian Czar was brought before him, and over the couch of the dying Amurath the eyes of Lāzar met those of Milosh. Then all was told, and the prince solemnly rendered thanks to God that he had been spared to find Murad fallen and Milosh true.

Furiously, Bajazet asked of him how he had dared to cause the death of his father. Undaunted, the Czar replied, "And thy father, how dared he invade my realm?" "Gospodar," interrupted an attendant, "are then thy neck and shoulders of willow wood, that thy head, if cut off, can grow again?" But not heeding him, Lāzar spoke on: "And thou Bajazet, son of Amurath, thinkest thou if I had at my side a certain thing which I have not, that I would now delay to send thee after thy sire?"

Bajazet commanded the executioner to strike. The faithful squire entreated that he might share the blow; and then, kneeling down before his master, held outspread the royal mantle to receive the royal head.

Such was the end of the last Christian Czar of Serbia ; her first Turkish Czar began to rule by causing his brother Jakub to be slain over the scarce cold body of their father ; and justified himself by a maxim from the Koran, to the effect that, rather than let a man cause dissension, it is better to put him to death.*

Thus was Kóssovo severed from Europe, and thus it became a pasture for Turkish cavalry.

* Hammer. "History of the Ottoman Empire," vol. i., book 6. Among his exonerating motives is also stated the following:—"He considered that it became him to imitate the example of God, who is alone and without rival. Wherefore God's shadow on earth, the Ruler of the Faithful, must be like God—alone on his throne, and rule without the possibility of rivalry."

CHAPTER XV.

WHEN, from the broken ground at the mouth of the
Pass of Katchanik, one has fairly emerged on the
plain of Kóssovo, it becomes possible to sit in the carriage,
and even to proceed at a sort of jog-trot. This, however, is owing to the level, not to any superiority in the
road, and the bridges are so rickety that one is recommended to take the precaution of getting out to traverse
them on foot.

As for the scenery at this part of the way, there is
nothing to be lost by passing it in a canopied coach. At
every step the wood becomes more sparse, and the grass
more mingled with sandy-looking soil, nor is this compensated by increasing signs of culture or human
habitation. We passed some poor khans, and near, not
through, a village said to be Albanian, its wretched huts
surrounded and almost hidden by a hedge of interlaced
roots and thorns. One of the khans is called by the
Turks the New or Yeni Khan, but it proved as dilapidated
as the oldest, and seems to retain its title only because
there are none newer. It stands on the bank of the little
river Neredimka, which we crossed immediately on leaving it. At mid-day we halted at the khan of Sasli, on
ground that in winter forms the bog of Sasli, whence
rises the river Sitnitza. On the brink of the stream

there rested a drove of cattle; and as the hour was about milking time, we were given delicious milk with our coffee. Afterwards we crossed the Sitnitza, and next passed the khan of Rupofzé, to be remarked by travellers as a half-way house, distant five hours from Katchanik, five from Príshtina. A little farther on, the side track leading to Gratchanitza diverges from the Príshtina road.

We may mention that, some distance to the left of that road, and on the right bank of the Sitnitza, is to be found a village, containing some thirty Christian houses and a church. Hilferding remarks that its name, Liplan, is mentioned by Byzantine writers as early as the eleventh century, and in old times it was sufficiently important to be the seat of a metropolitan. To the right of the road between Sasli and Rupofzé lies the Bulgarian village of Babush. Till lately this village was remarkable as wholly belonging to a single family, whose members were exempt from taxation because their ancestors rendered service as scouts to the army of Sultan Amurath. It is said that their privilege has ceased since the issuing of the Tanzimat.

Late in the afternoon we drew near to the spurs of those hills which bound Kóssovo on the east, and here, in a low and sheltered spot, we came upon the monastery and village of Gratchanitza. Previously we had passed a lately erected chapel, of which the extreme smallness and entire lack of ornament show that hereabouts the Christians are still afraid to offend the Mussulmans by display. In telling contrast to this poor little modern church rises the old church of the monastery, the noble *zadushbina* (work for the soul) of a Serbian king. Seen from afar, it appears a cluster of arches and cupolas, culminating in one large dome. On nearer approach, one perceives that the smaller domes are four in number, and

that among the curiously interlaced arches the higher
are pointed, and the lower round. The principal merit
of the structure is its general effect; and this, for
Byzantine architecture, is so unusually graceful as to
remind one of some churches in North Italy.

Evidence of Italian influence might doubtless be traced
also in the frescoes of the interior, but injustice is done
to these, as to everything else within the church, by
the numerous subdivisions necessary to accommodate the
inner to the outer form. Whether in the sanctuary, the
nave, or the porch, one is always in a dark compartment,
too narrow for its height. It would almost seem as if
this blemish in Gratchanitza had served for a warning
to the architect who built the church of the patriarchate
at Ipek, for there outward beauty has evidently been
sacrificed to giving the congregation a large well-lighted
nave.

Among the frescoes at Gratchanitza are portraits of
the founder, King Milutin, and of his queen, Simonida,
daughter of the Emperor Andronicus II. Paleologus
Milutin was the father of the king who built the church
of Détchani, and the grandfather of Czar Dūshan; he
reigned from 1275—1321, and it is said that he erected
no less than forty-eight buildings for religious or benevolent purposes. The privileges decreed to the monastery
of Gratchanitza are engraved on the wall of the church,
and the monks call this inscription their archive.

The figures of saints which form the subject of several
frescoes have suffered from the Turks, who fired pistols
at them, and were also at the trouble to poke out their
eyes. This latter injury evinced so much of the malice
of deliberate insult, that it riled the Serbians more than
wholesale destructions which might be supposed to have
taken place in the confusion and heat of assault. Besides,
the desecrated forms remain on the church wall, so that

o 2

their injury can never be forgotten; and their marred faces meeting the upturned eyes of the worshippers, seem ever to cry out for retribution. In the Principality of Serbia, where some ruined churches have been rebuilt, these blinded pictures are left unrestored. An old bishop said to us, " We still need them—they are the archives of centuries of oppression; and our people must not lose sight of them so long as the oppressor still keeps foot on Serbian land." For the frescoes themselves this feeling is most fortunate, as it has saved them from the doom of whitewash; and it is only to be wished that some similar protection could be extended to the exterior sculptures and walls. While the modern phase of taste in Serbia is represented by the new cathedral of Belgrade, such monuments of the mediæval monarchy as survived the Turkish deluge, have more to dread from the zeal of the restorer, than aught that befell them from the ravages of the foe.

Among the frescoes at Gratchanitza, one alone has been preserved by the height of the dome, or, as the monks say, by a mysterious terror which seized on the destroyers, and saved the church itself. This rescued fresco is the Head of Christ, which in Eastern churches is usually depicted of colossal size, and looking down in the act of benediction. The conception of the face here drawn is as superior to the stiffness of the Byzantine, as to the weakness of modern schools. The artist who painted it would be a contemporary of Cimabue, and Luccio of Sienna; and, like theirs, his genius was strong enough to infuse power and grandeur even into the then conventional forms. Indeed, the Christ of Gratchanitza is of so stern a type, that one could almost believe the painter to have had a foreboding of the dark days in store for the church. Those awful eyes look down from under brows whereof the frown might well strike terror into desecrators engaged in their unhallowed sport.

There are a few Roman remains at Gratchanitza, consisting of stones with inscriptions and two stone arœ, the latter preserved within the church. Hahn conjectures that these were brought from the station Vicianum, on the great military road between Lissus on the Adriatic and Nissus, a few days' journey from the Danube. Outside the church we saw the lid of a large stone coffin, marked with the cross.

From our experience of Serbian monasteries, we had hoped to find at Gratchanitza both comfort and satisfaction, but nothing could present a stronger contrast to the state of convents in the principality than the condition of the convent here. We came, indeed, at an unlucky moment, for the prior had just been carried off captive, —a fate which by all accounts he richly merited; but which served as excuse for every passing Mussulman to bully the monks, and extort what he pleased. Under such circumstances, the presence of our zaptiés was a terrible infliction, and it was revolting to behold their insolence, together with the cringing alacrity with which the monks made haste to satisfy them. After a while, the sub-prior got our dragoman into a quiet corner, and told him how matters stood. Of course we at once sent to assure him that we would take away the zaptiés next day, and pay for all that we consumed.

The story related by the sub-prior, as to the misdeeds and imprisonment of his superior, was bad enough, and we afterwards heard it confirmed with additions which were not improvements. The captured Hegumon was a man much too young for his post, and who would seem to have attained it by bribery; he was imperious and passionate, and made enemies in the village. On the occasion of a wedding-feast, when raki had got into the heads assembled, the abbot of Gratchanitza received a blow, and returned it with interest, felling his assailant. The man came down on some hard substance and was seriously hurt; his family demanded reparation, and also indemnification for the loss of his work during the time the wound would take to heal; altogether 2,000 piastres, about £20. This the Hegumon thought extravagant, and declared that it would be enough for him to pay the doctor, meanwhile lodging and supporting the patient; but the relations insisted, and the fine was paid. The man got better, and went out to work as before, but after a time he caught cold, the half-healed wound inflamed, and he died. The family having been paid for the wound, and recognising the death as an accident over which the Hegumon had no control, made no further demand; but the neighbouring Turkish authorities thought to improve the occasion and extort money from the monastery. They therefore interfered, and demanded a second fine; the Hegumon could not or would not pay it, so they seized what money they could find, and carried him off to Prizren. He was condemned to prison for seven years, and if any one could have relied on the sentence being carried out, the whole country would have rejoiced to be quit of him. Unluckily it was well known that he would only be kept till the authorities were sure that he had paid them all the money he possessed, and then he would be sent back to Gratchanitza on the condition of raising more.

The wretchedness of the monks at Gratchanitza extends to what they call their school. Perhaps, considering that they live in an out-of-the-way part of Turkey, are but four in number, and have the services of the church to attend, it is rather creditable that they have a school at all, and should they acquire a good superior, the germ may develop into real usefulness. At present, however,

their school is certainly far behind all others in the
country, and that in more ways than one. In an unfurnished cell we found five miserable children with torn
books under their arms. The books were the smallest
Belgrade chitankas, and the scholars read out of them
both old Slavonic and Serbian, but so glibly that we
could not but suspect they were repeating by rote. We
therefore opened the books at another place, and then
they could scarcely read a word. Their teacher, a kindly-
looking monk, apologized more candidly than many others
of his calling, by taking the blame on his own ignorance ;
"however," said he, "I only teach them the first rudi-
ments, and afterwards they will go to the good new
school at Prishtina. As their poor little chitankas were
torn, we gave them some, together with two New Testaments to the monks. Next day another monk came to
us at Prishtina, and asked if we would give a Testament
to him also, as he belonged to Gratchanitza, but happened
during our visit to be from home.

Before leaving the schoolroom we ventured a very
earnest remonstrance as to the mode in which the pupils
had greeted us. At our entrance they had literally fallen
down at our feet, and that with a sort of grovelling
action which, if not revolting, would have been ludicrous. We asked how in the world they came to suppose
we should wish to be thus received ? Their teacher
answered, "The Turks taught it us: their dignitaries
require us Christians to prostrate ourselves before them."
"But we are not Turks, and for Christians to enact or
to permit such self-degradation is not only a shame but
a sin. Have not some of you been in Free Serbia and
seen how the school-children behave there ?" "No,
none of them." But at these words they exchanged
glances, and began to cheer up a little. They invited us
to come into the church, and presently brought thither

a man from the village who *had* been in Free Serbia. This man wore a turban, was of uncouth aspect, and otherwise looked like the other rayahs; but he was far more outspoken than the monks. We desired him to say if the Serbian school-children prostrated themselves as these did. "Of course not," cried he, "but then in Serbia *everything* is different. There they have good roads, good judges, peace and prosperity; here there is nothing but disorder and zulum" (*Turk.*, violence and oppression).*

Prostrations like those of the school-children at Gratchanitza frequently greeted us during this journey, and we cannot think that any civilized traveller would see them with less distress than ourselves. But one's own feeling at thus witnessing the degradation of fellow-creatures and fellow-Christians gives but a faint idea of what is felt by the Serbs of the principality, to whom these rayahs stand in the relation of brethren of race, nay, often are near of kin. Monks, merchants, and emigrants of all sorts, constantly pass from the Turk-ruled districts to Free Serbia, and not even the accounts which they give of their position awake such indignation as the involuntary evidence of it afforded by their cringing demeanour, until they learn the manners of a new land. One instance among many may stand here. A young man working in Belgrade had committed some offence, and was sentenced to a term of imprisonment with labour. His old father, a Christian in Bulgaria, taking it for granted that the imprisonment would endure until he could be bought off, came to Belgrade, and found that the culprit, having served his time, was about to be

---

* For greater distinctness we shall use the term "Free Serbia" when speaking of the Danubian Principality, as distinguished from districts inhabited by Serbians, but ruled by Mahommedans. In the country, however, the name Serbia, without any prefix, is always understood to denote the free districts, the rest being called Old Serbia, &c.

set at liberty, and that there was no occasion for bribing any one. In his joy the father craved an interview of Prince Michael, in order to thank him for *pardoning* his son. This did not exactly please the prince, who is doing all in his power to break his own people of the habit of referring to him to comment on or change the sentence of the law ; he feels that such a practice as this testifies to a state of society where the caprice of the despot takes the place of justice. However, as the old man came from far, and would not be satisfied without seeing him, he agreed to receive him, and walked into a room of his palace where the Bulgarian had been told to wait. The moment the man saw the prince, he fell down and grovelled at his feet, again and again with out-stretched hand touching the floor and then his own brow. In vain he was entreated to rise, in vain assured that his degraded attitude inflicted on the prince the keenest pain ; poor rayah ! that was an idea which his mind could not readily take in. The scene was described to us by the prince himself,—the very recollection caused him to writhe : he added, " Je me suis dit, Voilà donc comment il faut se présenter devant un pasha."

As we were making our arrangements for departure from Gratchanitza, the new zaptiés who had come to meet us from Príshtina sent to say, that if we wished to continue the carriage they could compel the driver to go on with us,—we need not pay anything more. Of course we did not take advantage of this unjust proposi-tion, but having sent the poor man home, as previously agreed, proceeded on our own journey on horseback.

The ride from Gratchanitza to Príshtina is not reckoned more than an hour and a half. The town stands in the undulating ground where surrounding hills mingle with the plain. It is dirty and small, but makes a fair show in the distance, owing to the minarets of eleven mosques, said to have been erected by Turkish women whose husbands fell at the battle of Kóssovo. A picturesque feature is the little eminence to the right, which at the time of our visit was dotted with white and green military tents. There is generally a cavalry regiment stationed on the field during summer; and in camp, as in city, the Turk shows his taste by relieving the glare of white with green.

The kaïmakam of Skopia had despatched a letter re-commending us to the mudir of Príshtina; and this letter had an excellent effect, for besides sending to meet us at the monastery, he had provided us with capital quarters in the town. The house selected was that of the bishop, which, though not quite answering to the European idea of an episcopal palace (it boasted only four rooms, three small and one large), was neverthe-less an agreeable residence. The prelate himself, a Fanariote, was naturally away at Constantinople, and the community deplored not his absence; neither did we, since in consequence we came in for his large, cool, pleasant room, with its row of windows shaded by the projecting roof. From these windows most pleasant is the view: the house, standing on a slope, looks down on the clustered town, and beyond it far over the plain to a shadowy frontier of distant hills.

Immediately on our arrival, the mudir of Príshtina sent to offer a visit, and then appeared, not as usual in the form of an obese and greasy-uniformed Osmanli, but as a gaunt Albanian in a green robe lined with fur. He was a fine-looking old man, with silver hair, glitter-ing black eyes, a pale complexion, and with a look of blood unattainable to dignitaries who have earned pro-motion as a favourite pipe-lighter or café-gee. In a few minutes the companion of the mudir informed us that his superior came indeed of a noble race, and, as we displayed lively interest in the subject, the mudir himself took up the discourse, and told us the name of his family, adding that they were all Ghegga by race, and that in their country no one spoke a word of Turkish. Thus encouraged we proceeded to question him about other families of Northern Albania, and especially if he agreed with Consul Hahn's informant that the greatest houses were those of Ismael Pasha and Mahmut Begola. He said they were great, but that the last sprout of one of them had taken service under the Sultan, adding contemptuously, "He is a humpbacked little fellow," and imitating the humpback.

Referring to our journey, the mudir told us that he especially rejoiced to welcome us, inasmuch as at one time he had served under English command, and was well content with his treatment and pay. During the Crimean war he had accompanied an English consul through the districts of Ipek and Détchani in order to gain recruits. "The monastery of Détchani of course we knew—as it is the greatest in the world."

When the mudir was gone, the Serbian kodgia bashi came to ask us to visit the Christian school. After what we had seen at Gratchanitza our expectation was at the lowest ebb, and hence we were the more gratified with a very pleasing surprise. The schoolroom was large, airy, clean, properly fitted up, and embellished with texts from the Slavonic Bible written scrollwise on door and walls. These scrolls are the work of the schoolmaster, a Serb from Mitrovic, on the Austrian border of the Save ; and he has imparted so much of his accomplishment to his pupils that they not only write well, but also draw. Two wonderful pictures representing the Madonna and St. George were given us to take

away as keepsakes. The bright and vigorous-looking
children that filled the school then proceeded to show us
that they could read and cipher with ease; but they
proved unusually backward in geography—which surprised us, inasmuch as a set of good maps appeared on
the wall. In a while, however, we perceived that they
were fastened so high that no one could look at them
without getting a crick in the neck. The schoolmaster,
being of the tidy persuasion, affirmed that this was
necessary in order to keep them from being dirtied by
the children's fingers.

The books at Príshtina were from Belgrade, but as
they seemed only to have chitankas adapted for the
youngest children, we asked if they had not some
histories of Serbia. The master looked furtively around,
and then said that he had some, but dared not to use
them openly. "Why not?" "Because the officers of
the Turkish regiments frequently come and loll about
in our school, and the cavalry officers are often Hungarians or Cossacks or Poles, and can read the Slávic
books." "But these brief, dry histories contain nothing
revolutionary, and surely the officers who are your fellow-Christians would not wish to calumniate you." "The
rest would not, but the Poles are more Turkish than the
Turks themselves. One day a Polish officer looked over
the shoulder of one of the children, and called out,
'Halloa, master! what do I see here? These books are
different from those used in Bulgaria; they come from
the principality, and here is something about the history
of Serbia. If I catch you at this again, I shall report
you to the authorities.' I trembled from head to foot,
and knew not what I should say or do; but luckily there
was also present a Cossack, a deserter from the Russian
service, a good man who had always befriended us; he
got the Pole out of the room, and said to him in dis-

pleasure that they were not sent to Prìshtina to meddle
with the Serb school. Since then all reading of our
country's history has been in private." It need not be
pointed out what ill service this Polish officer was doing
the Sultan, in thus angering the Christians by suppressing the open school study of Serbian history, on a
spot where its most exciting details are known to every
man, woman, and child through the medium of national
song. Unfortunately such malevolent tale-telling is not
singular, and we have since heard how in one of the
largest Slavonic towns in Turkey, the school histories
of Serbia were seized. Of course the pasha had not
read them himself, but some one told him of their existence, and that they contained passages tending to
throw contempt on the Turkish government; fanatical
Mahommedans raised a cry, and the Greek bishop proved
a ready agent in the seizure. It is worthy of remark,
that one of the more intelligent local Mussulmans, himself Slavonic and possessed of the suspected histories,
objected to this measure on the ground that contempt
for the Turkish government was far more likely to
be engendered by such a step, than by anything contained in Serbian school-books. Having, like this
Mussulman, read the book in question, we can unhesi-
tatingly endorse his opinion.

Respecting the schoolmaster's assertion that Poles in
the Ottoman army are more alienated from their oppressed fellow-Christians than the Mahommedans themselves, we must confess to have heard it often repeated,
and with the bitterest emphasis. No doubt, at one
time, these exiles were too apt to hate the Slavonic
Christians in Turkey, inasmuch as they regarded them
as clients of Russia. Subsequently, however, they
showed more discrimination, and on the occasion of
the bombardment of Belgrade, Poles as well as Hunga-

rians offered their services to the Government of Serbia.

The school of Príshtina contains a second large room, which would just do for a class of girls ; but as usual there is the lack of a female teacher, and the customs of this part of the country would oppose boys and girls being taught in one room. There is also another obstacle. Even the boys on their way to and fro are insulted by the Arnaout *gamins,*—what would be the fate of girls ? This objection was urged by the kodgia bashi, and thereupon the schoolmaster said to him :—" Do you know what I have been told ? The new mudir has informed the medjliss that it is the Sultan's pleasure that the children of his subjects should go to school, not excepting the children of Arnaouts. Now if the young Albanians were shut up at their tasks, ours could get through the street in peace." The kodgia bashi gave us a look, as if to see how much we believed, and then said shortly, " When the Arnaouts become quiet and go to school like other people, it will certainly be an excellent thing."

The said kodgia bashi was not particularly liberal-minded in respect to female education. He observed to us, that in their community many of the boys were yet untaught, and it would not be well that the women should know how to read and write before the men. Thereupon we showed him some handsomely-bound books, and told him that the contents were histories and records of travel written by women. He examined the works narrowly, and called upon the schoolmaster, who knew Latin letters, to decipher the title, adding, " Are you quite sure that it is neither a letter nor a song ? " " Quite sure," answered we ; and the schoolmaster confirmed our statement. Then said the kodgia bashi, " If women will write such books as these, we must see what ours can do."

After he was gone, the schoolmaster told us that the inhabitants of Príshtina have generally the gift of improvising poetry, and that to the national songs which they constantly recite, they add others composed on divers occurrences of their own life. Of course this gift is turned to account in courtship, and hence a notion exists that if women could write they would be for ever inditing love-letters. Such ideas naturally prevail in a country long subjected to Mahommedan influence, but the old songs tell us of Serbian ladies who " wrote like men."

Yet, with all his prejudices, the kodgia bashi is at Príshtina an apostle of progress. It is owing to him that the new school was built, and by him the schoolmaster was found and brought. In default of the absent bishop it is he who leads the little community of Serbs; moreover, although one of their poorest members, he is chosen to represent them in the medjliss, because he does them credit by his demeanour, and dares to speak out before the Turk. Of course he has been in Free Serbia. You see it at once ; for, like the people over the border, he holds up his head and steps out like a man. The question is, Why did he return? This question we frequently put respecting persons who had similarly come back to their native town, although the state of things in it was one under which they groaned. The answer was as follows : In such cases all the family possesses— a bit of land, or a little shop—is in Turkey, and the Turks throw every impediment in the way of disposal of property for the purpose of emigration. Then, while some members of the family are willing to go, others cannot bear to leave their birthplace or the friends of their youth, and, rather than forsake their families, able-bodied men remain. Again, unless they go to Serbia before their mode of life is formed, they can seldom keep pace even with the workmen of the principality, and their habits are irregular and slothful; they cannot save enough to bring over their families, and rather than abandon these they go back to Turkey. But instead of themselves they send their children; the young son of the kodgia bashi was then on the eve of his journey.

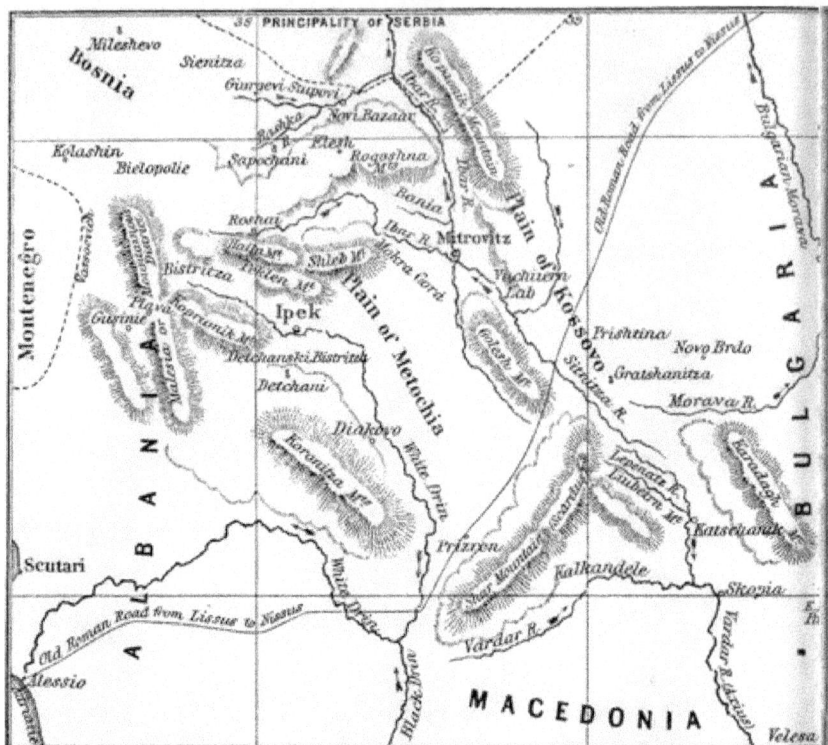

STARA (OLD) SERBIA

STARA (OLD) SERBIA.—A district between Macedonia and the south of the Serbian Principality. In consul reports it is included in Northern Albania, and the Mussulmans call it Arnaoutluk.

POPULATION.—Numbers very uncertain—some say about half-a-million.

RACES.—Serbian. Gheggha-Albanian. The Osmanlee is represented by a few troops and governors of to and some families in Prizren. The Greek only by the Bishops.

LANGUAGES.—Serbian and Albanian. Turkish spoken only by officials, and as one of three languages in Priz Greek only by Bishops and their Secretaries.

RELIGIONS.—Serbians, Christians of the Oriental communion. Albanians, mostly Mahometans, some Ro Catholic.

CHAPTER XVI.

"Where the sword is, there is the true faith."—*Albanian Proverb.*
"It is under the torture that the hero is shown."—*Serbian Proverb.*

AND now finding ourselves at Príshtina, in the very heart of Old Serbia, it may be as well to inquire what extent of country is included under the name, what is its history, population, and condition. And here let us give notice, that if once we attempt an explanation which relates to various and conflicting elements of race, language, religion, and political interest, we are likely to spin out a long chapter. Readers who have no fancy to go in for it, need not do so in order to understand the allusions throughout our future narrative, if they will but consent to look at the subjoined map, and charge their memories with its explanation.

Even in the days of the czardom, it would appear that Serbia Proper was distinguished from the "Serb lands." The latter appellation included all the countries peopled by the Serbian race—Zeta, Bosnia, Herzegovina, &c. ; but Serbia, in its strictest sense, denoted the tracts now comprehended in the Principality, together with those that intervene between the south of the Principality and Macedonia. Old maps of Turkey in Europe, which were drawn while all Serbia was subject to the Turks, give the whole of this country under its proper name ; but now that the portion nearest the Danube has thrown

off Mahommedan government, while the portion nearest
Macedonia remains enslaved, map-makers have restricted
the name of Serbia to the free districts, while the rest of
the country is called by its Christian inhabitants Old or
Stara Serbia.

This name is in use not only among the Slāvs in Turkey, but also with those throughout Austria and Russia,
yet it is ignored equally by the Turkish authorities and
by European Consuls in Turkey. The latter, with the
exception of an Austrian at Prizren, are indeed stationed
at too great a distance to know much of the local Christians; whereas they are aware that the Turks call the
country Arnaoutluk, and that it is partly inhabited by
Mahommedan Albanians. In the district itself both
names may be heard. If you notice any instance of ruin
or lawlessness, Turks and Serbians alike reply, "What
do you expect in Arnaoutluk?" If you halt in wonder
and admiration at the sight of an ancient church, and
exclaim, "Who would have thought to find such a
building hereabouts?" the priest who acts your cicerone
draws near and whispers, "*We* call this country Stara
Serbia."

The limits of Old Serbia have then no political definition, nor any definition except that which is assigned
them by their Christian inhabitants. This, again, depends on historical associations, so that it is not easy to
determine boundaries.

Yet, by way of giving some idea of the region, we
will indicate a few of its geographical features, and begin
with the frontiers as assigned by local tradition. On the
north, i.e. where Old Serbia meets the southern frontier
of the Principality, stands the town of Novi Bazaar;
whence westward runs a chain of hills (Rogoshna
Plánina), terminating in that mountain knot which
culminates in the Montenegrīne Berdas. At the *south-*

western extremity of Old Serbia lies Prizren, the former "Czarigrad," and behind it the Scardus range, now called Shaar Plánina. As on the *west* a line from north to south is marked by the mountains of Herzegovina, Northern Albania, and Montenegro, so on the *east* a line from south to north may be drawn from the castle of Marco Kralïevich at Prilip to Skopia, and thence, following the range of the Bulgarian Cerna Gora, to Nish. Nish stands a little outside the boundary of the free districts, but it owns a monument erected by the Turks with the skulls of Serbians who fell in defence of freedom; and this monument, as Lamartine observed, marks the true frontier of Serbia.

Mountains.

At the point where Old Serbia meets with Montenegro, we find the highest mountains in Turkey in Europe, and their most elevated summits, Kom and Dormitor, rise from 8,000 to 9,000 feet. Liubatern, 6,000 feet, we have already noticed as marking the western end of the Shaar Plánina, at the corner where the Pass of Katchanik debouches on the plain of Kóssovo.

Plains, Rivers, Towns, &c.

The heart of Old Serbia, both historically and geographically, is formed by the sister plains of Metóchia and Kóssovo. On or near Kóssovo are situated the towns of Príshtina, Novo Berdo, Gilan, Vuchitern, the monastery of Gratchanitza, and the site of the famous old church of Samodresha. The castle of Svétchani, once a residence of the kings of Serbia, occupies an eminence at the northern entrance of the plain.

The field of Metóchia lies west of Kóssovo, and is

separated by the low chain of the Golesh hills. On this
plain, as at once the centre of the Serb lands and a fertile
spot in a defensible position, the Nemanides fixed their
capital, and afterwards Stephen Dúshan transferred
thither the seat of the Patriarch. The Czarigrad Prizren
lay but a few hours distant from the ecclesiastical city
Ipek, and between the two stood the famous church of
Détchani, of which the king who built it felt so proud,
that he took his name from it, and has gone down to
posterity as Urosh Détchanski. Throughout national
poetry Kóssovo is celebrated as the battle-field, Metóchia
as the garden, of Serbia.

It would appear that the districts included in Stara
Serbia, together with the southern part of the modern
Principality, were in old times peopled by the richest
and most civilised portion of the nation. Most of the
higher nobles, whose family names are perpetuated in
the Book of Serbian aristocracy,* appear to have held
their residence in this part of the realm ; while the beautiful churches still remaining either as ruins or partially
preserved, show that a taste for the arts early penetrated
regions which now are all but a desert.

The native sovereigns of Serbia were evidently liberal
in their expenditure on works of piety or public usefulness. They took their surnames from the places where
they had founded some holy house, and the impression
left by their munificence on the mind of the people is to
this day traceable in popular songs. We cite as a specimen the following curious ballad, whereof the scene is
the convent of Gratchanitza, while the occasion is a
Sabor held after the death of " Czar Némania."

" Behold," says the minstrel, " the Christian gentlemen of Serbia hold parliament in the fair church of

---

* Said to be preserved in a monastery of Mount Athos. A copy was shown us
by M. Ljudevit Gaj, in Agram.

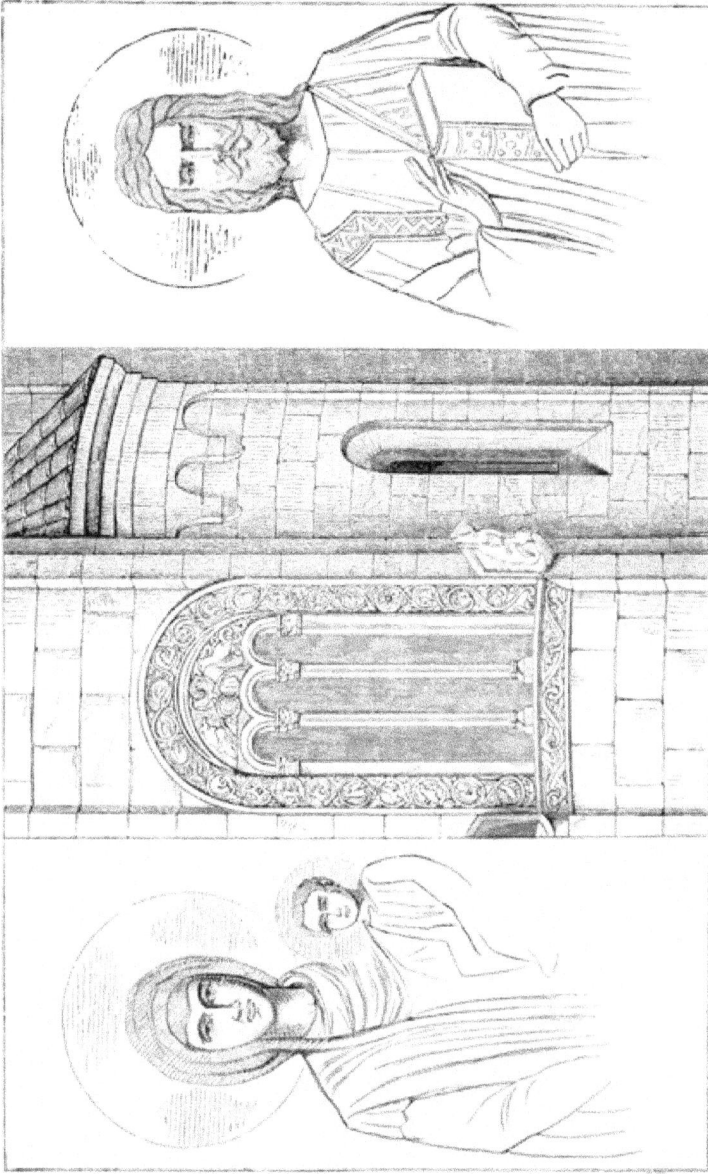

Gratchanitza, and they are saying one to another, Great
God! what a miracle is this! The seven towers which
Czar Némania heaped full of gold and silver now stand
empty. Is it possible that the Czar should have wasted
all this wealth on weapons, and battle-axes, and trappings for the war-horses?"

Then the Czar's son, Sava Némanjic, rises, and thus
addresses the assembly:—"Ye Christian gentlemen,
speak not foolishly, nor sin against my father's soul.
My father did not waste his wealth on weapon or mace
or trappings for the war-horse. My father worthily
employed his wealth on many and noble 'works for the
soul.' On the holy mountain of Athos he built the church
of Hilindar, and for that he emptied two towers of gold.
By the stream Bistritza he raised High Détchani, above
Novi Bazaar the columns of St. George, in Stari Vla the
white Laura of Studenitza; these cost him another
tower." (Here follows a long list of names containing
many churches really built by the descendants of Némania, but in this poem attributed to himself.) Then
Sava adds:—

"What remained of my father's wealth he spent in
making well-paved roads, in building bridges over the
rivers, he divided it among the sick and blind, thus
winning a place in Paradise for his soul. Truly several
towers of treasure were emptied by the Czar my father,
but on this manner was his wealth employed."

From Stara Serbia in the time of the Nemanides, we
pass to it in our day. Previous to 1389, it was the most
flourishing and favoured portion of European Serbia;
at present, excepting the neighbouring mountains of
Albania, it is the poorest and worst-ruled part of Turkey in Europe. The turning-point in its history is to
be found in the victory of the Turks on Kóssovo, but
the transformation of a fruitful land into a wilder-

ness was a gradual process, and came about as follows:—

According to the terms made between the Sultan
and the Serbians who first submitted to him, the church
and the mosque were to stand side by side, and men were
to worship in either as they might incline. But these
conditions met with no better observance in Serbia than
in Bulgaria. The moderation, the tolerance of the Turk,
lasted only till he got a firm grip on the country, and
then he appropriated to his own use whatever he did
not destroy. Of the children that were not slain, the
girls were dragged off to harems, the boys to the
janissaries, while their elders could only save themselves
by "ransoming their heads" (the original signification
of the haratch). Such churches as escaped being
destroyed or taken for mosques, owed it either to their
smallness or to their occupying sites not convenient for
Moslem worship, or finally because to save them the
Christians were willing to pay large sums of money. In
this manner Gratchanitza and Détchani still continue a
source of income to the Mussulman.

Nevertheless, except the Ottoman colonies sent soon
after the battle of Kóssovo to Skopia, Prizren, and Novo
Berdo, the Mahommedanisation of Stara Serbia went
on but slowly, so long as the population of the country
were Serbs. But in the latter half of the seventeeth
century, events occurred which nearly emptied the
country of its original inhabitants.

The Turks having carried their depredations into
the dominions of the Emperor of Germany,—having
installed themselves in Hungary and besieged Vienna,—
the House of Hapsburg took up the war against them
in earnest, and the Serbian Christians south of the
Danube were called on to lend their aid. At Adrianople the Patriarch of Serbia met George Brankovic,

last scion of her last princes, and anointed him ruler; then both the secular and the spiritual chief undertook to raise the people to arms. We have in another chapter noticed the result of this effort. Austria, having used George Brankovic as a tool, held him captive for life at Eger; her generals having penetrated to the Kóssovo Poljé, mismanaged matters and had to retreat. Thereupon the greater part of the inland Serbian population, finding themselves given over to the Turks, and judging further contest in their own country hopeless, resolved to accept the Emperor's offer and emigrate to his dominions.

In the year 1690, 37,000 families passed from their fatherland under the leadership of the then reigning patriarch, Arsenius Tsrnoïcvic; they were the remnant of wealth and valour in central Serbia, and preferred expatriation to unconditional submission. In their new settlements north of the Danube and Save they formed the greater part of that famous military frontier, which long served to protect Austria alike from the plunder of Oriental armies and from the contamination of Oriental disease.* The Emperor of Germany promised that their service in his dominions should be but temporary; that he would conquer their land back for them, and that meanwhile, if they would but help to defend his, they should continue to be governed by their own authorities, civil and religious.

But the old land has not been reconquered, and the

---

* In the rising of 1875 and 1876 the military frontier, which formerly served as the defence of Christian Europe against the Turks, has served as the bulwark of Islam against Christendom. Although it has been found practically impossible to restrain the sympathies of a kindred population, or to reckon upon the fidelity of every official, yet the northern frontier has been strictly guarded against the passing over of men with any sort of arms in their hands into Bosnia. Turkish barbarities have been committed within sight of Austrian soil, and attacks from Mussulmans on the lives and properties of Austrian subjects have been made with impunity, owing to the resolute determination of Austria-Hungary to keep peace with Turkey at any price.

new land was by no means freely accorded to its gallant defenders. The succession of the patriarchs was rendered dependent on the caprice of the cabinet of Vienna; the office of the Voivode was mulcted of real power; nay, some of the new settlers were so tormented in order to induce them to change their religion, that they left Austria for Russia.

At this moment, the Serbians under national government are not more enthusiastic patriots than those whose families have dwelt for 200 years on foreign ground; nay, young men among the Austrian Serbians take service in the principality rather than in the empire. Since the War of Liberation hundreds of families have passed over to Free Serbia, and should the Turks ever evacuate the more southerly districts, the bulk of the north Danubian colonists declare that they will return whence they came.

Significant of this unbroken adherence to their old fatherland, is the arrangement whereby the Austrian Serbs have consecrated a portion of their new territory *in memoriam.* The spot chosen is the so-called Frusca Gora, a hilly peninsula between the Danube and Save; there the newly arrived emigrants built churches named after those they had left behind them; thither they transferred their few treasures, and the bones of their last czar.

We visited the convent where Lázar lies. His body was carried from the field of Kóssovo first to Gratchanitza and thence to Ravanitza,—a church now included in the principality; finally to New Ravanitza, erected in the Frusca Gora. The day of the battle of Kóssovo is celebrated as the czar's anniversary; on it thousands of people make pilgrimages to his shrine, crowding around the open coffin wherein he lies, robed with the garments in which he fought and fell. A large picture of the battle is preserved in the same convent: it serves as a text for poems on the Turkish conquest, and for traditional descriptions of home.

Having now seen how Old Serbia lost her Christian and quasi-civilised inhabitants, we will examine how it came to be tenanted by barbarians and Islam.

The place of the fugitives who quitted the plains, both at the first emigration and afterwards, was filled up from the neighbouring hills by a descent of Skipetars, or Albanians, or, as the Turks call them, Arnaouts.

From the beginning of Serbian history there must have been districts where the Slavonic and Albanian elements existed side by side.* How far north the Albanians dwelt previous to their last ingress it is hard to determine; but it is certain that the Slavonians shared Albanian territory as far as Durazzo and Elbassan; also that, even before Némania's time, the little Serbian kingdom of Zeta united northern Skipetars and southern Slāvs. Afterwards, the laws of the empire speak of Albanians, both orthodox and catholic, as fellow-subjects with the Serb. Finally, after the breaking-up, first of the czardom, and then of Zeta itself, we find the Albanians under separate princes; but these princes—for instance, Scanderbeg himself—are relatives and allies of the Serbs.

Most of the northern Albanians dwelling near the Adriatic became adherents of the Latin Church. On the Mahommedan conquest it was the interest of the Otto-man to sow division between the Christian races. The

---

* M. Hahn is inclined to consider the Albanians as the aboriginal inhabitants, who vacated the fertile part of the country during the Serbian occupation for centuries. However this may be, both they themselves and the Slavonic inhabi-tants speak of their immigration as recent; in some places they have come down from the hills within the last fifty years, and constantly talk of returning thither.

Roman Catholics being in the minority were those to whom the most indulgences could be safely granted, and the mountaineers of Albania, unlike those of Montenegro, grew weary of acting breakwater to the flood of Turkish power. They therefore agreed to become subjects of the Sultan, on condition of a separate licence to maintain their religion and perpetuate their wild mode of life; these terms are still acted on by such tribes as dwell in the hills, and cannot well be reached by a Turkish army.

But when Albanians came down to live on the Serbian plains, they soon found that no better faith would be kept with them than with other Christians, and their fickle character and lack of definite purpose furnished poor stuff for patient endurance. Part of one tribe, called the Clementiner, did indeed emigrate with the Serbians; but those who remained in Turkey gradually yielded to the policy of the Porte, *i.e.* they became separated in interest from their brother-Christians, and purchased, at the price of apostacy, permission to hector over the rest of the population.

In Old Serbia the remnant of Roman Catholic Albanians is but small, although from time to time it is recruited by fresh arrivals from the hills. The newcomers usually follow the example of their predecessors, and after a while become Mahommedans. Even when they continue in the Latin faith, they compound for an exemption from haratch by lending the Sultan military service, and helping to keep down their fellow-Christians. Indeed, wherever the authorities are Mussulman and Mahommedan law is observed in courts of justice, it requires no small exertion on the part of the Roman Catholic priests, with occasional encouragement from foreign powers, to prevent all the so-called Latins in Old Serbia from going over to Islam. If once a few

families in a village become Mahommedans, they never
cease bullying the rest until they have made them follow
their example, for apparently nothing annoys a renegade
like the presence of constancy greater than his own.
Waverers attempt to bridge over the passage between
the two creeds by adopting Mahommedan names, and
thus passing for Mussulmans abroad, while they remain
Christians at home. We shall have occasion to speak
of these Romanists hereafter—their principal parishes
lie at Gilan, Ipek, Diakova, and Prizren.

As for the general characteristics and customs of the
Northern Albanians, there exists a full and particular
treatise on the subject, written by one who knows them
and whom they know well. We refer to the book of
M. Hecquard, late Consul of France at Scutari in
Albania. At present it suffices to remark that the
Arnaouts in Old Serbia belong to the division Ghegga,
and, like all Gheggas, entertain a strong aversion for
the southern Albanians, or Tosks. The Tosks are certainly very different from them, many being to a certain
extent Hellenized, and exhibiting both in physique
and character some affinity with the graceful, intelligent,
and fickle Greeks. The Gheggas, on the other hand,
are a sturdy and hardy type, and those settled in
Slavonic districts have a strong tinge of Slavonic blood;
indeed, some of their families are of Slavic descent, for
if a Serb forsakes his religion he at once loses the name
of Serbian, and is henceforth termed "Arnaout."

The Albanian in Old Serbia is taller and more stalwart than the Albanian of Epirus; he is cleaner in his
person, and his substantial and splendid dress displays
more analogy with the Montenegrine costume than with
the Tosk fustanella and dangling sleeves. But a cross
with the Serbian has not contributed to render the
Ghegga character more amiable. If more stately than

the Tosk, he is also more stubborn, and the Arnaouts
now installed in the old city of the Patriarch, fully
justify the merchant of Skopia's description, as the most
lawless Mussulmans in Turkey. Their antagonism to
the authority of the Porte is, however, quite as marked as
their arrogance to the Christians. " Fear God little,"
say the Arnaouts of Ipek, "and as for the Sultan, do not
know that he lives." They plunder the rayah, and are
glad of the excuse of their creed for plundering, but
they care about religion very little any way, and they
and the Serbs are certainly not separated by hatred of
race, as both are from the Osmanli. The Serbs look
down on the Albanians for their inconstancy, lawlessness,
and ignorance, but they admire their fighting qualities,
and they declare that many Albanians joined the War
of Liberation, and have since amalgamated with the
Danubian Serbs.

We now come to the remnant of Serbian families who
yet remain in the old country, and whom the emigration
of their countrymen and the apostacy of the Arnaouts
have left in the smallest minority formed by Christians
in any part of Turkey in Europe.

In dialect, dress, and physique, the Old Serbians are
identical with those on the southern frontier of the principality, and, like them, are as hardy a race as one could
wish to see. Even among Mussulman neighbours their
warlike qualities secure esteem ; but they are slow to
rouse, and this has often placed them at a disadvantage,
both with Turks and Albanians, in cases where sudden
and unscrupulous action wins the day. It is, however,
in time of peace that appears the radical distinction
between the Serbian and any of the Mahommedan peoples
of Turkey. His idea of order and right is not Oriental,
but European. In the principality, where he has his
own way, popular government is found compatible with

quiet and contentment; and his is the only country hereabouts where brigandage and official corruption are kept down.

In Arnaoutluk, and contrasted with the Arnaout, we have heard the Serbians called "good workers," but it is a comparison of laziness, for they certainly do not share the Bulgarian's disposition for agricultural labour. This lack of industry, together with a *dourness* which makes it difficult for them to yield in trials or to get on with others, constitute their most obvious faults. Fortitude, independent spirit, self-respect, and self-restraint, in fact a certain nobleness of character, cannot make up for such practical defects ; nevertheless, in the Serbian, such qualities have a special value, inasmuch as they are precisely those which the other Christians of Turkey lack.

The government of the principality discourages the Old Serbians from emigrating to seek a home with their brethren, because they would thus abandon the old country entirely to Mahommedans. Of course, however, the existence in their neighbourhood of a free state governed by Serbians helps to give them self-confidence ; and besides this, in Old Serbia, unlike Bosnia or Bulgaria, every proud memory is for the Christian.

The Asiatic Turk who conquered at Kóssovo has left few and sparse settlements in the country ; the Albanian Mahommedan represents a doubly conquered race. He is a European who has lost not only liberty but religion, whose past is barbarian, his present apostacy, and his future either a sneaking return to his former faith, or slavery to a despotic government administered by foreign officials. The Christians, on the contrary, meeting at their festivals under the walls of the grand old churches, claim as their own all traditions of ancient empire, and of such civilisation as distinguished Old Serbia so long as it was a part of Christian Europe. And if the past be theirs, they have only to look forward to be sure that the future is theirs also; that sooner or later they must become a part of Christian Europe once more. Their kindred of race—often their own near relatives—are living as European Christians in Serbia and Austria; hence they know what is meant by freedom, and there is no confusion, no uncertainty in their prospects for their children, who are educated in the conviction that they at least will be free. But all this ideal life (which, as it has been truly observed, one can only get at by coming among a people with some knowledge of its language and history) is not inconsistent with an occasionally despairing view of things at present, and an occasional temptation to throw up everything and be gone.

The condition of the country is indeed bad enough to reduce to despair all its inhabitants, excepting of course those evil men who thrive on it. The Porte, having exerted energies sufficient to extinguish national liberty in Albania, and to drive great numbers of Albanians to apostatise, has never carried its pains to the point of bringing its new adherents into the attitude of orderly citizens. Whenever authority is exerted over them, it is in order to obtain recruits, or to impose Turkish officials in lieu of the old hereditary governors—not to enforce a just treatment of the Christians. The mode wherein the administration is conducted gives so good an idea of the state of society, that we will describe it in a few words.

In the towns of Stara Serbia the governor is a Turkish official; sometimes an Osmanli who does not know the language of the country, sometimes an Albanian who has served in the regular army. This official supports his authority by aid of a few zaptiés and cavasses in his own service, and these useful persons derive their pay chiefly from what they can rob from the people. The mudir, kaïmakam, or pasha, buys his post to begin with, and is then left to enjoy it so short a time that his chief aim is to reimburse himself as quickly as possible. Every one knows this, so Mussulmans and Christians alike ply him with bribes. But, besides enriching himself, he has to raise the Sultan's taxes. If the Mussulmans will not pay their share he must doubly fleece the Christians; for the Mussulmans are not to be trifled with, as, should he offend them, they may bribe some higher authority to remove him from his post. At Príshtina this was constantly the case; the mudir we found there was the second in a year, and before we left the district he was already deposed.

Supposing, however, that a governor will not be intimidated, and having friends among the higher powers, cannot be got rid of by fair means, force must be resorted to. At Ipek the kaïmakam being resolved to raise taxes from Mussulmans, not only obtained regular troops to support his designs, but seemed inclined to circumvent the local Mahommedans by conciliating the rayahs. Thereupon the Arnaouts waylaid him, and shot him from behind a bush. This instance came under our own observation, inasmuch as while at Príshtina, we took it into our heads to inquire if we could make a detour by the monastery of Détchani. The mudir told us that he could not send us thither, the road being beset with Albanians who had lately murdered the governor of Ipek, and who would not even respect the Sultan's firman. If we were resolved to go, we must make a round by Prizren, and ask the pasha for a guard of Nizam.

Next in authority to the Turkish governor comes the town-council, or medjliss. The members of the medjliss are (with the exception of one Christian) **Mus-sulmans**, and in Old Serbia the post is filled by the most influential chiefs among the Arnaouts. In former days, when the governor was a native, he usually had a strong party in his council, for many of its members were his kin; hence the Christians had only to bribe him in order to secure a certain amount of protection. Nowadays, the governor must still be bribed, but being a stranger he has not the same power to shelter his protégés, so all the medjliss must be bribed too, and in this respect the Christians themselves told us that their present state is worse than the first. The only chance is to play the foreign governor and the local Mussulmans against each other; but it is a dangerous game, as whenever the two sets of plunderers find it their interest to make peace, they make it at the rayahs' cost.

The Christians could do far more to help themselves if they were worthily represented in the medjliss, but this is rarely the case. In Old Serbia, as throughout Turkey in Europe, the Mussulmans congregate in the towns, and in order to keep out of their way, the Christians dwell in the country and villages. Hence the town community of every Christian district is comparatively small, and furnishes the Turkish Government with a pretext for restricting Christian representation in the medjliss to a single member, or, if there are both Roman Catholic and Oriental Christians, to two members. Even this is a late concession, and certain Turkish governors, who would be glad to use the Christians against the local Mussulmans, have themselves described to us the treatment which deprives the rayah member of the medjliss of all power. In the first place, he is one against many; secondly, he is used as a servant to hand pipes and coffee to the Mussulmans;

thirdly, he is sent out of the room whenever anything of importance is to be discussed. In consequence, few Christians, except such as are willing to expose themselves to ill-treatment, will consent to sit in the medjliss. Sometimes a poor wretch is put in and paid for it; sometimes a creature of the bishop's or the governor's is got in by intrigue, and then becomes the scourge of his own community. In Old Serbia the courage of the Christians shows itself by better men offering for the post; and those who have been for a while in Free Serbia bring to their office a resolute demeanour and a definiteness of purpose which enable them now and then to hold their own.

Of the Christian community the principal representative is properly the bishop; hence nothing could more effectually take the heart out of the Slāvs in Turkey than the transfer of this important office to Greeks, who do not care a rush for Slavonic interests. In most parts of Old Serbia the idea we found associated with a bishop was that of a person who carried off what few paras the Turks had left. When at home he would occasionally exert himself to prevent Christian children being carried off and made Mahommedans, but he was too often absent to be available even for this purpose. Of course, in this case, as in that of Turkish governors and Christian representatives in the medjliss, there are honourable exceptions to the general rule.

Under existing circumstances, the actual head of a Christian community is its primate or chief elder, usually known by the Turkish appellation, kodgia bashi. This personage is supposed to be elected by the Christians themselves. He has little political power; but his social influence is great for good or evil, as he helps to apportion the taxes, and acts as judge in civil cases. In the latter function he is aided by the chief men, called

Kmets, a title general among Slavonic tribes, and which may be traced back in the ancient annals of Bohemia, even to the days of Queen Libussa. The room wherein we lodged at Prìshtina was used in the bishop's absence for the meeting of these kmets, who considered civil cases in the community itself; criminal cases are referred to the mudir's court, where, as we shall presently instance, Christian evidence is not received.

Having thus sketched the present condition of Old Serbia, we may conclude by quoting thereon the opinion of its inhabitants. This is,—that however in other parts of the empire improvement may be compatible with Turkish government, here that government is the very root of ill. The evils that desolate Old Serbia have their source in the antagonism of races and creeds: the first aim of a good government must be to appease these rivalries: the maintenance of Turkish rule depends on fomenting them. Hated alike by Albanian and Serb, the Asiatic conqueror, since the day he entered the country, has skilfully worn out the energies of his enemies by turning them against each other; should he ever allow them to make up their differences, their first act in concert would be to drive him from the land. That this will be the end of the matter is, in fact, the expectation of all parties; for the Arnaouts are only held to their present creed by interest; and the attempts lately made by the Porte to introduce the conscription and foreign officials have so disgusted them, that they have begun to ask themselves if they might not make a better bargain elsewhere. Their present profession of Mahommedanism is not an insurmountable obstacle: "they were all Christians once, and to gain anything they would be Christians again." During the last war with Montenegro it was very generally expected that a Serbian army would cross the border and co-operate with its kindred

in the hills. On this occasion the Albanians in Old
Serbia held assemblies and reasoned thus:—"We have
long been fighting the Montenegrīnes, and know that
they are good heroes; nevertheless we can hold our own
against them, for they have not Frankish arms. But it
is said that the Serbians on the Danube have cannon,
and officers trained in Frankish schools. If they join the
Montenegrīnes there will be another battle on Kóssovo;
we shall be beaten, and then we must make terms. Let
us seek persons who have been in Free Serbia, and ask
what taxes are there paid." They were told that the
Serbian government requires two ducats from every
householder. "Two ducats? We will give three, if
in return they will promise not to take us for nizam."
Answer: "The Serbians do not care to have nizam, their
soldiers are militia, who wear the national dress, and do
not go on foreign service." "Good, good," cried the
Arnaouts; "why, we should be better off under the
Prince than we now are under the Sultan. Let but the
Serbs march over the border, and we will negotiate with
them through the Abbot of Détchani."

But a Serbian army could only cross the border in
event of a Christian rising throughout Turkey—a rising
which, even if successful, must entail massacre and
pillage. No wonder, then, that some persons would
desire to avert such extremities by diplomatic arrangement. According to them, we must find an agent for
bringing this part of Turkey under civilisation, without
necessarily detaching it from the Ottoman empire; such
an agent is to be found in the native Christian government of Free Serbia. That government manages to keep
order; and were the southern frontier of the principality
extended so as to include Old Serbia, we should soon see
brigandage put down, and all clans and classes equal
before law. The present population is sparse, idle, and

disorganized ; but once let life and property become
secure on the fertile plains of Metóchia and Kóssovo, and
their inhabitants would be recruited from beyond the
Danube by industrious and well-ordered colonists, able
to retrieve their fathers' exile, and give back to Europe
the Old Serbian land.

CHAPTER XVII.

AT Príshtina we dismissed the kiradgees who had accompanied us from Monastir. Their grass-fed horses were becoming knocked up, and we spent so many days in resting, that it was bootless expense to pay for them when not in use. Scarcely had we parted, when the poor fellows met with a grievous mischance. As usual, to save paying for their horses in the khan, they drove them out to pasture. At nightfall, in a lonely place, they were accosted by some Arnaouts, who, pretending to be zaptiés, found fault with them for letting their horses graze in such and such spots, asked their names, and otherwise bothered them. When at last the kiradgees contrived to satisfy these tormentors and drove their horses together, they found that three were missing. At once they suspected that the *soi-disant* police were but members of a party of horse-stealers, and that they had engaged them with questions merely that the rest of the crew might have an opportunity of making off with the beasts. But it was now dark, no search could be made; and next morning at daybreak a diligent quest succeeded in recovering, not the horses, but the horses' tails—cut off, and left on the ground. On this discovery, the kiradgees considered it certain that their beasts had not merely strayed, and they repaired to the town to see if anything could be done towards reclaiming them from

the thieves.   To swear to the horses having been in
their own possession overnight, they called in the evidence of our cavass, *" because his oath, as that of a Mussulman, would be received, and theirs would not."*   This he, a
Mussulman, explained to us, when requesting leave to
go with them.

So soon as the mudir heard what had happened, he
determined to give the passing Frankish travellers a
proof of his zeal; therefore he sent out into the bazaar,
and captured the first two stranger Albanians on whom
his zaptiés could lay their hands; then he let us know
that the thieves were caught, and that he would
send them, loaded with chains, to Prizren.   Through our
dragoman we questioned the kiradgees, if they thought
the imprisoned Albanians were really the thieves.   They
answered that it was most unlikely, as the men who stole
their horses would not be found next morning dawdling
about the bazaar; they had doubtless made off, and the
horses were with them.   Besides, the poor kiradgees remarked, that what *they* wanted the mudir to catch was,
not the thieves, but the stolen animals, and to this end
no steps had yet been taken.   We thought of a law of
old Czar Dūshan, which ruled that if the magistrates and
nobles of a district did not keep that district free from
robbers, or, when a theft had occurred, could not find the
robbers and force them to make restitution of stolen goods,
they, the nobles and the magistrates, should indemnify
the plundered voyager.   It seemed that some law of this
kind was still needed to quicken the execution of justice
in Stara Serbia.

However, we asked the kiradgees whether, since they
believed the captured Albanians not to be those who had
stolen their horses, they would not say so, and have them
released.   But this no one would hear of: *" All* Arnaouts
were thieves!   If those now imprisoned had not stolen

the horses in question, they had stolen others, or were
about to steal them. The mudir himself had pronounced
them *maurais sujets*, their teskérés were not in proper
order, and their testimony concerning themselves agreed
not together. Let them stay in prison by all means;
doubtless the mudir would let them out as soon as we
were gone."

As the horses were not ours, nor any longer in our
service, we did not see that we could intermeddle further,
and we really dreaded to do so for fear of causing other
persons to be thrown into jail. Evidently *justice* was
beyond the mudir's functions, and all representations on
our part would be considered simply as cries for vengeance. In this part of the world, if a privileged person
demands justice, somebody is sure to be punished, and
that promptly—whether he be the culprit or not is a
matter of comparative indifference.

The road between Prishtina and Vuchitern lies over the
actual battle-field of Kóssovo, and crosses the river Lab,
which flowed between the hostile camps. To the right
are passed the ruins of the old church of Samodresha—
identified with many Sabors (parliaments), and with one
account of the last sacrament partaken of by the Serbian
army. The spot where Sultan Amurath was assassinated
is covered by a small mosque, and all the neighbourhood
between it and Prishtina is associated with legends of
Milosh. By the Turks themselves a house is shown
containing the tombs of the Vizier, and his companions
slain by Milosh in his death-struggle. They also point
out a mound on the top of which they say he planted
himself, and killed all who attempted to approach.
" All the graves around it are graves of Turks whom
Milosh slew." But the most interesting monument has
perished ; three large stones placed at equal distance,
and each marking the spot attained by Milosh in the

three bounds that almost carried him to his horse's side.
The third stone marked where he was cut down. Some
years ago, when the mosque of Murad was rebuilt, these
stones were removed and used as materials. Considering,
however, how long they had been suffered to remain, it
would not appear that the Turks intended, when removing
them, to insult the Serbians; any more than the British
peasant intends to insult the memory of the Druids
when he breaks up their stone circles to build his
cottage walls.

The hospitable sheikh from **Bokhara**, who entertained
the winter travellers Zach and Hahn with tea, is still
guardian of Amurath's tomb; but at the time of our
visit he was absent at Prizren, and his black *locum tenens*
was not communicative. He demurred at first about
letting us enter, but whether as women or as ghiaours
we knew not. However, the Usbashi gave a positive
order, in the name of whom we also knew not; and the
result was that not only were we admitted, but nothing
was said about taking off shoes. There is little to be
seen. The so-called tomb is a shabby likeness of some
of those in Constantinople, *i.e.*, simply a room containing
a large coffin. The body is not there, having been carried
to Broussa, but over the coffin hangs a scarf, and at the
head of it is fixed a sultan's turban. Once the actual
vestments worn by Amurath when he received the blow
were kept here; but the attendant assured us that the
"old soiled ones had been thrown away, and that those
we saw were bran new and sent from Stamboul." The
turban is on the pattern of those worn by the lay figures
in the hall of the Janissaries, a pyramid of linen coils
monstrous to behold, and as unlike as possible to that
most stately and simple of headgears, the turban, as it is
still worn in Bosnia. At the top stands a little red fez,
stiff and crimped as if with irons; this again is totally

unlike the fez with its long flowing tassel as sported by the Albanians and Greeks.

It is said that the sword of Milosh Obilic used also to be kept here, but this we did not see, and the guards said it had been taken away. Having left the mosque, we remounted and rode onward for about half an hour, when the zaptié stopped to point out what the Turks call the site of Murad's tent; he showed us also a heap of stones where some Beg or other had fallen. Apparently the latter was of late origin, and referred to another battle on Kóssovo. Then we crossed the Lab, but not having with us any Christian from the neighbourhood, we could identify no spot connected with the Serbian battle array except the hills of Golesh (Slav. *gol*, naked), where Vūk Brankovic is said to have been stationed, and which have been cursed with barrenness for his sake.

But if the remembrance of their army's station is faded from all but uncertain local tradition; Serbian minstrels have not forgotten the order and manner of their heroes' fall—old Iūg Bogdan early in the day; eight of the brothers Iugovic side by side; the brave Ban Strahinia "where blood flowed knee-deep;" last the Standard-bearer Bosko is seen "chasing the enemy in flocks as a hawk chases pigeons, and driving them before him into the Sitnitza;" and where "the broken spears are strewn thickest and the bravest warriors lie slain," there is the spot where fell the Czar. Thus in the ever-darkening twilight we passed over that fatal field where once on the warm quiet Sabbath morning came forth the ministering "maiden of Kóssovo," with water to wash the blood of the wounded, with wine to freshen the lips of the faint, while still she sought her gay bridegroom of yesterday among the mangled corpses of to-day.*

* See one of the most touching Serbian ballads, "The Maiden of Kóssovo."

CHAPTER XVIII.

WE had lingered so long on the way that it was dark when we reached Vuchitern, and then our dragoman, who had ridden on before, met us with a face of dismay, saying, "They have nothing for supper." However, it seemed that quarters had been bespoken, and we presently found ourselves in the house of the Serb pope, and in a room which, though it lacked window-panes and even shutters, was provided with a substantial goat's hair carpet. While we were improvising curtains the popadia entered, and by the time the luggage was brought up, we had made friends, and she whisperingly informed us that "a fowl was in the pot." Why then had they not said so at once? For this very sufficient reason. The pope and the kodgia bashi were standing without when the dragoman rode up and accosted them abruptly—behind him they saw Turkish horsemen. "You know," said the popadia, "we had not enough for all, and if those Turks had heard of supper in our house, they would never have gone to the khan."

The peasants from Prîshtina went no farther than Vuchitern, and we sent back the postman with his obstreperous steeds, so that the operation of getting horses had to be performed all over again. We knew this would prevent us from starting in good time, and as our hosts appeared the sort of people likely to give information about the country, we agreed to spend next day where we were. This resolve we communicated to the mudir's son, who was in attendance the evening we arrived, and next morning at an early hour the mudir himself came to visit us. Our room was not yet arranged for the reception of company, so we agreed to receive him on the chardak,—a sort of covered balcony in form like a small room, which forms the outer saloon of most houses hereabouts, and where guests may be received without entering the house. However, when we came forth, we found him not reclining on the cushions of the chardak, but seated at the head of the stairs on a chair. The Arnaout or Bosnian Mussulman rarely affects foreign fashions, so we saw at once that this must be an Osmanli desirous to be thought cognizant of European manners. An Osmanli he was, and dressed in European costume, with an enormous pink waistcoat, which set off his *embonpoint* to the full. But an Osmanli shows much better when he is surrounded by menacing Arnaouts than when he is fattening on Bulgarian and Fanariote bribes; in the post of danger he is forced out of his sloth, his courage is called into play, his will too puts forth its real strength, while its imperiousness is restrained. Moreover, we found the mudir at Vuchitern both obliging and intelligent, and willing to tell what he knew about the place, though being himself a foreigner he had to call in assistance before replying to any question. Especially he was anxious to let us know that he had not always lived among barbarians. No—he had been mudir in the Roumelian provinces, and his son spoke Greek well. Encouraged by his amiability, and appealing to his civilised sentiments, we asked if we might visit the Mahommedan girls' school. The countenance of the mudir fell, and all present looked one upon another. This was not the first time we had made the request, but it was the first time we had asked point-blank ourselves. Our former messages had always met with some excuse : the schoolmaster was ill, the children had a holiday, or, as at Príshtina, it was Friday, and the school was not held. Yet we kept hearing of Arnaout girls' schools, and in the same breath that their women lived in gross ignorance. How were these accounts to be reconciled ? Evidently we must see the schools.

The mudir of Vuchitern having no time to frame an excuse, waited only a minute to take breath, and then replied, that the request we had made was such as might be expected from civilised and enlightened travellers ; further, he was well aware that it would be cheerfully complied with in Constantinople. But we were now in Arnaoutluk, and he regretted to say that the Mussulmans were fanatical and rude. However, he would take steps to secure that we should see what we desired ; the girls' school was next door to his harem, and if we would condescend to visit his khanum (lady), she and his son would escort us to the school. The visit was fixed for the afternoon, and all preliminaries were nearly settled, when we called to mind the slovenly déshabillé of the women at Katchanik, and therefore remarked to the mudir that we had heard much of the beauty and splendour of Albanian costume, and that we had long wished to judge of it for ourselves. He took the hint, and promised that in his harem we should see the best-dressed women in the town. At the same time, the cloud on his face gave way to a good-natured smile, as if this last trait had served to assure him that whatever we might ask or attempt, we had no motive deeper than feminine curiosity.

When the time for our visit came, the popadia offered to accompany us, and for that purpose arrayed herself in

black serge; her tight-fitting garment reaching to the
ankles, and scarcely differing from a long pelisse. We
were heartily glad of her company, for such was her
quickness of comprehension, that she contrived not only
to understand our broken language, but also to interpret
it to others. At the gate of the harem we found a sort
of lodge, where we had to leave our cavass and dragoman, and where we were met by the Greek-speaking
son, a dreadful little fellow in shabby uniform. He conducted us through a court to the chardak, on which
carpets and cushions lay prepared. At the foot of the
stair we were received by his mother. The khanum was
a fat old Turkish woman, frightfully like an overfed bird
of prey; her dress showed the same Frankish taste as her
husband's pink silk waistcoat, for it was of brown European muslin, but its thin trousers and scanty bodice
could hardly be said to become a corpulent and withered
form. None the less, she was not emancipated from the
fear of exciting dangerous admiration. While we sat
sipping coffee, it happened that a zaptié having some
message for her son, poked his head out of the lodge.
Far off as he was, a hue and cry was raised, and the old
dame ducked under the side of the chardak with all the
haste that might have beseemed a fair one of eighteen.
This incident recalled to us certain reflections that had
occurred frequently in the female compartment of the
steamers on the Bosphorus; namely, that if Turkish
women value their prestige as beauties, they must oppose
every attempt to draw them into public view; and for
the following reasons. Most Oriental women have dark
eyes, bright enough to look bewitching through the slit
of the yashmak, and all can paint well enough to produce
a complexion which seems roses and lilies when half seen
through muslin folds. But alas for their charms should
the veil be torn away, and the wearers be called on to

show their faces honestly beside those of European
women—the whole face, in broad daylight, exposed to
sunshine, wind, and rain! Of course in the wealthy
harem, where a high price is paid for beauty, and the
faded rose is discarded or passed on, one sees exquisite
forms arrayed with taste and splendour. But many of
the officials in the European provinces cannot afford
polygamy, nor to buy Circassian slaves; or as sometimes
happens, they have inherited the favourite of some higher
official—hence in this class, as a rule, the women are
unpleasing to behold. Indeed it is hard to see how they
could be otherwise. They destroy their teeth by smoking
and eating bonbons, even when they do not blacken them
on purpose. They dock their hair, they cultivate fatness,
they bedaub their finger and toe nails with a coating
that looks like red mud. Then, unless they have what
is much admired, a broad, flat, featureless countenance,
they exhibit the Turkish long nose, retreating brow, cut-
away chin, and sallow complexion. Absence of intellectual occupations, and exclusion from cultivated society,
deprive plain faces of a redeeming expression of intelligence, while even fine features bear the stamp of sloth,
triviality, and too often of unbridled passion.

While we were at Constantinople, some persons who
should have known better spread the report that a fête
given by Fuad Pasha would be signalised by the eman-
cipation of Turkish ladies—to wit, by their appearance
outside the harem and dressed in Parisian toilettes. Of
course, when the fête took place, there was nothing of
the kind. Supposing, however, the report had proved
true, is it not a question how far the moral elevation
of the Turkish ladies would have been advanced by their
mingling in Pera society, or by exchanging the dress of
their country and climate for the foreign artifices of
Parisian mode? Till the Mahommedan woman can receive

an education calculated to arm her with self-restraint
and self-respect, those would indeed assume a grave
responsibility who should turn her loose on Oriental
society, or suddenly divest her of her present guardians,
the veil and the sacred walls of the harem. One might
say more than this, and assume that until the women of
Christian communities situated in Levantine cities shall
make a more creditable use of their liberty, Mussulmans
can hardly be expected to believe that the Eastern female
possesses powers of self-guidance sufficient to justify a
husband's confidence.

Such were our reflections while the khanum put num-
berless questions to the popadia: they were interrupted
by her son taking leave, and then the door into the
house opened, and a troop of ladies crowded in. In a
few moments all were squatted on the chardak, staring
at us, and we at them. Many of them were old and
withered, and wore a heterogeneous costume; others
were gaily coifed with seed-pearls and coins, but enveloped in a black serge pelisse like that of the popadia,
and unlike any other dress that we saw in Turkey.
These younger dames were painted to such a degree that
at first we really thought they wore masks, and as their
mask-like faces represent the ideal of beauty in this part
of the world, we may state that this consists of cherry
lips and cheeks, a very fair complexion, and jet-black
eyebrows, strongly drawn. Among them all stood one
unpainted fresh-looking girl—a bride—and, as we understood, the bride of the mudir's son; she it was who
produced the fine clothes. Her trousseau was brought
forth, bit by bit, and all wrapped in pretty handkerchiefs, for it is a *coquetterie de toilette* that the handkerchief should be handsome enough to correspond with
the garment it enfolds. After a little coaxing she went
in and dressed, reappearing in a suit of rose-coloured

under-robes, with the over-robe of dark green velvet; a charming ensemble of which the idea seemed to be taken from a rosebud half folded in its leaves.

The details of the costume were as follows :—First, a garment of white silk gauze, the lower part of which disappears in voluminous trousers of rose-coloured silk, while over the upper part is worn a waistcoat of ruby-coloured velvet, showing the shirt in front and at the sleeves. Waistcoat and trousers are connected by a girdle, which, to match the dress, should be of the richest material ; maybe the bride had a silver one at home, but that which she here wore was a piece of stuff. Over these garments, and open down the front, hangs a robe of silk, also rose-coloured, but lighter in shade than the trousers and vest; this robe has long sleeves. Lastly, comes the green velvet paletot, falling backwards and without any sleeves. Consisting, as this dress did, of so great a variety of parts, no portion of it was hidden by the rest, no item appeared *de trop.* As for the work on the robes, it was all in gold and exquisitely embroidered ; yet when with pride they told us its enormous price, this did not exceed what is paid every day in Paris or London for perishable garnitures composed only of artificial flowers, ribbons, or tulle. The young girl's headgear consisted of a fillet of coins and seed-pearls, with a natural rose stuck behind the ear.

The dress being duly complimented, handmaidens brought forth bundles of handkerchiefs worked by the ladies present. They were of muslin or something like it, and embroidered in coloured worsted with a slight admixture of gold thread, but displayed little taste in hue or design. We supposed these handkerchiefs were worked at school. " No, at school the ladies did not work." " What ! did they only read and write ? " " No, all those present had been to school, but none of

them could write or read." "Then what is it that you
do learn there?" "To say our prayers, Turkish
prayers."* "Can you understand these prayers?"
"No." "Do any of you speak Turkish?" "No, no."
Here the khanum interfered, highly amused at what she
considered an enforced confession of inferiority. "*I*
speak Turkish," quoth she, and then bursting out laugh-
ing, and spreading her hands over the assembly, she
added, "but these women are every one of them
Arnaouts."

Becoming wearied of this society, we at length proposed to adjourn to the school, when the khanum
answered carelessly that there was no object in doing
so; the school was empty, and the pupils were here.
Former pupils, perhaps, but there were no little girls
present; however we were about to yield the point
when the good lady turned to the popadia, and with a
wink at us and a scornful laugh said something about
ghiaour. At the sound of the word *ghiaour* there
flashed on our minds a recollection of the manifold
excuses by which hitherto we had been dissuaded from
seeing Mahommedan schools; we felt we were excluded
as unbelievers, and that the cause of our exclusion was
fanatical contempt. At once we determined to see the
school. With a changed voice and frigid manner we
turned to the popadia and said, "The mudir promised
us to see the school, so be it full or empty we go there
now." With these words we rose to our feet. What a
hubbub in the chardak; the khanum exchanged her
malicious triumph for a look of real alarm, and with
deprecatory gestures hurried into the house. The
Arnaout women scattered before us, as followed by
the popadia we descended the stairs, walked to the
lodge, and summoned our attendants. With them

* By *Turkish*, the Albanian and Bosniac mean Mahommedan.

came the mudir's son. "We are going to the school,"
said we, and therewith walked to the next door in the
wall; it stood open and we passed in. Before us lay a
sort of garden, and in the garden were a number of little
girls who, half-frightened and half-curious, ran before
us and showed the way. *En route* we came to an
aperture in the wall between the school garden and
that of the harem. It was stuffed with heads, among
which we recognised those of the khanum and her
visitors. Scarcely had we passed when the whole
party, frantic with curiosity, clambered through the gap,
and appeared in our train.

At the further end of the garden stood a house, with
one door on the ground floor and another in the upper
storey, the latter reached by an outside stair. At the
top of the stairs we beheld a tall figure completely
enveloped in mantle and veil, but at the sight of us she
vanished instantly, and her place was taken by two
unveiled women, who hurried down the stairs to meet us.
And now the popadia, who evidently enjoyed the dis-
comfiture of her fanatical neighbours, took the command, and laying hands on the little girls nearest her,
began to push them in at the lower door. The other
women called out to her that many of those children
did not belong to the school. "Never mind," cried
she, "scholars or no, let them get in and fill the room."
In a few minutes we were invited to enter. To be sure,
there was the school, *i.e.*, a little low den, with earthen
unsmoothed floor, and a few broken benches. Of the
scholars of course we could not judge, as many of those
present were unaccustomed to attend, but in the front
row sat some elder girls holding in their hands books
dirty and torn, and written in Oriental characters.
These girls were reciting or rather humming while they
swayed their bodies to and fro. "You see," observed

the popadia, "it is as they told you, what they learn
here is to say the Turkish prayers." At that moment
a voice sounded behind us, and one of the women of
the house appeared. Her demeanour was nervous, and
she asked very humbly what we were pleased to desire.
" Here was the school, here were the scholars, as for the
teacher (hodgia) she hoped we would not call on her
to appear, she was a very reverend person." "She is
sick," screeched a voice from the upper storey, "she
cannot come : why don't you say she is sick ? " " Ah,
yes," said the former speaker, " that is it, she is sick,
and very old too. Will you then be pleased to excuse
her ? " This we did gladly, and had they not betrayed
themselves we never should have known that the
hodgia did not choose to see us, any more than why
they kept us from the school. It was only because we
were excluded as ghiaours—a character shared by all
the non-Mussulman inhabitants of Turkey—that we felt
bound to carry the point. What right have they to
shut Christians out of their schools, while Mussulmans
walk into Christian schools without so much as asking
leave ?

The son of the mudir waited to escort us home. He
seemed much agitated, and several times repeated, "O,
this is not Constantinople, this is Arnaoutluk, Arnaoutluk ! " But the grievances of Arnaoutluk were not at
an end, our cavass had his story to tell. The horses sent
in the morning for us to choose from were all miserable,
and we had charged him to inquire for better. On our
way to the harem we had encountered a drove, all strong
and well-looking. He had been to inquire about these,
and had found that the mudir dare not serve the firman
on them because they belonged to Mussulmans. This
story and the discussion thereon took us to the end of
the bazaar, and then the popadia begged us to come with

her and visit the Serbian kodgia bashi. On taking leave
of the mudir's son we charged him with the following
message:—All due thanks and compliments to his father,
whose good intentions we fully recognised; but we were
much surprised to find how little his Mussulman subjects
cared either for the Sultan or for him. In spite of his
order, the hodgia had refused to show us the school, and
at this we were not so much angry as hurt, for we had
intended only to show a friendly civility such as we
were in the habit of paying to Christian schools. The
Christians invited such visits, and took them as compliments, hence we perceived that hereabouts the Christians
were the most enlightened and dutiful part of the community. Moreover, we were indignant to find that no
good horses could be obtained for our journey, inasmuch
as the Mussulmans would not obey the Sultan's firman,
and give their horses for fair payment. The whole bur-
den fell upon the Christians, who, being the poorer,
could least bear it. Were the Mussulmans not also subjects of the Sultan? Had not the firman equal claims
on them? As we finished these words we became aware
that the end of the bazaar was filling with Arnaouts;
and the thick gossamer veils which we wore as protection against sun and dust, could not altogether screen us
from the flashes of angry eyes.

The mudir's son saw the eyes too: he was terribly
frightened, flung his arm caressingly over the dragoman's
shoulder, and speaking in a low voice assured him all
would be well, his father would see to all. He then
almost ran homewards, leaving for our protection a stout
zaptié, who strode before us out of the bazaar; our
cavass brought up the rear.

But a troop of urchins followed in our wake, and
before we reached the kodgia bashi's dwelling we had
ample grounds to credit the complaints made of the

aggresive habits of these Mussulman gamins. Lurking
in a body behind to watch favourable opportunities, they
detach parties to run in front. These parties station
themselves on each side of the way, and then first from
one quarter and then another the victims are assailed by
a pelt of small stones. In vain the zaptié swore and
threatened, till at last, being struck himself, he furiously
drew his hangiar and dispersed the tormentors with a
sudden charge. Our cavass, a southern Albanian, was
excessively incensed, and again and again assured us
that in his part of the country the Mussulmans were not
half so bad.

No wonder that the kodgia bashi's door was barred,
and that cries from without afforded no inducement to
undo it. At length the popadia caught sight of one of
the family passing by, and asked him to use his voice in
our behalf. When we had entered, and the door was
closed behind us, what a change, and what a pleasant
change! Instead of the parrot screams and excited
gesticulations of the Arnaout females, or the khanum's
medley of compliments, disputes, and insults, we were
met by the sedate and hospitable greeting of a Serbian
"house-father," and coffee was served by a gentle
slender woman, modestly attired, and with unpainted
face. Then came a half-hour's conversation, into which
one could enter with earnestness and cheerfulness while
resting in the well-cushioned "chardak," and looking
down on the large and quiet garden.

Another interesting conversation was held that evening
in the house of our host the priest. Pope Dantcha is a
person well known throughout Old Serbia, and looked
up to as he deserves. Without being previously aware
of his reputation, we were much struck by his intelligence, his facility in communicating what he knew, and
his courageous and upright bearing. In the presence of

the mudir he showed none of that timid obsequiousness too common among the Christians in Turkey, while behind the mudir's back he abstained from reviling him, and did full justice to his difficult position. "There," said he, "the mudir sits—one man with half a dozen zaptiés—what can he effect? There are here but 200 Christian houses, and from 400 to 500 Mussulman, so the Arnaouts have it all their own way. They rob the Christians whenever and of whatever they please; sometimes walking into a shop, calling for what they want, and carrying it off on promise of payment, sometimes seizing it without further ado. Worse than this, their thoroughly savage, ignorant, and lawless way of living keeps the whole community in a state of barbarism, and as the Christians receive no support against them, no enlightenment nor hope from Constantinople, they naturally look for everything to Serbia;—to the Serbia of the past for inspiring memories, to the Principality for encouragement, counsel, and instruction."

The town of Vuchitern must needs have been once more important than it is at present, for it formed the seat of a bishop, and its old castle, whereof the ruins are used for the mudir's konak, was the residence of the hero Voina, brother-in-law of Czar Dūshan. One of the most fanciful of Serbian legends relates the feats of Voina's youngest son, and how he saved his imperial uncle "from the false friendship of the Latins." The old church of Vuchitern was destroyed, but a new one has been built. Not only is it of the plainest exterior, but lest it should overtop the houses of the Arnaouts it is sunk some feet in the ground. A similar church, but still further underground and almost dark, is to be seen at Nish, a town on the high road between Constantinople and Belgrade; but at Nish the Christians, having of late years got leave to build another church, have shown the

joy of their hearts by beginning it on so large a scale
that it towers over every building in the town.
At Vuchitern there is a Serb school containing about
sixteen children. We saw it, and though small it was
clean and orderly, with an intelligent-looking lad for a
teacher. A girls' school they have not, for the same
reason as at Prishtina, but with a little encouragement
they would be likely to start one, for the wife of Pope
Dantcha would do her utmost, and is as energetic and
clever as himself.

She said with pride, " I come from Ipek, and at Ipek
there is a girls' school." We exclaimed, " But are
not the Arnaouts of that district the most lawless in
Turkey ? " " So they are, but, on the other hand, the
Christians of Ipek are the 'greatest-hearted' in Old
Serbia. They have amongst them the church of the
Patriarchate which is so stately and venerable ; they
have amongst them 'Katerina'—a woman whose equal
is not to be found in the land. It was she who founded
the female school." The pope added with pride, " My
wife is her relative ; " and feeling this a great recommendation, we asked many more questions about the
school at Ipek. They said that it was provided with
books, but not with maps, so we gave a set to be taken
by the popadia on her next pilgrimage to her native
town. Expecting soon to be in Free Serbia, we also left
nearly all our remaining books to supply Pope Dantcha's
school.

By way of rewarding us for these evidences of sympathy, the pope sat down on the carpet and gave us a
sort of *catalogue raisonné* of all the churches, monasteries, and schools in the neighbourhood of Vuchitern.
Most of them we shall presently have occasion to describe
or allude to. All or almost all of the churches are old,
some royal chapels and some formerly belonging to large

convents. Many exist now only as ruins, but the people
make pilgrimages to them regularly, and it is on or near
their sites that new churches will rise. Unfortunately,
while enumerating the ruins, the pope did not specially
insist on the church of the old castle of Svétchani, and
thus we passed it over on our way.

The glowing and affectionate praises bestowed by the
popadia on the old city of the Patriarchate, and her
husband's description of the church of Détchani, again
roused our desire to go to Ipek; and we resolved to ask
whether the route between it and Vuchitern was as
dangerous as that from Prishtina. It was agreed, to try
the effect of the firman, to send the servants early next
morning with it and our request to the mudir. In order
to give instructions to the dragoman we opened the door,
and stood for a moment on the head of the stairs. He
came, but with him Pope Dantcha in great apprehension,
solemnly conjuring us not to appear outside with a light.
" For fear of fire?"   " No;" but the Arnaouts had
been rather excited in the bazaar; some of them would
now be lolling about on their way home, and talking
angrily of our visit to the school. In that case our light
might serve to " direct their mark!" In a room without shutters, this was no pleasant idea to sleep upon, so
we put it out of our heads, assuring ourselves that the
pope's apprehension led him to exaggerate. But we
afterwards received the same warning from Mussulmans; and found that to take a suspicious stranger for
a target is one of the recognised freaks of the Arnaout.

Next morning all was bustle, and by the time we had
dressed and breakfasted the servants returned from the
mudir. The firman had been read in full medjliss; to
show proper dutifulness, the principal councillors declared that if we would go to Ipek, they would raise
100 Arnaouts and take us there. On the other hand,

the mudir sent us his earnest advice by no means to make the attempt. According to the most recent tidings, the kaïmakam of Ipek had been murdered by the local Mussulmans while in the act of raising the Sultan's revenue, the whole district was in confusion, and who would receive us he could not say. As for himself, his zaptiés were few, and necessary for his support at Vuchitern; he could not give us enough for protection, and we should be at the mercy of an Arnaout guard. With less than 100 men the Arnaouts would not go, as they had feuds all over the country, and certainly would not return without a fight.

To such representations there was of course but one reply. "We grieved to find the Sultan's dominions in such a state, but as his officers were responsible for our safety we could not act against their advice." The fact was, that we might have got over the murdered kaïmakam and the general confusion, but we could not have answered it to ourselves to make a two days' journey through Christian villages, and to have halted at the monasteries described by Pope Dantcha, with a retinue of 100 fiends.

Scarcely was this matter decided when the mudir himself appeared. He enforced the arguments used by the dragoman, and further took occasion to express his regret at the discourtesy of the Arnaout hodgia. Now, he assured us, she was convinced of error, and he would be much obliged to us to give her an opportunity of proving penitence. Would we go to the school once more? The khanum was coming to return our visit, and would conduct us thither herself.

But we had had enough of the khanum; and hastened to deprecate her coming on the ground that we were engaged in packing and had not a room wherein to ask her to sit down. As for the school, for sake of precedent we thought it better to act on the mudir's invitation, but we intimated that, as we could not come forth expressly to pay it a second visit, we would take it on our way out of town. This we did, and experienced a reception so strongly contrasting with that of yesterday, that we could scarcely suppress a smile. At the first tap at the garden door, it was opened by a man in a turban who bade us welcome, and even carried his courtesy so far as to draw water from an adjacent well and offer it all round. He then led us into the school, which was this time filled with scholars, all duly rocking to and fro, and humming the prayers they did not understand. Even the recalcitrant hodgia was present, but with ill grace enough. Wrapped in yashmak and mantle as if for a walk through the crowded bazaar, she crouched against the wall in front of the first row; her back turned to us in the peculiar attitude adopted by Mahommedan women when desirous not to be seen. At our entrance she gave no sign, but about a moment later, espying one of the children raise its head to look at us, she dealt it a slap—such a vicious slap, its very sound spake of spite and rage.

Scarcely were we remounted, when, followed by his zaptiés, the mudir walked forward to bid farewell. He asked us formally if we were satisfied, and carried his pink waistcoat with additional dignity in the consciousness of having made himself obeyed. We did our utmost in the way of acknowledgment, feeling sincere admiration for his firmness, bearding the very Arnaouts whose brethren had just attacked his compeer, the luckless kaïmakam of Ipek. Poor old mudir! his post was not enviable, and probably offered but little emolument to reconcile him to its danger: apparently he had not even the luxury of a horse, or else, as a Turk, he would scarcely have presented himself to mounted strangers on

foot.   At the moment he turned to go, there appeared
to escort us two of the principal members of the medjliss,
so splendidly accoutred that we involuntarily thought of
old Voina and his son.   One of them bestrode a magnificent white horse, and the pistols in his belt were richly
worked and gilded.   These grandees rode speechless on
either side of us, and as soon as we were out of town
they turned back with a silent salute.

CHAPTER XIX

FROM Vuchitern it takes but four hours to reach the northern boundary of Kóssovo, formed by the convergence of mountain ranges through which flows the river Ibar. The gate of the plain is the Castle of Svétchani, which rises from the banks of the stream, and, as seen from a distance, appears to fill up the angle between closing chains of hills. The eminence on which the castle stands is now richly clothed with wood; its sides, steep and tapered like a pyramid, look as if (like those of the hill of Castle Vissoko in Bosnia) they owed something of their form to art. In truth, the first dawn of history in these regions shows Svétchani as a fortified point, and it was probably a castle of the East Roman Empire before the immigration of the Serbs. In the beginning of the eleventh century all the surrounding country owned the sway of Samuel of Bulgaria, and when he was overthrown by the Byzantine Emperor Basil II., Svétchani was probably one of the numerous fortresses which sent its keys to the conqueror.[*]

The last Byzantine governor of Svétchani was ejected by Stephan Némania; and it was under the Serbian dynasty that this castle earned its tragical renown.

---

[*] In one district alone thirty-five are mentioned.—Hilferding's "History of Serbs and Bulgarians." See also Finlay's "Byzantine Empire," p. 450.

First a royal residence, it became a royal prison, and
there King Urosh III., called Detchanski, was detained,
and mysteriously died. Stephan Dūshan, the son of
Urosh, who had superseded his father in the government,
has been accused of giving the order for his death; but
a cloud rests upon the whole transaction, and the Serbs
are naturally anxious to exonerate their great czar. It
is alleged that the sainted Detchanski, in his old age,
fell under the power of the clergy, whereas his son, the
strong-willed Dūshan, never was a favourite of theirs,
—and the monks have had the telling of the tale. The
most probable opinion is that cited by Mr. Finlay,
viz., that nobles who had rebelled against the father
murdered him to prevent a reconciliation between him
and his son.

This tragedy in the Nemanjic family has furnished
a topic to the modern Serbian poet, M. Iovan Subotic.
His poem, called "Krāl Detchanski," tells its story
simply and picturesquely in the easy language and
metre of the popular songs;—language and metre so
suited to each other that it almost seems as if good
Serbian naturally utters itself in rhythmical flow. In
this story the mischief-maker is Dūshan's stepmother,
who, moreover, causes the death of his young bride, the
daughter of a Zetan noble. The brothers Merliávche-
vic and other evil counsellors goad on the prince to
take up arms, and then hastily murder the king, knowing that should he and Dūshan meet, their mutual affection would cause them to make peace. The scene of
the king's death is laid at Neredimlïë, a country palace
in the neighbourhood of Prizren; but history places it
at Svétchani, a stronghold where it would be likely for
the old monarch to retire with his treasures and wait
for an opportunity of coming to terms with his son.
Perhaps M. Subotic may have taken one idea in his

narrative from the charter of the Detchansky Monastery, wherein Urosh himself, with touching words, refers
to the misunderstanding caused by his Greek stepmother between him and his father, King Milutin.
Naturally enough, the Serbians lay on these foreign
consorts the blame of all quarrels in the Nemanjic
family ; for whatever may have been the faults of that
dynasty, its members were certainly benevolent to the
people, and left among them a memory of strong personal love.   Not so the later and lesser rulers.   Irene,
the consort of one of the despots, has left a name
proverbial in hatred, and her husband is allowed to
bear his full share of blame.

At the foot of the hill of Svétchani lies the little
town of Mitrovic, and at a short distance outside the
town a khan marks the boundary between Bosnia and
Arnaoutluk.   Near the khan stands a great stone, and
here it is customary for Mussulmans passing from one
district to the other to slay a sheep, by way of thank-
offering for the safety of the journey thus far.

The boundary represented by the stone of Mitrovic
does not apply to the Christian population, which on
both sides is alike Serb, calls its country Old Serbia,
and insists that Bosnia does not properly begin till
much farther to the north-west.   But for the Mahommedans on either side Mitrovic the sacrificial stone
marks a real frontier ; the Mussulmans in Arnaoutluk
being Albanian immigrants, while the Mussulmans in
Bosnia are the renegade descendants of a native Slavonic
aristocracy.   In Bosnia the Mahommedan has not only
more *prestige* than in Arnaoutluk, but his tenure of
the land is far older ; for the greater part of the Bosnian
nobility became Mussulmans towards the end of the
fifteenth century, whereas the Christian emigration from
Old Serbia did not occur till the end of the seventeenth

MUSSULMAN BEYS AND CHRISTIAN PRIEST.

century, and the Arnaout renegades did not become
masters of the soil till then. The relative position of
Christian and Mussulman is also different in Arnaoutluk from what it is in Bosnia. In Old Serbia, where
such noble families as did not perish in war gradually
amalgamated with the people, they inspired the mass
with their historic recollections, their proud obstinacy,
and warlike spirit. Thus, although at a later period
the Arnaouts obtained supremacy by adoption of the
conqueror's creed, the Serbian still continues to feel
himself their superior; and the renegade's slight at-
tachment to his new faith causes him to be hated less
as a Mahommedan than as a barbarian and a brigand. In
Bosnia things went very differently. There the Christian
population consists of that part of the nation which
already before the Mahommedan conquest occupied the
lowest room; while the Mahommedan represents the class
which from time immemorial has been man-at-arms
and lord of the soil. Hence in Bosnia antagonism fixes
itself far more specifically on *creed* than in Arnaoutluk
—difference of creed, not difference of race, being the
barrier between the Bosnian Christian and Mahommedan : remove this, and they are one people.

It is curious to remark that the Croatians, and even
the Serbs of the Principality, who are no longer
oppressed by Mussulman landowners, look on the
Mahommedan Bosniacs with great philosophy and even
complacency as brethren of race, and the remnant of an
old Slavonic nobility. They take a certain pride in
observing that the Bosniac used to be the "Lion that
guarded Stamboul;" that some of the greatest Turkish
viziers were Bosniacs; nay, they glory in the Bosnian
gentleman's superiority in stature and manly bearing as
compared with the Osmanli official. It would not be
hard for the Bosnian Mussulman to obtain good terms in

a political arrangement with any South Slavonic community which is already free; but woe betide the
haughty and oppressive landlord should he be left to
the mercies of a successful rising of his own rayahs.

For ourselves, having travelled throughout the greater
part of Bosnia, we have not to complain of the Mussulmans, who generally infused into such civilities as they
rendered us a frankness and courtesy which savoured of
the old noble. On the present occasion, although the
orders to receive us with due observance had been the
same to Mitrovic as to Vuchitern, at Mitrovic we met
with a reception which showed how different was the
disposition to interpret them.

The first thing we saw on approaching the Bosnian
frontier was a troop of horsemen, richly dressed and
armed; and soon we discerned that these included not
only the mudir, but also the cadi and the whole medjliss.
They were magnificent-looking fellows, and their welcome was full of hospitality. When to their salutation
in Arabic we answered by a salutation in Slavonic, the
ice was at once broken, and they talked away with real
cordiality. They insisted that, if we would not pass the
night at Mitrovic, we should at least halt there, and
take some refreshment; and for this purpose conducted
us, not to a Christian's humble dwelling, but to the best
Mussulman house in the place, and there sat in state
with us and drank coffee. The room in which we were
entertained was very handsome, and bore every trace of
belonging to old landowners, being filled with old arms
and china and other family valuables. We conversed
some time pleasantly, and among other questions asked
our entertainers whether they had served in the last
Montenegrine war. As usual, the answer was, "No;
the Albanians did, but not the Bosniacs." "Had the
Sultan gained anything by the war?" "He had got

back a *little* bit of Vassoïevitch." " Had he not got Cetinje?" " Certainly not."

No one made himself more agreeable than the cadi, a personage who in other places seldom came near us at all. He was a tall, fair man, with European features, and gave one an idea of the knights his forefathers, when they first put on the turban. He valued himself on his Arabic learning, but had a thorough abhorrence of Turkish and a strong love for his own language. As we were tolerably well up in the conventional phrases exchanged in Serbian meetings he imagined that we knew more of his language than we really did, and exclaimed: " It is a great pleasure to me to hear you speak Bosnian ; *I* am a Bosniac (*Ja sam Bosniak*)." When we departed he and all the rest accompanied us, and before mounting our horses the mudir presented us with a bunch of roses.

But these Mussulman civilities cost us dear, and placed us for once in the position of those travellers who in passing through Turkey in Europe held converse only with Mahommedans. The same feeling which induced the Bosniacs of Mitrovic to deem it an honour to entertain us themselves, caused them to exclude the rayah from joining in the intercourse. We passed some Christians, standing near the road to have a look at us, and stopped to ask them about the castle on the hill, but they said they were strangers, and evidently did not choose to speak. In Mitrovic no rayahs appeared, and thus we heard nothing about their school, nor about the old castle, for the Mahommedans were of course oblivious of all local curiosities, and especially of Christian ruins. We afterwards heard that the Castle of Svétchani contains the remains of a church and several tombs, that it commands a magnificent view over the plain and the mountain ranges, and that the ascent is by no means so long and arduous as it appears from below. But all this was learned too late; our quarters for the night had been fixed for Banska, so we went on thither, and passed Svétchani by. This mistake caused us so much chagrin that we would do our best to secure other travellers against it by counselling them to divide their journey thus:—from Príshtina to Vuchitern in the morning, from Vuchitern to Mitrovic same afternoon; spend the night at Mitrovic. Next day go up to the castle and spend the night at Banska. If an extra day can be passed on the way, let it be at Mitrovic, not at Vuchitern.

When issuing from the street of Mitrovic we finally passed out of the plain of Kóssovo into that range of forest-mountain which divides it from the valley of Karanovac and the basin of Novi Bazaar. This so-called Zélena Plánina, with its long-drawn furrows, forms the natural bulwark of Danubian Serbia; Sultan Bajazet, though victor on the plain of Kóssovo, durst not attempt to cross the hills, and attack the Czarina in the town of Krushevac. Therefore he at once offered her favourable terms, and by his fair words opened the door he could not storm.

For some distance the road runs along the right bank of the Ibar and winds round the base of the castle hill, affording a striking view of the ruin. The change in scenery is attended by an equally sudden change in climate: one passes from hot and brilliant sunshine into the chill shadow of the hills.

At a turn of the winding road the way was stopped by a group of armed horsemen drawn up behind a tremendous figure, who was clothed from head to foot in crimson and mounted on a huge black steed. This red trooper proved to be the Bosnian chaoush of the little station of Banska, who had duly come out to meet us.

As he rode home before us, we rejoiced in having so fine
a piece of colouring to relieve the grey rocks and droop-
ing green boughs.

Near Banska the green became sparse, and the rocks
began to assume a volcanic form and hue; the place is,
as its name indiates, the site of a bath or mineral
spring.* It is also a defensible point of the pass, and
in Serbian times was held by that brave Banovic
Strahinia who was killed on Kóssovo, and whose adventures and generosity form the subject of a stirring poem.
While the inhabitants of all the neighbouring villages
are Christians, those of Banska are exclusively Slavonic
Mussulmans: may be the descendants of her ancient
garrison, if, like some others, it apostatised to avoid
laying down arms. The bath establishment at Banska
is small, and as it was evening we did not go in; but
we made the tour of the old citadel, now in the last
stage of ruin. The high-walled enceinte contains
nothing except the kula of a few zaptiés, who have also
a watchman's post on the wall, uninhabited houses, and
a deserted mosque; twenty years ago, they said, the
houses were inhabited and the mosque used for worship.
But traces remain of an earlier stage. From the ruined
wall project the heads and forepaws of two stone lions,
the rest of their bodies having been built up with the
gate or pillars to which they belonged. The mosque too
is in the form of an Eastern church, and the lower part
of its apse displays some rows of beautiful masonry,
marble of red and gray ranged in alternate layers and
polished, like that which we afterwards saw at Détchani.
Both church and castle appear to have been stately

* It seems however, doubtful whether it takes its name, like so many other
places, from Banja, a bath, as it certainly possesses mineral springs, or, as is
sometimes alleged, from its having been the residence of the Ban celebrated in
Serbian song. A district ruled over by a Ban is called Banovina.

structures when in Serbian hands; indeed King Milutin, their founder, took from them his surname of Banski.

Here, on the subject of ruins in Bosnia, we may remark that the description which Mr. Paton gives of that country, from what he heard of it on the borders, though probably applicable at the time he heard it, is not so now. Omar Pasha, when putting down the last revolt, did much to reduce the Begs, who no longer occupy feudal strongholds, but live more or less meanly in towns, going into the country only to collect their rents; even when in the country they inhabit white houses, neither old nor of castellated exterior, though probably capable of being defended. Castles of the size and age of that of Marko Kralïevitch, at Prilip, may be seen near some of the towns or guarding the most important mountain passes; but they are either, like Marko's, totally ruined, or still nominally defended by a few rusty cannon and local guards under the name of Imperial fortresses. In fact, anything of a feudal residence on a large scale in Bosnia is so dilapidated as to give less idea of having been lately inhabited than the castles on the Danube and the Rhine. Such relics of architecture as the older castles exhibit, such legends of warlike owners as lend them a romantic interest, mostly refer to ante-Turkish times.

Our night's lodging had been prepared in the house of the chaoush himself; and though the room was small, it was interesting from its primitive ornaments in carving, old pottery, and arms. The officer himself received us with great hospitality, and presented to us with his own hand a large round cake (Släv, *kolatch*), which he evidently thought a great dainty. We longed to bestow it on the poor Christian drivers, who must have spent an uncomfortable night. There are no fields near Banska, and it was hard to get forage for the horses ; moreover, as the small khan would not hold them, they had to remain in the court of the chaoush's house.

But one good result accrued from their discomfort— they were ready to start at break of day. This is very necessary when the journey is from Banska to Novi Bazaar, for, although nominally only nine hours, it is nine hours of such mountain travelling as may be indefinitely prolonged. Not but that there is a road, *soidisant tel*, made by the Turkish government, and, like others, answering its end so far as to serve for the transport of cannon, but extremely rough withal, and uncompromisingly steep both up and down hill. In every part it is wide enough for two bullocks to pass abreast, and we met several patient couples dragging the elementary cart of the country laden with the stems of trees. Altogether, we cannot quite endorse the opinion of the Polish officer who pronounced this road passable for a carriage containing ladies, *because* it is passable for wood and guns; but we are none the less obliged to him for his verdict, without which, in our then state of health, we should not have dared to attempt this route at all.

A day's riding in the Zélena Plánina (green forest-mountain), such as we came in for here and elsewhere, left us each time the richer by a memory of delight. It brings a fresh breeze over one for ever after, only to think of those forest hills, green as they are and windy as the summer downs in England, and yet with almost Grecian sunlight pouring on their brows. Greece herself has lost her forests, and so has beautiful Dalmatia, which the Venetians robbed of fertility when they bared her hills and left them to dry and bleach in the glare. It is well that the Serbian ranges did not share this fate, for they present comparatively little picturesqueness of

form wherewith to atone for bleakness, and their inland
scenery lacks the thousand charms inalienable from
countries washed by a southern sea.

In the hills between Kóssovo and Novi Bazaar the
grand monotony of greenness is only broken here and
there by the grey walls of a far-off ruin. Svétchani is
seen again and again as you round each new ascent; and
farther on, the lone castle of Yelic appears on its eagle
crag.

There would seem to be Roman remains in this neighbourhood; at a roadside fountain where the horses
drank we descried on the trough a Latin inscription,
and found that it was an ancient sarcophagus. After
much questioning, which (no Christian being present)
was difficult and unsatisfactory in the extreme, all we
could elicit was, that this sarcophagus came from a
village called Séochanitza. Séochanitza is said to lie two
hours from the Kadiaschi Khan near the fountain where
we saw the sarcophagus, six hours from Novi Bazaar,
and four hours from the Serbian frontier; moreover
many other stones covered with writing have been found
there and walled into the little village khan. By all
accounts the place is very small, and not abounding in
konaks or food for horses, so we dared not turn out off
the road to explore it.

Our chaoush, who had provoked us greatly by his
"know-nothingness" about the Roman remains, was
more communicative on the subject of the population
here and on the Serbian border. He denied that there
were any Albanians to be found in the neighbourhood,
and said that from Banska to Novi Bazaar all the villages
were Christian, or, as he called them, "Serb." On the
other side of the border, as we doubtless knew, the
Serbians had set up a state of their own. Last year they
and the Sultan quarrelled; and he, the chaoush, and

many other persons, had expected to see a Serbian army
re-appear on the field of Kóssovo. The men on the
Serbian border were fine fellows, and so were those on
the Bosnian side ; in fact "borderers always are the
finest people of any country, as they are kept in fighting
practice." We told him that one reason why the Serbs
had not crossed the border was, that last year they had
not good arms, but that now they had received a supply
and had drilled 200,000 men. He answered, "We all
know that quite well. They have also plenty of cannon;
and, as I heard, not less than 300,000 men." "And
how many fighting men do you think there are in
Bosnia?" He answered, "They say 50,000 ; but they
could never bring that number into the field."* Being
a Bosniac, he spoke on this subject quite dispas-
sionately, having probably made up his mind that,
whatever the chances of a second battle of Kóssovo,
he, like his forefathers, would make his terms with
the victor.

With the chaoush and his fellow-borderers we must
confess to have shared the anticipation of seeing the
Serbs reappear on Kóssovo, when, the road attaining its
highest bend, we turned back to take our last view of
the field. We left our horses and walked to a little
eminence where, resting under the trees, we could look
over the winding of the mountain ranges, and past the
spiral summit of Svétchani down on the far-off golden
plain.

How many and divers travellers must have halted on
this spot and been moved by this view ! Here the con-
tingent from Rascia and Bosnia, on their way to join the

---

* The immense disproportion between this number and that in the principality
of Serbia, which has not a much larger population, is accounted for by remem-
bering that in Bosnia the Christians, who form over two-thirds of the population,
are not counted as fighting men.

camp of Czar Lāzar, must have seen the spot that was to
behold their fall.   Here the Mussulmans of Bosnia—all
renegades and traitors as they be—when marching to
vindicate against the Sultan their claim to govern their
own provinces, broke out into the gloomy chant—" We
march, brethren, to the plains of Kóssovo, where our
forefathers lost their renown and their faith; there it
may chance that we also may lose our renown and our
faith—or that we shall maintain them, and return as
victors to Bosnia." Here, day by day, the passing
rayah prays, " that God will hasten the hour when a
Christian army shall cross these mountains, to deliver
Old Serbia, and redeem what their fathers lost on the
old battle-plain of Kóssovo."

CHAPTER XX.

THE middle of this day we spent under the trees, near a dirty khan without any separate room. After leaving it we commenced the descent towards Novi Bazaar, passing by a short cut through a wood, of which the paths were spoilt by late rain, and so slippery that our horses could scarcely keep their feet. Emerging thence on the main road, we found ourselves at a beautiful point of view; we looked down on Novi Bazaar, lying in a basin of hills, traversed by the road that passes from Constantinople to Serajevo, and overtopped by a steep eminence on which rose the dome of a church.

At the foot of the last descent we met a zaptié, who instantly galloped off to give notice of our approach, and soon after we saw coming to meet us a train of horsemen, so numerous as to reduce that of Mitrovic to comparative insignificance. At their head rode three personages, all so portentous and dignified that for some time we could not discover which of them was the greatest. The most solemn wore plain clothes and a fez, and appeared to be so precious that, in case he should fall off his horse, a man walked at its side all ready to catch him; the handsomest and most brilliant wore a splendid Turkish uniform; while the fattest—and in Turkey this is often a criterion of high position—had what looked like a French uniform with voluminous

scarlet trousers. In due time we learned that the civil
governor of Novi Bazaar was gone on business to
Seraïevo, and that the man in plain clothes was his
locum tenens. The handsome soldier was military
kaïmakam ; the fat officer, a cavalry bimbashi ; in their
tail followed the medjliss of Novi Bazaar. Though
heading the native Mussulmans in the ceremony of hospitable reception, the three superiors were Asiatics, and
could speak nothing but Turkish, which our dragoman
imperfectly understood. Hence the procession moved
on in silence, the Turkish dignitaries acting as our out-
riders, the Bosniacs bringing up the rear. In this order
we entered Novi Bazaar, and rode very slowly and very
solemnly through the long charshia (market-place), round
the foot of a hill covered with the houses of Mussulmans,
and on and on, till between the holes, the stones, and the
weary-footedness of our sorry steeds, we began to get
into despair. At this juncture an incident took place
which among any west-European crowd would have
been saluted with roars of mirth. Down the central
gutter of the sloping street flowed a brisk stream, swollen
by recent rain ; our poor horses were thirsty, one of them
suddenly got his head down, stopped stock still, and
drank. It was hopeless to get him to move till he had
his fill ; officious blows dealt by the cavass from behind
only served to make him kick ; so there we stuck fast,
while the unconscious dignitaries rode out of sight, and
the wondering Bosniacs pressed one upon another. On
each side the shopkeepers sat cross-legged on their boards
and stared at us—stared, yet did not smile. But from
the lattice windows above peered down a galaxy of female
eyes, and it was from these hidden spectators that the
only expression of amusement at our ludicrous position
escaped : almost on a level with our ears bubbled out
the irrepressible giggle of a girl.

On rejoining the vanguard we found that it was leading us, not up the hill to the large houses of the Mussulmans, but down a narrow street to the marshy land near the river, *i.e.*, to the Christian quarter. Here we stopped before the dwelling of the Greek bishop, who, like his *confrère* of Príshtina, was spending his time more pleasantly at Constantinople. In his absence, the house was kept by his servant's family, and they had received orders to prepare the best room for our use. Bad's the best; small and unfurnished, it is like a slice off a passage, and has no glass in any of the four windows. Worst of all, these apertures look towards the street, whereby we are exposed to the observation not only of passers-by but also of the dwellers on the opposite side; the latter, stationed at their windows, stare at our doings as from the boxes of a theatre.

In places where we stayed more than one night it was customary for the Turkish authorities to appoint a zaptié to remain in our house, in order that we might send him to say if we required anything and have his protection if we walked abroad. For all these purposes one man was sufficient, and one could be managed without much inconvenience by the Christians with whom we lodged; give him good food and drink and a comfortable corner, and he would sit all day in a state of kef, or discuss horses and arms with our cavass, when the latter had time to attend to him. But in order to do us especial honour the authorities of Novi Bazaar left us, not one zaptié, but three, and these three proved an attraction to their comrades, who came constantly out and in. They were a terrible nuisance—those imperious, rapacious men turned loose in a rayah's dwelling; no part of the lower house was free from their presence, the women had to hide from them, and the young father of the family was ordered about as their slave.

We soon perceived that something was amiss by the repressed cringing air of the man, and sent our dragoman to say that we only wanted one zaptié and would only give bakshish to one. However, the other two would not stir, so all we could do was to ask the master of the house into our room, and try to reassure him with kind words. But the sound of our voices caused him to shake like a leaf, and to the most indifferent question he would only give a whispered reply.

The dragoman then told us that the zaptiés were sitting in a room just below our own; the man was in agonies lest they should hear us talking with him. Immediately we too whispered, assured the poor fellow that the obnoxious guards remained in his house contrary to our express desire, and that our inquiries proceeded from the sympathy we felt for the Serbian Christians, who through all our journey had treated us with hospitality and kindness. We then told the dragoman to ask him a few questions as to the state of the Christian community in Novi Bazaar, and meanwhile we talked to each other in a raised voice, for the benefit of the guards below. How curious a picture was the group in that little room! At one end, in the candlelight, we sat talking cheerfully on each side of our little table covered with English books and work; at the other end, where the shadow fell darkest, crouched the dragoman and the rayah, the former with his keen swarthy face bent down to catch the whispers of his companion—that companion a young man with the fresh colour and rounded contour of an European, but quaking, almost convulsed, with fear.

The whispers became quicker and more eager; our question as to the state of the Christians had acted like the sudden withdrawal of the dam from a stream, the pent-up waters overflowed, the rayah was pouring forth

his tale. " The Christian community of Novi Bazaar is
at the mercy of the Mussulmans; they enter houses
both by day and night, take what they choose, and
behave as they will. Raise an arm or speak a word,
and you bring on yourself death or the loss of a limb.
Make a representation to the authorities, and you are
ruined by the revenge of those of whom you have dared
to complain."

We asked if within the last few years things had
become better or worse.

" In so far they are better, that the officials now sent
from Constantinople are jealous of the Beys and the Beys
of them, and the two opposing cliques act as some sort
of check on each other. The Christians are less perse-
cuted in their dress and other trifles, and they may enter
their own quarter of the town on horseback, though it
would still not be safe to ride past a Mussulman in the
road or the bazaar. On the other hand, since last year
great repression has been exercised, for fear of the
Christians rising to join the Serbians over the border.
We have been obliged to do forced labour in raising
defences, and to contribute both in food and money to
the maintenance of troops; and such troops! Do you
know that last summer Bashi-bazouks were sent to Novi
Bazaar? But no insult, no injury is so hard to bear, as
that of Mussulmans carrying off Christian girls. Lately
a maiden of the rayah community was servant in a
Mussulman family. Suddenly her parents were informed that she had become a Mahommedan; she was
not suffered to return to them nor see them, but was
secretly sent off to Saraïevo. She escaped, came back
to her family, and they ventured to give her shelter,
but the Mussulmans tracked her home and their vengeance fell upon the whole Christian community. Out
of its 110 houses at least 100 were, in their estimate,

connected with the escape of the poor girl ; all felt the weight of their wrath, and several were completely ruined."

This calamity was of recent occurrence, so it appeared uppermost in the narrator's mind ; but when questioned as to whether he could say that a similar outrage had ever actually occurred in his own family, he answered straightforward that it had happened to his wife. Being a handsome young girl, the Mussulmans got hold of her, and she only escaped because the bishop was at home and took up the matter himself. As soon as she was released, the bishop married her to her present husband ; when he left the town he put them in his house as one mode of providing for her safety.

Thus ran our landlord's tale, but he was not the only sufferer whose story came to our ears at Novi Bazaar. On the morning of our departure an old man knocked at our door, pushed into the hand of the dragoman a paper, and then turned and ran away. It contained some sentences in very crabbed Serbian written characters, which we could not decipher by ourselves, and knowing it was out of our power to redress the injuries of the writer, we deemed it wiser not to expose him to a risk of betrayal by showing it to any one in Turkey. We took it to Belgrade, where we were helped to read it, and found the meaning to be as follows :—" Gracious ladies, in God's name I welcome your visit to our town. Have pity, and save my unhappy daughter, whom the Mussulmans have carried away."

It has been said that the Christians in Turkey invalidate their complaints of Mahommedan oppression by the very fearlessness with which they complain, also that travellers detailing the grievances of these Christians have seldom had their stories first hand. We leave candid readers to judge whether either the one or the other of these explanations can be applied to the cases just detailed.*

At Novi Bazaar we passed three days, and one afternoon went to see the Serbian school. The zaptiés were left at home, our cicerone being the master of the house. Indeed he had volunteered to be our guide, and since last night appeared another man. He walked at our side stoutly, and spoke—although still in an undertone —cheerfully; neither did he show us any more of that servile homage which indicates terror mingled with hate. Such other Christians as were now presented to us, also opened out with friendly confidence, and one after another at convenient opportunities would whisper, "So you have been in Serbia?"—meaning the principality. The word "Serbia" is the Open Sesame of hearts between Prizren and Novi Bazaar.

Approaching the school our ears were saluted by a not inharmonious burst of children's voices singing "Welcome"; but when we reached the door we saw that the poor little choristers looked very miserable and ill. The atmosphere of the school was certainly not bracing—an exception to the rule hereabouts, where you find in every room open windows and draughts *ad libitum*. At the further end of this school we perceived a row of holy pictures with lighted lamps hanging before them, and we were told that the room was also used for a church. Hence the sickly after-smell of incense (worse even than that of tobacco) mingled with the unhealthy closeness of the air. We did not venture to remain more than a few minutes, and were glad to be invited to a stone seat outside, where we looked over the books, which were all from Belgrade. Meanwhile the schoolmaster released

---

* Consular reports testify that, so far is the offence here alluded to from being punished, that the man who carries off a Christian girl, and can make her become a Mahommedan, is rewarded by exemption from the conscription.

the poor children, who had been called together out of
hours for us to see.

The bench assigned to us was an old tombstone, and
others similar stood against the wall ; but neither the
priests nor the kodgia bashi could tell us anything about
them.   They cared rather to show us the town, of which
this spot commands a view.   Lovely it looks, in the
narrow wooded valley, with its clustering white houses
bedded in rank green ; but evidently it lies in an airless
caldron, and its inhabitants say that it is cursed with
bad water and ague-breeding swamps.   Smallpox had
raged throughout the winter, and now the summer fever
was in full force.   Six persons of the richest families in
the town had died of it lately within a few days.   We
now knew why that morning we awoke with the heavy
feeling we hoped to have left behind at Skopia.

"To whom belong the houses on the hill ?"   "All
to Mussulmans."   "How many may there be ?"   The
rayahs looked at each other, and hesitated, as if talking
treason, then said in a low voice, "About 800, _we_ believe.   But the Turks themselves say 1,200 or even
1,400."   "How many Christian houses ?"   "That is
soon told ; 110."   "So few ?"   "Say rather, so many.
God knows why any of us live here ; better for us we
should dwell in the woods and never see a town.   Look
at our quarter, in the lowest ground close to the river ;
the garden of the house where you are staying is all but
a marsh."   We turned our eyes to a high breezy terrace
immediately above the town, and asked, "Why do you
not build there ? the Mussulmans have not taken that."
The rayahs exclaimed, "We build there! the Begs dare
not build there themselves.   It is vakouf."   "Vakouf"
means that it belongs to a mosque, and thus at Novi
Bazaar, as at Volo, on one pretext or another, the Turk
has tabooed the most healthy site in the town.

We afterwards took a walk in this vakouf land, and thence perceived—rising on the top of the hill immediately above us—that beautiful light dome of a church which we had already admired from a distance on our approach to Novi Bazaar.

We were now told that this was the celebrated Giurgevi Stūpovi, or Monument of St. George,* built in the latter half of the twelfth century by the first Némania as a thank-offering. The church is supposed to cover the mouth of the cavern where that prince was confined by his elder brothers : St. George was the good friend who delivered him from their thrall. Two Serb priests had joined our party, and one of them, an outspoken intelligent person, offered to show us the church ; our host persuaded some of his friends to lend us horses, and we set out forthwith.

The hill, which, from its steepness and commanding situation, appears from a distance of considerable height, may be ascended from the town in less than half an hour. The church stands on a point of rock ; a little below it one arrives at a rough plateau, where from time immemorial it has been customary for pilgrims to leave their horses and approach the shrine on foot. This spot is marked by a large stone cross, strangely like some of the Celtic crosses, and also by three of the beacons erected last year by the Turks all along the frontier range of hills. The sight of the cross called forth the priest's enthusiasm at the humility of the Némanjic sovereigns, who dismounted thus far from the church door ; the sight of the beacons elicited a cry of reprobation on the profaners of Némania's shrine. "Oh!" he exclaimed, "those Bashi-bazouks! God knows how they treated us here!"

---

* Stūpa, in Serbian, means literally "pillar" or "column ;" but is also used in the sense of monumental erections that may consist of more than a mere column.

The shell of the church is still so far intact that until one is quite close it preserves a stately effect. First we reached a small building open on two sides and vaulted within; the pope supposed it to have been an outer chapel or a porch, but Hilferding describes it as the base of a campanile. Its walls are covered with frescoes, of which the colours are still in part fresh and the inscriptions legible; on one side is a picture of the Last Supper, and of SS. Cosmo, Damian, Pantaleon, &c.; on the other, portraits of the Némanjic family, in long gem-bordered garments and with glories round their heads. The priest declared this porch to be of later date than the church, and his opinion is confirmed in so far as that the royal personages there represented belong to a generation later than the first Némania.* In the church you see himself, represented as founder, holding the model of the building; there too is his son and coadjutor, St. Sava, depicted with a long fair beard; also his patron, St. George, with the dragon. The relics of another Némanjic used to lie in a side chapel, but were stolen thence some time ago; we saw the broken tomb, but did not distinctly gather who the occupant had been nor whither the body was gone. Hilferding calls him King Dragutin, and heard that his bones had been " lifted " by the family Znobic of Novi Bazaar, who thereby brought a curse on themselves and their posterity.

From the outer building it is some paces to the west door of the church, and on the way the priest pointed out a shattered column of red stone, which had formed

---

* We had unfortunately left pencils and notebooks behind us, so could not write down the names on the spot. Hilferding enumerates among the frescoes the following names:—1. Saint Simeon, Némania, lord of all the Serbian lands, 1159—1195. 2. Stephen Pervovencani, Simeon Monach, 1195—1228. 3. Stephan Kral Ourosh, Simeon Monach, 1240—1272. 4. Yelena Velika Kralitza, daughter of Emperor Baldwin, who then lived in Constantinople, and wife of Ourosh. 5. Stephen Ourosh, called Dragutin, 1272—1275. 6. Katherina Kralitza, daughter of Stephan V., King of Hungary, wife of Dragutin.

MANASSIA

INTERIOR OF SERBIAN CHURCH.

part of the doorway. He said, "This was thrown down quite lately by Turkish soldiers from Prizren."

The church of Giurgevi Stūpovi is one of the oldest specimens of Serbian architecture, it is also one of the most simple ; the numerous little domes of other churches are wanting, and thereby the large dome in the centre gains infinitely in effect, its full swell reminding one of those island churches of Venice which look like bubbles blown from the sea. But while the outer shell is nearly entire, within the building is completely gutted, its pillagers having helped to exhibit its fair proportions by carrying off those doors and screens wherewith most Serbian churches are encumbered. In the principality, we know only Manassia where the interior proportions receive justice, and that because funds are still wanting to raise the picture-screen (iconostasis) to the wished-for height. The interior of Giurgevi Stūpovi must have been covered with frescoes, but it is only on that part of the walls which cannot well be reached, either from above or below, that any traces of painting remain. To obliterate the figure of Christ, the destroyers have broken up the plaster of the dome, while all the lower part of the frescoes has been picked off by mischievous hands. The paintings still extant are attainable only by throwing stones ; and while we were in the act of look- ing at these a pebble rattled in through the door, and left its mark on the painted wall. Turning round, we perceived our zaptié, whom we had left with the horses, and who, striding in at the shattered entrance, rudely asked the priest, "What was here?" Our wrath was only increased by the civil and deprecatory tone in which answer was returned, and we peremptorily inter- fered, demanding of the intruder how he dared follow us, and ordering him back to his charge. Our cavass, who at first was in ecstasies of wonder and delight over the

beautiful colours, on the entrance of his co-religionist,
the zaptié, thought fit to adopt a nonchalant and scornful mien ; finding the latter contemptuously expelled,
he changed again, and exclaimed, " Really the Turks
here surprise me ; they are extremely mischievous, and
destroy beautiful things." Then, with an after-thought
highly creditable to his former employers, he added,
" But you see, at Novi Bazaar there are *no consuls.*"
From this date to the end of our journey, whenever he
was struck with a case of Christian suffering, we used to
hear him promising the people that the Queen of England
would send a consul to their town. The behaviour of his
co-religionists in these parts was not, however, without
effect on our Albanian attendant, and we had to watch
constantly to prevent him from making all sorts of unjust
requirements in our name. On the way to Novi Bazaar
he thought he recognised the lost horses of the kiradgees,
and forthwith dispatched zaptiés to bring the drove and
its drivers before the kaïmakam, when, by his own ad-
mission, he found that the horses were not the same.
After this he made an attempt, unknown to us, to
obtain for our journey the good horses lent to us to
visit the church. So far as we could learn the price and
quantity of what we used, we were most anxious to pay
for it, but from time to time it came to light that the
zaptié sent on beforehand ordered seven chickens where
we ordered and paid for one, &c. Indeed, one of the
great discouragements to travelling in these parts is that,
with the best intentions, one cannot avoid being constantly oppressive to the inhabitants.

On the floor of the church we observed a piece of
marble beautifully carved with old Slavonic letters.
Outside the south door we discovered a fresco, with its
colours as fresh as on the day when limned, but half
smothered in a heap of rubbish ; better that the whole

had remained concealed, for doubtless it has only become visible to be destroyed.

On the north side of the church, and as it were hidden behind it, is a small plot, used as a Christian burying-ground. Before the south door there is a larger space, where the pilgrims assemble on St. George's Day, and where we found numbers of faded oak-boughs, which they bring along with them for shade. Here the pope showed us a small hole in the rock, hollowed as a reservoir for rain. The women of the district have a superstition that water from this sacred hole is a cure for fever, and the plants near it are decorated with scarlet threads, sacrifices drawn from holiday aprons in testimony of supposed cures. It is to be hoped that the inhabitants of this feverish district will not lose their faith in the rain water at the top of this rock until they have learnt how much fever patients may be benefited by a change from valley to hill air; especially during such short cheerful journeys as their holiday pilgrimage to the church of St. George.

From the rock of Giurgevi Stūpovi there is a fine view towards a range of hills, of which the names were written down for us by the priest. We give them here for the benefit of future travellers, who may thus be enabled to judge of the excursions best worth making from Novi Bazaar. Towards the north and east are the mountains Sokolovitza and Kopaonik; from the latter of which there is an extensive view of the lands between Macedonia and the Danube. Among the hills to the south lies Yelic, with its old castle just visible. South-west are the hills where the river Rashka has its source; among them lie the monastery of Sapotchani, and the so-called castle of Relja. North-west is seen a picturesque gorge in the hills, called the Ludsha Clissura; and further north rises a summit, conspicuous for its rich

covering of grass and wood; it is called the Czerveni
Verh (or Red Height).

The plain which stretches towards the Serbian frontier is called Dezevo Poljé; and one can see Dezevo,
now a village inhabited by Mussulmans, but formerly
a town "where the family of Némanjic loved to
dwell." The road which leads thence in the direction
of the hill Sokolovitza is called to this day the "Tsar-
ska Ulitza," or the "street of the Czar;" and it is
said that hereabouts lay the *divor* or country house
of Czar Dūshan. The village Sudsko, also inhabited by
Mussulmans, lies about a quarter of an hour from the
"street of the Czar;" it marks where in old times the
Serbian rulers used to hold their court of justice (Slāv,
sud).

A heap of stones on the bank of the Rashka is called
by the country people the house of Relia, and belonged
to that hero in the winged helmet who appears in every
gallery of Serbian worthies. Winged Relia is sung as
the bond-brother of Marco, and one of the paladins of
Lāzar; like Milosh Obilic, he was of unknown parent-
age, and was rejected by a haughty damsel as a found-
ling picked up in the streets of Novi Bazaar. There is
a certain popular song which seems to have been composed in order to contrast the merciful rule of the native
sovereigns with the tyranny of foreign lords, and in it
Relia is intrusted with the punishment of the Czarine's
own brothers, because they kept back the pay of the
Czar's workmen. But in this song, which is very old,
Relia lives, not at Novi, or New Bazaar, but at Stari, or
Old Bazaar, the ruins of which were afterwards pointed
out to us. This Old Bazaar would appear to have been
no other than the capital of the so-called "kingdom of
Rascia," one of the zupanias most frequently spoken
of in Serbian annals, and by some supposed to have

included the greater part of the country now known as
Old Serbia.

Rascia is mentioned as a Serbian government by
Byzantine historians as early as the ninth century; and
in 1143 its bishop, Leontius, was one of the few prelates in Serbia belonging to the Orthodox Church.
The father of Némania was zupan of Rascia before he
succeeded his cousin Bodin, king of Zeta; afterwards he
does not seem to have changed his title; and according
to some reports, he continued to reside in Rascia. In
the government of that district he was succeeded by his
son Némania, though not till after a struggle with those
relatives who are traditionally said to have imprisoned
him in the cave. The prisoner, released by miraculous
intervention, and abhorring the heresies of his rival
brethren, was admitted by Bishop Leontius into the
Orthodox communion in a little church near Novi
Bazaar, still called by the country people the "Holy
Metropolitan Cathedral of Rashka." Afterwards arriv-
ing at supreme power, he erected as a monument of his
deliverance the large and beautiful church of St. George.
Some writers say that the old capital of Rascia was destroyed in war: the legend says that it was overthrown
by an earthquake. In either case, the new zupan would
have to build a new town, which, lying like the old on
the frontier between Serbia and Bulgaria, and succeeding
to its position as a rendezvous of merchants, would, like
it, be distinguished by some such name as the Turks
have translated by *bazaar.**

When the seat of Serbian government became fixed at

---

* In early Serbian history it is mentioned that an exchange of prisoners
between Serbians and Bulgarians took place at this town of Rascia, as being then
the frontier between Serbia and Bulgaria.

The Serbian name for that part of a town where the citizens live is *varosh*, in
contradistinction to the *grad*, or citadel. *Terg* is the immediate market-place,
whence *tergovac*, a merchant.

Prizren, Rascia gradually lost the position of a separate state, and its name is now associated only with the river Rashka, with the little metropolitan church of St. Peter and St. Paul, and with those emigrants who passed in the seventeenth century from this neighbourhood into Hungary, where to this day the appellation Rashki denotes Serbians of the Eastern Church.

According to the plan of journey made out at Monastir, Novi Bazaar was our last stage on the Mussulman side of the border; but the ride over Kóssovo and the Zélena Plánina had so far restored our health, and the descriptions of Ipek and Détchani had so strongly excited our interest, that we could not bear to leave all this unexplored country behind us and cross into the principality, where we knew every step of the road to Belgrade. Rather we bethought ourselves of a long-cherished scheme, viz., so turn back at Novi Bazaar, cross the hills to Ipek, and then pass viâ Prizren to Scutari in Albania.

Novi Bazaar is a principal station on the road between Constantinople and Seraïevo, and it was evident that the authorities were not ill-off for troops; no doubt they could spare us such an escort as was required. On the other hand, if we could not get to Ipek at least we might go a two days' tour further westward to Senitza, and cross thence to Serbia, in which case we should visit Uzitza, a part of the country we had not already seen. Of this change of plan it was necessary to apprise our friends at Belgrade, lest, should we not appear at the date when they expected us, they might express anxieties, which the Austrian papers would take up and cook into some absurd report or other.

At our request the kaïmakam of Novi Bazaar sent to the Serb capitan at Rashka to ask if some one would come over and speak with us. Forthwith, two Serbians

SERBIAN PEASANTS AND CITIZENS OF A COUNTRY TOWN.

rode across the border; not military men, for that might have excited suspicion, but quiet "house-fathers," members of the national guard.

These good people brought us pleasant tidings. They said we were expected, and orders given for our welcome. They told us that we should lodge in a good house at Rashka, and that if we would fix a day for crossing, the frontier capitan and his followers would meet us and bring us over with rejoicing. From Rashka onwards there is a good road, but the country is mountainous, and they added, that if we wished for a carriage they must send for it to Karanovac. The men looked peaceful and good-tempered, clean, calm, and comfortable, like the members of a well-ordered community, unlike either terrifiers or terrified; it really cost an effort to turn from them and their hospitable offers, and plunge again into a country where every one's hand is against his neighbour. However, as Serbians, they could not but highly commend our idea of a pilgrimage to Ipek and Détchani, and they promised that, lest after all we should be obliged to give up our plan and cross to the principality by Senitza, the capitan of adjacent Uzitza should be duly prepared to receive us.

Having sent news of movements to Belgrade, the next thing was to communicate with the Turks. The three dignitaries had duly sent to ask at what hour they should call, and we had appointed the afternoon, adding, that as there was not in the house a room large enough to accommodate them we would receive their visit in the garden. This garden was decidedly swampy, nevertheless cushions and carpets were carried into it; punctual to the hour, the Turks arrived with a numerous suite, and were conducted to the spot prepared; then we were apprised; but when we came down and found so many grave personages enthroned in the long grass, and

surrounded by their attendants stooping under the
boughs of the low fruit trees, we could scarcely suppress
a smile. The dignitaries smiled too, and observed that
like ourselves, they were strangers to Bosnia, and
considered its climate and accommodation as things to be
rather endured than enjoyed. On this we became quite
grave, and assured them we prayed God that on the first
convenient opportunity they all might be transferred to
Asia. "Please God," responded they fervently, thus
probably expressing the sentiment of every unlucky
Turk quartered in the Slavonic provinces, and certainly
that of their still more unlucky harems. The wife of a
high-placed official once said to us, "Such Osmanlis as
are sent to these parts are sent by their evil fate. This
is Bosnia: every one knows what that means, and that
it does not mean *our* land." We most heartily agreed
with her.

After the usual round of compliments and coffee, we
began to tell our visitors of the difficulty we had met
with about going to Ipek, and how two governors
had refused to send us there. The military kaïmakam
observed superciliously, "that those little mudirs probably had no zaptiés to spare, but that *he* could provide
us with an escort with which we might go whither we
pleased." The civil officer further remarked that no
doubt the mudirs were themselves Arnaouts, and did
not wish us to penetrate into their country, but that,
bearing with us the Sultan's firman, we should be properly received everywhere. As to the road from Novi
Bazaar to Ipek, it certainly passed over the mountains,
but the inhabitants were Bosniacs, and *konacs* could be
secured. He also recommended us to go by Roshaï, a
station on the frontier between Bosnia and Arnaoutluk,
for there we should find a new mudir, a talented and
liberal-minded person, who would receive us with every

distinction. At this juncture some of the attendants interfered, and began telling a long story, when it appeared that, although living only two days' journey from Ipek, the governors of Novi Bazaar had not yet heard of the attack on the Ipek kaïmakam. At this news they rather abated their zeal, and the civil officer remarked that the mudirs who had warned us not to venture, might possibly, from their proximity to Ipek, be acquainted with sufficient reasons for their advice. However the military kaïmakam repeated "that with a Bosniac guard nothing was to be feared; those wretched Arnaouts were altogether barbarous, but Bosniacs could be depended on." At this point the matter was deferred for further reflection.

Wishing to know something about the state of the Montenegrine frontier, which is here but twelve hours distant, we asked if they could send us to Berda.*

The Turks replied that they could send us to the border, but that on the other side they could answer for nothing: even our firman would be of no use to us there. It was evident that whatever might be pretended in Constantinople, these officers of the Porte were well aware that Montenegro had not been compelled to acknowledge the authority of the Sultan. We replied that we knew Montenegro perfectly, and that therein everything was quiet and well-ordered; our anxiety for safety referred solely to this side the frontier, and if they could guarantee that, well and good. However, we

---

* B'rda, or rocky mountains, is the name given par excellence to the north-eastern portion of Montenegro; Cerna Gora, or black-wooded mountain, being properly applied only to the part nearer the Adriatic. Both alike were included in the government of Zeta, of which the present principality of Montenegro claims to be the representative; but during the greatest distress of the Christians the champions of independence could only maintain themselves in a very small district, and it is under their present reigning family that they have re-asserted bit by bit their old territory, as one tribe after another dared to join them and openly to disclaim allegiance to the Sultan.

would think over our plans and let them know. Soon
after they were gone our cavass came to us with a
message from a Bosnian Mussulman. He had just come
from the neighbourhood of Ipek, and could answer for
it that at Roshaï we should find Bosniacs willing and
proud to take us into the Arnaout country. Whatever
information we wanted he could give us, and would tell
us to whom to apply for help. "On no account," he
said, "be persuaded not to go to Ipek; all the alarm
about danger is a pretence of those beggarly Arnaouts."
This was the only communication we had with native
Mussulmans at Novi Bazaar. We should much have
liked to find out some connections of our friends made
in Bosnia the previous year, but we dreaded to remain
longer in so unhealthy a spot. Then, too, we had no
personal introductions, and under the circumstances it
would have been difficult to adjust amicable relations
with the Beys, considering our intercourse with their
adversaries on either side—with the Turkish authorities
and the Christian Serbs.

However, from the message now received it was
evident that the Bosniacs thought there was no reason
we should not go to Détchani; so we forthwith sent to
the kaïmakam, saying that we had quite made up our
minds to go to Ipek, unless he could formally declare it
to be unsafe. He replied that he would take steps to
make it safe, and that we had only to fix the day.

CHAPTER XXI.

THE BOSNIAN BORDERS.

" Little heart ! do not get angry with me ;
For if I were to get angry with thee
All Bosnia and Herzegovina
Could not make peace between us again."

Bosnian Love Song.

NECESSARY preliminaries having been adjusted, on
the fourth morning after our arrival at Novi Bazaar
we turned our horses' heads, not, as hitherto, towards
Belgrade and the Danube, but towards Scodra and the
Adriatic.

The first stage was to be Tutin, a Mahommedan village
in the mountains; thither we sent our luggage on peasants' horses, and ourselves were lucky enough to follow
on decent animals furnished by the menzil. The two popes
came to escort us, as before leaving Novi Bazaar by the
western end we were to ride a quarter of an hour to the
east, and visit that little church of St. Peter and St.
Paul, called by the country folks the cathedral of Rashka.
Just as we were starting the kaïmakam was announced—
come in person to accompany us out of town. What
was to be done? We would not for the world miss
seeing the place where Némania was baptized; so there
was nothing for it but go thither, kaïmakam and all.
Having slowly proceeded to the church, we entered it
in company with the popes, but were well satisfied to
remark that the official and his Turks remained outside.

The church is very small, with windows like gun-holes. It was built at least as early as the eleventh century, but was restored in 1728; owing probably to its un-ostentatious exterior and its situation without the town, the Christians have been allowed to retain it in use. A small side chapel contains the tomb of a Serbian patriarch; we were shown also part of a patriarch's staff inlaid with mother-of-pearl, an old candelabrum, in form like a griffin, and a curious little tryptich in gold. Lastly, the popes brought forth a Serbian copy of the Gospels, sent from Ipek, and began to explain the sig-nification of some handwriting on the first page; but they moved and spoke nervously and hurriedly, ever with one eye on the door. And with good reason. While we were thus engaged the sound of tramping caused us to raise our heads, and behold the church fast filling with the figures of the kaïmakam and his train. Possibly they were only tired of waiting outside; more probably they suspected and hoped that some treasures were being brought from their hiding-place; but what-ever the motive the entry was made with rude careless-ness of all feelings except their own. Without speaking to the priests or waiting for guidance, the Turkish official walked straight through the church and through the principal door of the iconastasis into the sanctuary, where even Christian laymen may not enter without special invitation. Our first sight of him was when the tassel of his fez was already disappearing behind the screen, so all we could do was to get him out again as fast as possible by instantly quitting the church ourselves.

We had mounted our horses when the dragoman called our attention to the Turk, who had followed us and was striving to make a speech. He evidently saw that some-thing was wrong, and therefore told us that he had been impressing on the priests the necessity of always keeping

this church smart and clean, that it might remain a show
to strangers. We replied that we hoped he would extend
his solicitude to the beautiful church on the top of the
hill; and in order that it might be preserved for admiration, that he would desire the Mussulmans to cease
pulling it to pieces. To this the Turk answered, with
some peevishness, that the church on the hill had been
ruined ages ago, and turning to the pope he demanded
what we meant. But the pope stood his ground, and
declared that part of the building had been destroyed
quite lately by the rude soldiery from Prizren; he also
took occasion to inform the governor that near the very
church where we stood the Christians had lately begun
to build a little house for a priest, but that the Mussulmans had pulled it down. The governor was evidently
not prepared for this statement of grievances before
strangers, and he looked all the more cross when he saw
that the priest's outspokenness pleased us well.

The procession now resumed its march, and the kaïmakam, with admirable patience, escorted us to the other
end of the town. At parting, we offered him very sincere thanks for having secured our journey to Ipek;
and contrasting the mode of our exit from Novi Bazaar
with that of our countryman Mr. Paton, we felt that the
introduction of a rival element, in the shape of officials
from Constantinople, had here acted as a much needed
curb on the fanaticism of the native Mussulmans.

Scarcely had we parted from the Turks when down
came a pelt of rain; no one seemed to know where the
next house stood, and for some time we galloped pell-
mell along the road. Meanwhile the priests underwent
a sudden metamorphosis; each drew from behind his
saddle a wide red mantle, and flung it over, not only
himself, but the greater part of his horse. Thus accoutred they looked so exceedingly like the heroes whose

portraits adorn the walls of Serbian taverns, that we had only to strain our fancy a little to see old Relia tilting along on his own ground.

The first attempt at shelter was under a tumble-down shed, literally so called, for part of it tumbled on ourselves; while we were there the zaptiés discovered a Mussulman's cabin, and prepared it for our reception in the following manner. They caused the proprietors to make a good fire and then turned them out of doors, the father of the family improvising a harem by barring his women up in the maize shed. When we arrived nothing was to be seen save a hen hatching in the corner of the inner room, and on the floor a wooden trough of the favourite plant basilica. Before departing we got them to call the master of the house, in hopes that a bakshish might console him for his trouble.

The rest of this day's journey proved unexpectedly interesting, partly because the chaoush of the Bosniac guard turned out a great talker and knew something of the local traditions. Our way first pursued the left bank of the Rashka to a point where it is joined by another mountain stream. The angle between the rivers is occupied by a huge rock, and on the opposite side of the Rashka lies a small plain covered with low ruined walls. "Here," said the zaptié, "stood Stari Bazaar, which was a great town before Novi Bazaar was built. There are the stones of some of the houses, and in that great rock lived the king's daughter, called Morava. One day an earthquake destroyed the city, and shut the king's daughter up in her cell."

This, then, is the traditional site of the ancient town of Rashka, to which we have alluded in the preceding chapter.

Some distance up the glen to the right are the ruins of the famous church of Sapotcháni. We had much

wished to see it, but were told this was impossible, as
there were no konaks within several hours. Let not
other travellers be thus deterred. Sapotcháni cannot be
more than three hours distant from Novi Bazaar. It
might be visited thence in one day, but if taken on the
way to Ipek there is a house belonging to a certain
Murad Bey, where one would probably find as good
quarters as at Tutin.

Our way now left the course of the Rashka, for that
of a smaller stream to the left ; after a while we crossed
this also, and struck over a wooded hill. Here all
around is forest-mountain, its wild stillness broken only
by the gurgle of unseen brooks, or by the fitful sobs of
the breeze when rain is in the air. But though no
human habitation is to be seen, the region is not
really uninhabited; through these glens the Albanians have pushed from the borders of Montenegro
to their north-western limit, namely, Senitza, a small
town on the Serbian frontier. The Bosniac guards
called our attention to one hill in particular, and said
that in its glens lay ten villages which had never
obeyed the Sultan nor paid tribute till some ten years
ago. Then Reschid Pasha was sent to quiet the
country. There was a great war in the glen, and the
villagers lost many of their men, some being killed
and some sent prisoners to Stamboul. We asked, "Do
the villagers pay tribute now ?"

"Not very punctually," he answered; "but they
cannot rob their neighbours and go on as they used
to do."

"Were the robbers Bosniacs or Albanians?"

"Mixed. The real boundary between Bosnia and
Arnaoutluk is Roshaï, but you will find Albanians
mixed with Bosniacs on this line as far as Senitza."

"Are there any Christians hereabouts?"

"Yes; but few, very few."

Finding the chaoush so communicative, we questioned him about the country through which we rode. Passing a beautiful ravine on the left one heard the sound of a descending torrent; thereupon he declared that not far off, in a spot called Ostravitza, was to be found an intermittent spring; he further told us that the hills we had passed were called Yelak and Ruya, and that we should next cross a high ridge named Kanima—all before we reached Tutin.

A new theme was then started by the menzilgee, who suddenly burst into a wild song, whooping exultingly such words as these: "I am a Bosniac, I carry shining arms."

We asked the chaoush, "What kind of military service do you Bosniacs prefer, the Nizam or the Bashibazouks, *i.e.*, regular or irregular?"

He answered, impetuously, "Not the Nizam; we will have nothing to do with Nizam; but the Bashi-bazouks are fine fellows, and have always good horses and fine clothes."

"Has the Sultan yet raised Nizam in Bosnia?"

"No, nor can he; the Bosniacs will not give him Nizam."

"How is that?" we asked; "the Arnaouts furnish Nizam."

"So they may, but the Bosniacs—no."

"And which, then, do you consider the best heroes—Albanians or Bosniacs?"

"Listen," he said. "The Albanians are heroes with guns, whereas with guns the Bosniacs are worth nothing; but the Bosniacs are heroes on horseback—hu!—such as there are not in the whole world."

The distant view of the Vassoïevic Mountains here suggested a change of subject, and we asked whether he

or any of his people, had been fighting there last year.
He said, "No, but the Albanians were."

" And what sort of heroes are the Vassoïevic?"

" Good—very good: heroes, and like the Albanians,
with guns."

" Are they as good as the Arnaouts?"

As a Mussulman he would not allow this, and said
the Arnaouts were better. Wanting to hear what he
would say, we asked if it were true that Vassoïevic
used not to belong to Montenegro, and if it was only
during the last thirty years that even the Berdas had
become free.

" Yes," he answered, "they do not belong to the old
Montenegro, but now they are all free together."

We asked if they heard anything about the Danubian
Serbians arming lately.

" Oh, yes," he cried, "but we don't care about them.
It is true they have good cannon, but they are not
heroes."

" Were they not good heroes in Kara George's time?"

" Yes, that they were; but now we know that they
cannot be, for this reason, they have not fought these
thirty years."

The sun was setting as we emerged from the thick
woods of oak and beech. Before us lay the little mountain plain of Tutin, traversed by a stream, on the banks
of which rise wooden houses with peaked roofs. At the
entrance of the meadow, two well-mounted Bosniacs with
their attendants were drawn up to await us. The elder
was a fine old man in turban and robes; the other,
middle-aged, wore over his linen tunic a crimson jacket
lined with fur. The former led the way in silence; the
latter said, "Dobro doshlé," and rode into the village at
our side. At the door of the largest house the cavalcade
stopped, the crimson jacket alighted, and seizing the

nearest of his guests, literally *sous le bras*, half carried her up-stairs. All was dark, the steps broken, and the general impression that one would land in a granary. With pleasant surprise we found ourselves in a comfortable room, thoroughly carpeted, and containing a fireplace as well as a stove. The windows were very small, but the wooden walls were literally perforated with loopholes, whence to fire on a besieging foe; some of these were large, some small, and most covered with thick white paper, so as to exclude the air.

That evening we amused ourselves with recalling what we had heard about a personage whose forest realm we were now traversing, *i.e.*, the *vila*. Of her presence in the surrounding mountains the chaoush had spoken without a shade of doubt. He affirmed that she was frequently seen both by Mussulmans and Christians, provided they were natives of the country; but he did not think she vouchsafed to appear to strangers, whether Franks or Osmanli. "And what is she like, when seen?" asked we. He answered, "She does not always appear in the same way. Sometimes she looks like a fair maiden riding on a good horse." Such, indeed, is the usual description, with the further details that her dress is white, her bright hair flowing, and her steed swift as the wind. When not riding, she is represented with white wings. Albanians talk of her as well as Serbians, yet she would seem to be of Slāvic origin, for she is found in most Slavonic countries, and even in that half of Germany of which Latham says that "if it did but know, or would but own, it is Slavonia in disguise." Famed as are the vila's horses (a vila steed being proverbial as a good one), she has been seen mounted on other animals; for instance, on a stag, with a snake for bridle. But this is told of an eccentric old vila, who used to make travellers pay for troubling her woods and waters, and got her quietus from Marko Kralïevitch.

The supernatural maiden on horseback reminds one of the Scandinavian *valkyr*, who rides wind and storm, and from whose horse's mane the drops fall as dew into the valleys, producing fertility and freshness. But the valkyr, though more than human, is human still; though termed the Maid of Odin, the Fair One of Valhalla, the Chooser of the Slain, she may also be the daughter of an earthly chief, the bride of an earthly hero.* In fact, the valkyr is the conception of a race whose christianized descendants carried the idealization of woman both into religion and daily practice, and as such she is the legitimate precursor of the high-bred, high-spirited, yet gentle "ladye" of chivalry. But the Serbian has no such female ideal. His free, powerful vila is one thing; his submissive, affectionate wife another; the former has no link with humanity save that of *posestrima*, or bond-sister, whereby certain heroes engage her, in order to secure aid in the hour of need.†

But if the vila has not the idealized humanity of the valkyr, as little has she the demoniacal taint of the northern race of elves and gnomes. We hear of no "tithe paid to hell," no uneasy forecasting of future condemnation, no terror of holy signs, no deceitful pomp and private wretchedness. Indeed the Serbians have not the same intimate acquaintance with demons as the Germans. The devil in person is not a hero, either of popular legends or religious epics; he is distinguished by a simple and awful name, "the Foe," while human enemies are merely called "not-friends," or, in Turkey, by a Turkish word—*dushman.*

---

* See "The Story of Svava and Helgi" in the Edda.

† That some vilas have domestic ties among their own people may be inferred as allusion is occasionally made to their children, though not to their fathers and mothers, brothers, lovers, or husbands.

Perhaps, although with important differences, the vila has most in common with the nymph of classic heathendom. We hear of her sleeping at mid-day in the deep shade of fir trees, while her feet are washed by the wavelets of a forest tarn. Near her the swans build their nests, and so do the *utvas*, or gold-winged ducks. In her realm the wild deer let themselves be tamed and bridled, and the lamb grazes confidently by the wolf's side. She has too her cloud-castle built on the hill-top, with its gates, one of scarlet, one of gold, one of pearl. In some cases she is even the "cloud-compeller,"—storm and thunder come at her call.

Now-a-days the most frequent appearance of the vila is as a spectator of human concerns. In that capacity the nymph most celebrated is she who dwells on the mountain Lovchen.

The peak of this hill overlooks Montenegro, and a poetic chronicle of events in that country usually begins by announcing that they were witnessed, heard of, lamented over, or predicted by the Lovchen vila. We happen to have seen two little modern poems, the one written by a poor Montenegrine, the other by the present prince. The prince's poem describes the battle of Grahovo; that of his subject, the death of Prince Danilo; but in both the first lines introduce the vila, and throughout you are supposed to hear with her ears.

One might go on for ever instancing the actions attributed to the vila by the more ancient popular songs. We will merely give that which at this moment we can remember as her most purely benevolent deed.

The eyes of a poor lad have been put out with the connivance of his own mother, and he is left alone weeping among the hills. The vila washes his wounds in the brook, and then, " having prayed to God," she proceeds to make him new eyes. The ballad recording this is too long to stand here; it is called "Iovan and the Elder of the Deevi" (giants). We could fancy its scene among the weird caves of that deev-haunted region we afterwards traversed between Montenegro and Old Serbia.*

On the other hand, the most purely malevolent action we can remember of the vila consists in watching the hasty temper of one of two brothers; setting those brothers, who really loved each other, fighting, and when one is killed mocking the survivor with false hopes only to goad him to despair. The heroes of this legend are Slavonic Mussulmans, and it originates in a region bordering on Montenegro; hence the remarks of our Bosnian chaoush naturally introduce it here. We will give it under the name of

HASTY WRATH;

OR, THE VILA AS MISCHIEF-MAKER.

There were two brothers, Muyo and Ali, who lived together in wondrous love.

So lovingly did they live together that they changed horses with each other, that they changed with each other their shining arms.

One day they arose, and went together to the dark mountain-lake to chase the utva with golden wings. Muyo loosed his grey falcon. Ali sent forth his well-trained hawk. They caught the utva on the lake.

---

* There is much to be said about this word *deev*, or *div*, and its forms in different languages from Sanskrit downwards. In Serbian it is given to mythic giants to denote, not their size, but their supernatural character. *Divno*, adj., in Serbian expresses "wondrous," and when used for "wondrously good" or beautiful, the words "good" and "beautiful" are understood. The Albanian giant is also called *dev*, *def*; (see Hahn's "Journey from Belgrade to Salonica," p. 39;) he and the Serbian have several localities and exploits in common.

Muyo cried out, " The falcon struck it ;" but Ali said,
" Nay, it was the hawk,"—and his words vexed Muyo
to the soul. And now they sat down under the trees,
under green fir trees, drinking cool wine : over the
wine sleep surprised them.

All this was seen by three white vilas, and the eldest
of them said to the rest, " Behold two marvellous good
heroes. A hundred sequins would I give to the vila
that could set them quarrelling."

Then flew off the youngest vila—off she flew on her
white wings, and alighted at Muyo's head. Burning
tears she wept over him, wept till they fell on his face
and scorched him. Up sprang Muyo, startled to fury ;
but when he looked, behold a damsel ! Loud called
he to his brother, " Rise, Ali, let us get home !" The
young Turk bounds from the earth to his feet (but still
half asleep and the wine dazing him ; he sees, not one,
but *two* damsels). " Ho, Muyo !" cries he ; " may evil
befall you ! Two maidens for thee, and for me not
one !" Again Ali's words stung Muyo, vexed him to
the very soul. From his girdle he snatched the
hangiar, and struck his brother through the heart.

Ali falls on the green grass. Muyo seizes his white
steed, and throws the fair damsel behind him ; off they
go to his home in the hills. Ali's black steed neighs
after them. Then wounded Ali calls to his brother,
" Ho, Muyo, brother and murderer ! Turn thee again,
and take my little black horse, that it be not left
uncared for on the hill. Else, better pluck out thine
own eyes than meet such praise as thy comrades will
give thee." Muyo returns, takes the black horse, and
sets the fair damsel on its back ; off again they go
among the hills.

But lo ! in the middle of the road there meets them
a raven without its right wing. " Alas ! poor raven !"

cries Muyo, "how wilt thou fare without thy right
wing?"

With a loud croak the bird answers him, "I shall
fare without my right wing, as a brother without his
brother: as *thou*, Muyo, without Ali."

Then doth the Turk begin to say to himself, "Ill
done, oh Muyo! was to-day's exploit. If the very
birds upbraid thee, how much more thy kinsmen and
comrades!" Thereupon out speaks the vila: "Turn
thee again, oh Muyo! Once I knew something of
leechcraft; maybe I could heal thy brother's wound."

Back they ride towards the dark lake; back they
ride till now they have reached it. Then Muyo looks
behind him; he beholds the black steed—the vila
is gone.

Muyo falls on Ali's body, but already Ali has
breathed out his soul. When the young Turk, Muyo,
sees this, from his belt he snatches the hangiar, and
plunges it into his own breast.*

* Parentheses mark where we have interpolated a line telling how Ali came
to see two maidens when there was but one. Such an explanation we ourselves
required, and think it likely others may need it also; but in the written version
of the legend it is omitted, perhaps because the audience to whom it is usually
recited know well enough that after drinking wine a man sometimes sees
double.

CHAPTER XXII.

THE BOSNIAN BORDERS—(*continued*).

FROM TUTIN TO ROSHAÏ.

NEXT morning we started for Roshaï, but before departing we asked to speak with our host. He looked very sulky, and took our expression of thanks without any return of Oriental compliment. We asked whether the *pushki* (gun) holes with which the chamber was studded were still necessary for defence. He said, "No; but ten years ago they were constantly in use. In those days the Arnaouts plundered the country, and haunted the village to that degree that we and our rayah dare not stir beyond doors." "Who put an end to this state of things?" "Reschid Pasha—he who made an expedition into the mountains and erected so many kulas." "Was that the same pasha who fought with the ten villages that would not pay tribute?" At the mention of these villages the brow of the aga became still darker and his utterance slower; he knew nothing about *ten* villages; something like that to which we alluded had been spoken about in his hearing, but it only concerned *one* village, not ten." "Did he know the name of the village?" "No, he did not; it had no name." We then asked him some questions as to the road we were about to travel and the names of rivers and mountains. He told us that in winter the roads between Tutin and Novi Bazaar were filled up with snow, but the snow froze so hard that communications could be carried on without difficulty. Further, he said that the whole substance of the village consisted in cattle, the mountains being unfit for cultivation, but, as we saw, well-watered and abounding in pasture. "How many houses are there in Tutin?" He took up the string of beads which he was twirling in his fingers, and counted thus: "There is my house, and my uncle's, and Abraham Aga's—that makes three"—and so on—"in all seven." "And to whom does the village belong?" He again became sulky, and answered that he did not know what we meant, but that this village and all the district stood under the kaïmakam of Novi Bazaar. This struck us as a strange reply, for besides that the Bosniacs do not in general like to be reminded of the central authorities, in what country would a proprietor be likely to describe his estate as standing under the governor of the nearest town? Suspecting something amiss, we only added that we should much like to know his name, as that of a person who had entertained us hospitably. Without seeming aware that he thus replied to our former question, he answered readily, "I belong to the family Hamsa Agitch, and so do the other proprietors of this village, who are all my brothers and cousins—we and our rayah are the only people here." On coming outside the gate to mount our horses, we saw the representatives of "our rayah," in the shape of three or four supremely ugly women, clad in shirts and aprons and adorned with silver coins. They looked at us in a friendly and confiding manner, and smilingly stood forth to let us examine their weird head-gear and necklaces. It appears that they had inquired of our dragoman if we were really Mahommedans, as the aga had told them, and when they heard we were Christians they rejoiced greatly, for "was it not a fine thing to see

Christian women received with honours and lodged in
the aga's house?" But if the rayah were glad to
see us, so was not the old uncle in the turban. This
morning he looked grimmer than ever, and again escorted
us without uttering a word. We could not but marvel
at this demeanour, as opposed to all we had formerly seen
of Bosnian Mussulmans. But in due time the pheno-
menon was explained. The possession of a firman, the
journey to Ipek at this crisis, perhaps also some expres-
sions in the letter of the kaïmakam of Novi Bazaar, had
given rise to the impression that we were emissaries from
Constantinople. This was made known to us by our
dragoman the moment we had taken leave of our host.
Like us, he had been struck by the exceeding reserve and
suspicion shown by all at Tutin. But during the evening
one person after another had come to ask him if we were
really the persons sent by the Sultan to investigate
matters at Ipek. "This," he added, "was the reason
they would tell you nothing more about the contumacious
villages, indeed they were very vexed you should have
heard of them at all." We asked the dragoman if the aga
really thought we were Mahommedans? He answered,
"Who knows? The kaïmakam probably did not tell
to the contrary, for otherwise they might have objected
to lodging you. At any rate they did not wish their
rayah to think that they had been forced to receive
ghiaours." We were by no means satisfied with this
story. The sullenness of these Bosniacs was no good
omen of the temper in which we should find the Arnaouts, who had an attack on the Sultan's representative on
their consciences. If we were taken for emissaries at
Tutin, how much more at Ipek! We had not forgotten
that the Arnaout, when uncertain of the good intentions
of strangers, is apt to quiet his mind by taking a shot at
them, and under such circumstances we could not but

fear lest the mudir of Roshaï should forbid our going farther. To be turned back a third time would have been too bad. All we could do was to bid our servants din in the ears of future inquirers that we were from England, not from Stamboul; and that we were not Mahommedans but Christians, on a pilgrimage to Détchani.

What a day's ride between Ipek and Roshaï! Here is again Zélena Plánina in all its shades—from fir to hazel; in all its forms, from the park-like valley to the grim ravine. Then ever and anon some break in the dark woods, opening like a break in rain-clouds, shows sunlit vistas of the eagle's realm, — of Montenegrine summits streaked with snow. It is in such scenes . that one identifies the epithets wherewith the Slāvic language characterizes, and even seems in sound to describe, the varieties of highland landscape. There is the *shuma*, or great forest ; the *plánina*, or mountain-chain ; the *berda*, or knot of rocky mountains; the *cerna gora*, or black-wooded hills; and lastly, the *verh*, or individual height, whose huge grey shape, rising out of the blue-green, looks like the giant shepherd of the forest-mountain, his head enveloped in a misty *strooka*.*

A peak wherewith we made acquaintance to-day for the first time is Haïla, immediately above Roshaï. Rising as it does to the height of nearly 7,000 feet, its limestone crags retain even in the end of July a partial covering of snow, and it forms a magnificent feature in the landscape as seen at intervals from this forest ride. Presently our path emerged on a lovely little valley, its lawns strewn with fresh-mown hay and sloping to a rapid stream. At its farther end appear two twin

---

* *Strooka,* the plaid of the Montenegrine highlander ; in tempestuous weather he wraps it about his head; in colour it is usually grey, black, or brown.

hillocks covered with the dark wood, while darker still
—*cerna gora* in its gloomiest form—rises behind them
the hill of Soko. Having traversed the valley we
crossed the stream, and began climbing the fir-clad
ascent.

Some years ago this region was so infested by robbers
that none could pass it except in a large company;
and the "thousand shining-armed wedding guests"
celebrated in Serbian poetry would scarce have been too
strong an escort for a bridal party between Tutin and
Roshaï. Whether in self-congratulation on their present
safety or from old habit, our zaptiés began to fire off
their pistols and to whoop and shout with giant voices;
the cavass, who, being badly mounted, had fallen back,
came rushing up on foot, sword in hand, expecting
to find us in a fray with haïduks. The dragoman
was also behind, but did not rejoin us till long afterwards; he then told us that, like the cavass, he had
dismounted, and, believing us attacked, had turned "as
green as death." Here, however, the story broke off,
and we were at liberty to suppose that the end of his
exertions was to creep into a bush.

A long ascent brings you to the top of the pass—
unluckily, not to the top of the hill, from whence the
view must be magnificent. We saw the summit rising
on the left, its apex a large rocky fragment, whereon a
shepherd was keeping watch. We would fain have
climbed this eyrie, but the wind blew chill and the
horses were heated; the zaptié would scarcely let us
halt even for a moment, whereas, we could have sat for
hours to feast our eyes on the vale of bowery wood we
were leaving behind. But a greater feast awaited them
on the other side, when we began the descent towards
Roshaï. This frontier hamlet, built of the rough wood
of its own forest, lies at the foot of a deep glen, and

" in the water and out of the water " of the Ibar, which here, near its source, is a powerful mountain burn. Right in front rises the peak of Haïla, now golden with the sunset on its snows, while on each side the woods open, showing pastures scattered over with herds, and glades dotted with heaps of green hay. Near the head of the glen a few roofs peep up from a Bosnian Mussulman village. There are Christian villages among the hills, but none in sight from any point of our way.

Within half an hour of Roshaï the mudir met us with all his following in full array. He bestrode a great black steed, and managed it in the Turkish style, *i.e.*, causing it to rear and bounce as if in conflict with a swarm of wasps. This looks very fine, till the poor brute becomes covered with foam, and one perceives that, being all the while perfectly quiet, it has been heated and wearied by the rider for show.

The whole population of Roshaï turned out to see us, and a truly picturesque community they appeared : many wore turbans, and all wore white and red garments that well set off their stalwart forms.

The dwelling prepared for us belonged to a Mussulman. We were not a little surprised at its size, cleanliness, and the proportion of glass to paper in the window frames ; above all, there was a regular fireplace, such as one still sees in mediæval houses in England, with a peaked stone canopy for chimney-piece. The young mudir ushered us into the room and then seated himself á la Franca, threw off his fez, and ran his fingers throught abundant hair, which showed small sign of the Mussulman tonsure. He then began to talk at a great rate in Slavonic, and called to his counsels, *not* the master of the house, a dignified Bosniac, but the Christian kodgia bashi and pope, both of whom he introduced to us in a perfectly conventional style. In

return, those representatives of the rayah treated the
mudir with ease; nor could we discern in their behaviour
anything of the usual traces of fear. The text of
their discussion was the letter of the kaïmakam of Novi
Bazaar, which had not been sent forward to the mudir
as we expected, but reached him first by the zaptié
who accompanied us. Hereupon it appeared that the
mudir had not the slightest knowledge of such a place
as Détchani, although the far-famed monastery lies but
thirteen hours from Roshaï. Neither did he at first see
any difficulty in our going to Ipek; but on this subject
a second thought struck him, and he suddenly exclaimed, " By-the-bye, the last thing we heard from
Ipek was, that the mudir and all the medjliss had been
called to Prizren to answer for murdering their kaïmakam. It is a question who may now be there in authority, or in a temper to obey the Sultan's firman." Here
was a difficulty. The Bosnian master of the house
came forward, and said that he and his friends would
take us to Ipek, maugre all the Arnaouts in the hills.
But the mudir dismissed this idea rather impatiently,
deciding that as we wished to go not only to Ipek but
beyond it, it was peremptorily necessary to know how
matters stood. Hereupon we suggested that he should
send a messenger with a letter, enclosing the order
of the kaïmakam, and we would await the answer at
Roshaï.

This proposal found favour with all parties, and we
ourselves were not sorry to have a day's rest. But now
a fresh solicitude arose. Where was our luggage? We
had not passed it on the way, and hence expected to
have found it awaiting us, but no; and after the mudir
was gone some time passed without its appearance. At
length unpleasing ideas suggested themselves; either
the drivers must have mistaken the road, or else some

accident having happened, they had quietly resolved to
wait where they were, counting that we should send to
look after them. At last the mudir did despatch some
zaptiés, but not till it was already dark and we had
made up our minds to an uncomfortable night. However, about nine o'clock the wished-for tramp of horses
was heard, and the drivers being called to account,
explained that there had been no accident, nor had they
lost their way, but they had taken a different road from
ours, and in the middle of the day had indulged in a
long rest. Roshaï was the limit of their district, so
next day they and the Novi Bazaar zaptiés went home.
So did the menzilgee, though we had engaged the
menzil horses to Ipek; he insisted on returning with
the guards, because, should he return alone, he was
certain that the Arnaouts would shoot him and make
off with his beasts.

Of the two days we spent at Roshaï waiting for an
answer from Ipek, the first was unpleasantly taken up
in getting over the effects of a chill caught the evening before. When it became known to our host that
we were taking remedies for fever he begged us to prescribe for his eldest son, who had been suffering from
it for a year, and a lad of fifteen was brought before
us, terribly green-faced and glassy-eyed. We gave
him some of the simple medicine we had found most
useful, and thereupon the father applied for himself.
Though a stout, well-built man, he had, like all the
inhabitants we saw at Roshaï, an unhealthy, livid hue.
After nightfall there came a message from the harem,
hoping that "if we came back this way" we would
prescribe for a woman who suffered much from her
head. We were really glad not to be asked to see her
this time, being afraid of doing mischief; nor did we
ever attain the happy confidence wherewith so many

amateurs can prescribe in total ignorance of a patient's constitution. With such scruples it is painful to be asked for medical aid, in a country where to refuse it would be considered irreligious as well as unkind.

There is not much to be seen at Roshaï, except the picturesque Ibar Glen and slight remains of an old castle. The pope told us that at some distance there lie the foundations of an ancient church, and that hither on great feast days the Christians gather, and hold divine service among its grass-grown stones. Making inquiries as to the road to Senitza, we heard of two ruined castles on the way. The convent of Biélopolyé lies also in that direction, and the pope said that its monks keep a school.

The kodgia bashi and the pope were loud in praise of the new mudir, and gave the following story of his appointment. Last year, during the Montenegrīne war, numbers of Christians were arrested on suspicion, and it was believed that the Mussulmans hatched a plot to kill, imprison, and exile every energetic and intelligent rayah; in fact, a plot similar to that which, in the beginning of this century, gave rise to the war of liberation in Serbia. Then came the bombardment of Belgrade, to which the Serbs replied by an unexpected show of teeth and claws, and the spirit of the rayah hereabouts was roused by the hope of a kindred army crossing the frontier. The Turkish government, having its hands full with Montenegro, dared not drive the Slavonic Christians to desperation, and orders were sent to let them alone. At the same time the late mudir of Roshaï was displaced and succeeded by the present. Now the former mudir was a fanatic Turk, and in all things went hand in hand with the native Mussulmans, but the present governor had come with instructions to conciliate the Christians, and was a man whose temper and antecedents disposed him to carry his orders out. For this very reason he was odious to the Mahommedans, and the Christians expected to see him murdered by these Bosniacs, as the kaïmakam of Ipek had been by the Arnaouts. The first part of this story we had heard before, for we had ourselves met with exiles from this part of the country at Travnik in Bosnia, and we now delivered their messages to their families, who thus first learned what had become of them. The second part of the tale, namely, the efforts of lately-appointed governors to win over the Serbian population, was also corroborated by several instances of our experience. Everywhere, however, with a like result, *i.e.*, while it fails to diminish the legitimate longing of the rayahs for a Christian administration, it has the effect of rousing the native Mahommedans to ominous discontent. The agent of this policy, now at Roshaï, may be taken as a superior specimen of his class. He also represents another remarkable though not numerous type, namely, the young generation of Bosnian aristocrats when transmuted into Turkish officials; thus furnishing an illustration of what bureaucracy, centralisation, and Stamboul life make of the tough old Slavonic Bey.

The day after our arrival the mudir came again to see us, and this time chose to talk Turkish, falling into Slavonic when necessary to make his meaning clear; probably he did not wish the people of the house to understand him, for he had much to say, nor did the deficiencies of our dragoman in Turkish discourage him from a conversation of some hours. This may be partly accounted for by the circumstance that he was talking of himself and his ancestors. Like Bosniacs in general, he had "ancestors," and no sooner knew that we had been in the Herzegovina, and seen Mostar, Blagaï, Stolac, than he poured forth their history and

his own. He came of the house of Rizvan Beg, a
relative of the famous Ali Pasha of the Herzegovina.
The family seat was Stolac, and had been so ever
since the Turkish conquest, but the rank and power
of the family dated earlier; they had been great
people in the days when Herzegovina was called the
Duchy of St. Sava, and they came to Stolac when
the last duke was driven from Blagaï by the Turks.
One branch of the family renegaded to save its
lands, the other followed the duke into exile, and
became nobles of the free city Ragusa; but between
both branches friendly intercourse continued, and the
family of Rizvan Begovic always remained on good
terms with the Latins. At last came the grand revolt
of the Bosnian Mussulmans against the Porte; one
after another the great families found their ruin,
and the turn came to that of Rizvan Begovic. Advantage was taken of its old connections to accuse
it of treasonable negotiations with the Latins, and a
firman of the Sultan empowered Omar Pasha to deprive
its members of their lands and bring them captive to
Stamboul.

At the end of this story the mudir drew a long breath,
and then asked—

"At Stolac did you see a factory built by an
European merchant?"

"We did."

"Well, the merchant who built that factory agreed
to set it up at his own expense, on condition that for a
certain number of years he should hold it free of rent.
During the war the factory could not work, the merchant lost money, and he called on my family to indemnify him. But at that time all our rents were
paid in to the Sultan, and we lived on a yearly allowance from the treasury; therefore it was settled that the

Sultan should indemnify the merchant, and stop the amount out of our revenue. Thus ever since we have been shut out of our estates; but they say that by next year all will have been repaid, and that we shall get our lands again. Meanwhile my father lives in Constantinople, and there I was born and educated. My mother was a Circassian : it was from my father I learned the Bosnian tongue. I spoke it when I was a child, but I never had occasion to speak it since, till I came here two months ago."

We told the mudir that much of his story was already known to us, and that we had met other families of Bosnia and the Herzegovina in the same position as his own.

"Yes," he said, "in Bosnia and the Herzegovina there is scarcely one whole family spared. Do you know any of these ?"—and he named one after another the great Bosnian houses.

"Yes, we know some of them, and also some of those that went over to Ragusa and have fallen under Austria ; and a Herzegovinian family we know that would not submit either to the Turks or to the Latins, and are now princes of Montenegro."

"Ah !" he exclaimed with a start, "ah, indeed ! Well, my family was once almost as great as princes, and when Montenegrines came to Stamboul, they always visited my father. Pray tell me what sort of place is Montenegro."

Thinking of the adjacent Arnaoutluk, we answered, " It is a place where robbery has been put down, and where even a woman may walk in safety by day or night, carrying any property she pleases."

He interrupted impatiently, " I don't mean that kind of thing: is it a comfortable place to live in? I have heard that it is all mountains. What sort of house has the prince ? "

We answered, that the prince had a good house, but that the most of the country was mountainous, and that to preserve their freedom the people were constantly at war.

"Yes, yes," he said, "that is just as it was described to me; but now tell me, have you been at Bucharest?"

"No."

"Well, that is a delightful place; it would surprise you to see such a European-looking city in this out-of-the-way part of the world. Now that is the sort of place I should like to live in. The truth is, I have become used to large cities, and if to-morrow the Sultan were to give me back all our estates, and say, 'Now you may go back to the Herzegovina,' I would beg him to keep them. I could not go."

These last words he said with a tone and air absurdly like *blasé* young gentlemen elsewhere, and apparently like them he believed that his utterances bore the impress of great mental superiority. As, however, we gave no sign of admiration he changed the subject, and began thus:

"I have been in England. One of my relatives is attached to the embassy, and I was sent to him on business. What a great city London is! but when I was there it was almost as dark as night."

We asked him if the climate had not disagreed with him.

"No, indeed; the climate of England is not bad, but it is a climate wherein it is necessary to drink a little spirits."

We asked him if he had ever seen English people in this part of the world before.

"Not here," he answered, "but once, while I was mudir in Caramania, an English gentleman came to dig for antiquities. He had a huge train of servants and

BOSNIAN RAYAH PAYING TRIBUTE.

baggage, and like you he carried a firman. I went out to meet him as I did to meet you, on my best horse, with all my people, but the English gentleman coming thus suddenly on a great company of armed men took us for robbers and turned to flee : with difficulty he was persuaded to return. Ah ! " added the mudir, presently, " Asia Minor is a much nicer place than this. There, if I wanted any number of horses I had only to send out a zaptié, and the people brought them at once ; here, if I require horses, I may send a dozen zaptiés and not get them after all. The people here are headstrong to a degree ; they do not even care to earn money. If horses are wanted for travellers, the travellers pay for them at a fixed rate ; if they are wanted for government service the owners receive in exchange a receipt, and when the tax-gatherer goes round he remits the equivalent. Yet rather than thus gain money the people of this district will let a horse stay idle at home."

In qualification of this statement we were aware, first, that the government pay is too low to defray the expenses of horse and man ; secondly, that the receipt is not always honoured by the tax-gatherer, while the horses are starved, overdriven, and not unfrequently taken away altogether. However we only remarked that so far as the Christians were concerned they felt it a hardship to be called on for horses when the demand was not equally served on Mussulmans.

"That," said the young governor, " is the fault of the mudirs : they are afraid of the Mussulmans and do not force them to do their duty. But I am not afraid ; they may kill me if they will; but I have the Sultan's authority for it, and I will make them obey. Why should there be any difference between men of one faith and another ? For my part what do I care who is Christian and who is Islam ?"

We remarked that with such sentiments it was a pity he did not live in the Herzegovina, for there the Mussulmans in their fanaticism were always goading the Christians to revolt. He answered, "It would do no good; nothing can make these Mussulmans act otherwise."

"But your ancestors used to make themselves listened to, why should not you?"

"True," he said, "you are right. If I were restored to the Herzegovina, it might be an excellent thing for the people: but you see, it would not be at all pleasant for myself." Presently he added, "To show you what a set of people I have to deal with, I must tell you that the Christian pope finds a better friend in me than among his own flock. His dues are small enough, but the rayah would not pay him unless I forced them. What do you think of that?"

We thought that, whatever it proved for the mudir, it told very badly for the priest.

The conversation finally turned on Serbia. Of the new roads and schools the mudir had heard, and he much wished to visit the country. He said, "I have heard that Serbia has kept up the old ways, and has not, like Bucharest, become *European*. But they say there is justice for the poor in Serbia, and that rich and poor are equal before law." Then he added, "I did not mean that Bucharest is a *good* place, only that it is a place where a man can enjoy life. They say there are good schools in Serbia. I was at school in Constantinople; my brother went to a school where he learned French and Greek, and I should have liked to have learned Greek, for it is the most beautiful of all languages; but in the Mahommedan school there is nothing taught but Turkish."

"Is nothing taught but Turkish in the Mahommedan schools in the Herzegovina?"

"Nothing," he replied; "but the Christians are taught Serbian, and we will send our children to the Christian schools rather than they forget their fathers' tongue."

The morning before we left Roshaï, the mudir, who was evidently a great dandy, sent to ask if we could spare him a pair of gloves. At first we feared that none of ours would be large enough, but as he was a little fellow, with the hand and foot of his Oriental mother, we decided to try a pair of ample German gloves we had bought for riding—the only specimens to be got at Salonica. Of course we supposed they were to be kept for his next visit to Novi Bazaar; so, conceive our amusement when, at the door of our house, we found him on his prancing charger, and with the great black *handschuhs* carefully buttoned.

Early on the morning of Monday a message came from Ipek to this effect: "The pasha of Nish holds court in Prizren, and thither all holders of authority at Ipek have been summoned to answer for the attack on their kaïmakam; meanwhile, in the room of the kaïmakam a new mudir has been appointed at Ipek, and he will be glad to receive you with honour, in obedience to the Sultan's firman." Hereupon we made ready to depart, the master of the house at Roshaï hospitably inviting us to return. "Only," added he, "this thing I pray you: when you think to come here write not to the mudir, but to me; and if you want horses apply not to him, but to us residents. This time, if you had asked me, I would have procured you capital horses from my friends; but you have applied to him—see what miserable beasts he has got!"

END OF VOL. I.

LONDON : PRINTED BY VIRTUE AND CO., LIMITED, CITY ROAD.